Economies of Desire at the Victorian *Fin de Siècle*

T0382665

This volume marks the first sustained study to interrogate how and why issues of sexuality, desire, and economic processes intersect in the literature and culture of the Victorian *fin de siècle*. At the end of the nineteenth century, the move toward new models of economic thought marked the transition from a marketplace centred around the fulfilment of 'needs' to one ministering to anything that might, potentially, be desired. This collection considers how the literature of the period meditates on the interaction between economy and desire, doing so with particular reference to the themes of fetishism, homoeroticism, the literary marketplace, social hierarchy, and consumer culture. Drawing on theoretical and conceptual approaches including queer theory, feminist theory, and gift theory, contributors offer original analyses of work by canonical and lesser-known writers, including Oscar Wilde, A.E. Housman, Baron Corvo, Vernon Lee, Michael Field, and Lucas Malet. The collection builds on recent critical developments in *fin-de-siècle* literature (including major interventions in the areas of Decadence, sexuality, and gender studies) and asks, for instance, how did late nineteenth-century writing schematise the libidinal and somatic dimensions of economic exchange? How might we define the relationship between eroticism and the formal economies of literary production/performance? And what relation exists between advertising/consumer culture and (dissident) sexuality in *fin-de-siècle* literary discourses? This book marks an important contribution to nineteenth-century and Victorian literary studies, and enhances the field of *fin-de-siècle* studies more generally.

Jane Ford has taught across the undergraduate English Literature curriculum at the University of Portsmouth, UK and, more recently, Keele University, UK. Her current work focuses on metaphors of economic exploitation and domination in *fin-de-siècle* writing and she has written chapters and articles on Vernon Lee, Lucas Malet, and Bertram Mitford.

Kim Edwards Keates is a sessional tutor at Liverpool John Moores University, UK. She has published in *Dickens and Modernity*, recently co-edited the *Victorian Periodicals Review* special issue, "Digital Pedagogies: Building Learning Communities for Studying Victorian Periodicals" (2015), and is Bibliographer (with Clare Horrocks) of *Dickens Quarterly*.

Patricia Pulham is reader in Victorian literature at the University of Portsmouth, UK. She is author of *Art and the Transitional Object in Vernon Lee's Supernatural Tales* (2008), and has published articles on a range of nineteenth-century writers including William Hazlitt, Thomas Hardy, Nathaniel Hawthorne and Olive Custance. She has co-edited several collections of essays, most recently "Decadent Crossings," a Special Issue of *Symbiosis* (October, 2012); and she is the editor of a four-volume Routledge facsimile collection, *Spiritualism, 1840–1930*, published in 2013.

Routledge Studies in Nineteenth-Century Literature

Economies of Desire at the Victorian *Fin de Siècle*

Libidinal Lives

Edited by Jane Ford, Kim Edwards Keates, and Patricia Pulham

Routledge
Taylor & Francis Group

LONDON AND NEW YORK

First published 2016 by Routledge

2 Park Square, Milton Park, Abingdon, Oxfordshire OX14 4RN
52 Vanderbilt Avenue, New York, NY 10017

Routledge is an imprint of the Taylor & Francis Group, an informa business

First issued in paperback 2019

Library of Congress Cataloging in Publication Data

    Economies of desire at the Victorian fin de siecle: libidinal lives / edited by Jane Ford, Kim
    Edwards Keates, and Patricia Pulham.
       pages cm. — (Routledge studies in nineteenth-century literature; 16)
    Includes bibliographical references and index.
      1. Desire in literature. 2. Sex in literature. 3. English literature—19th century—History
    and criticism. 4. Literature and society—Great Britain—History—19th century.
    5. Economics in literature. I. Ford, Jane, 1983- editor. II. Keates, Kim Edwards,
    1984- editor. III. Pulham, Patricia, 1959- editor.
    PR468.D45E37 2015
    820.9'3538—dc23   2015021678

ISBN: 978-1-138-82634-2 (hbk)
ISBN: 978-0-367-87126-0 (pbk)

Typeset in Sabon
by codeMantra

Contents

PART III
Queer Performativity

List of Figures

Acknowledgements

We would like to thank John Redmond for his unstinting encouragement, advice, and assistance throughout this project. Matthew Bradley also provided much support and guidance for which we are especially grateful.

Thanks to Bodleian Libraries, University of Oxford for permission to print material from their special collections, including their Michael Field Collection.

Introduction

Jane Ford, Kim Edwards Keates,
and Patricia Pulham

H. Rider Haggard's 1887 best-seller *She: A History of Adventure* contains what could be taken as a byline of *fin-de-siècle* market society; according to Ayesha, immortal queen of the civilisation of Kôr, "the world is a great mart ... where all things are for sale to whom who bids highest in the currency of our desires" (1998, 182). Of course, remarking that "woman's beauty can ever be bought with gold," Haggard's goddess notes what must be painfully clear to an immortal—that the economic structures that underpin sex relations are as old as sex and exchange themselves. But there is something strikingly current in this statement that emphasises the boundlessness of human appetites and a freer, more capacious definition of the commodity. As existing scholarship spearheaded by Lawrence Birken (1988), Regenia Gagnier (2000), and others demonstrates the move, at the end of the nineteenth-century, toward new models of economic thought that presented "economic man" as an unproductive, self-maximising consumer marked the transition from a marketplace centred on the fulfilment of "needs" to one ministering to anything that might, potentially, be desired. Ayesha's mart, actuated by desiring subjects who select from an infinite range of terrestrial pleasures, goods, and services, provides a fitting sketch of a late nineteenth-century marketplace in which—at least as far as (neoclassical) economists were concerned—"value," or more fittingly "price," was determined by a subjective and theoretically insatiable consumer. As Regenia Gagnier remarks, "new" economic man's "advanced stage of development was signified by the boundlessness of his desires. He must choose from a whole universe of goods on display" (Gagnier 2000, 20). In an economic milieu popularly defined by the escalation of human appetites, "desire" itself had effectively become an economic category.

The emphasis on desire in the arena of economics ran roughly parallel to an inclusion of economic principles in the study of desire. In his seminal 1988 study, *Consuming Desire,* Lawrence Birken shows that "consumerist values [were] already evident in Freud's preanalytic work" (43); Freud's "Project for a Scientific Psychology" (1895), for instance, mapped patterns of nervous discharge (culminating in pleasure), which closely resembled patterns of consumer spending—a bias that anticipates the "economic point of view" developed in his later work, *Beyond the Pleasure Principle* (1920). Birken, however, points out that sexology took slightly longer than economics to fully establish a model of individualistic desire. His study describes a three-phase transition (1870–1895; 1895–1915; 1915-beyond) from productivist to consumerist patterns of thinking in the discipline. As he explains, in the early stages of sexual science, heterosexual reproduction (a functional analogue of economic productivism) was interpreted as a "normal" expenditure of sexual desire; homosexuality, on the other hand, was regarded as a perversion. The discovery "of ever more complex and subtle forms of sexual variation" led, in the latter part of the nineteenth century and opening decades of the twentieth, to the abandonment of this "idea of sex as social need in favor of the idea of sex as individualistic desire" or "object-choice" (indicative of a consumerist ethos) (95; 99–100). Ayesha's maxim, presented here as a striking exemplar of the primacy of individualistic desire within the *fin-de-siècle* economy, arguably substantiates the residual productivism described in Birken's chronology; indeed, that the immortal queen's object of desire is the reincarnated lineal ancestor of her long-dead lover might well gesture towards the (re)productive imperative seen as the natural product of heterosexual desire.

Constituting some of the major developments in late nineteenth-century economic and sexological thought, the cross-fertilisation of theories relating to idiosyncratic desire and consumer choice is both indicative of the kinds of questions that inform this volume and a springboard for more conceptual readings of the late-Victorian "economy of desire." Principally, the question this book aims to address is: how and why do issues of sexuality, desire, and economic behaviour intersect in the literature (and culture) of the Victorian *fin de siècle*? Among the range of implied "hows" are matters tropological (how, for instance, does the period's literature articulate desire through the motif of economy?); contextual (how do fully-embodied economic phenomena relate to literary representations of sex, pleasure, and desire?); and formal (how do *fin-de-siècle* writers deploy poetic/narrative/metrical economy to articulate various forms of "unacceptable"—often homoerotic—desire?). The "whys," on the other hand, pertain to those political, theological, and aesthetic ends that the dialogue between "economy" and "desire" employs.

Because sexual science locates a particular kind of economy within the unstable somatic territory of the desiring body, critical studies of the last twenty years have chiefly schematised "libidinal economies" as a favoured trope of the modernist "fiction of interiority," the formal experimentalism of which would seem to replicate the psychoanalytically-conceived libidinal impulse. Joseph Allen Boone's influential 1998 study *Libidinal Currents: Sexuality and the Shaping of Modernism,* for instance, has done much to establish a connection between the "radical subjectivity" of modernist aesthetics and sexological theories of libidinal energy/economy. Boone's professed aim is to investigate how the "techniques and strategies whereby something like 'consciousness' and something like a 'stream' of libidinally charged thoughts, images [and] desires ... are insinuated into the trajectories of an array of more or less experimental fictional narratives engaged in exploring the inner life ..." (5). Though Boone is prepared to accept that the roots of this form of narrative and sexual economy are pre-twentieth century—for instance, he reads Charlotte Brontë's *Villette* (1853) as a "'Victorian' precursor" to the "quintessentially unstable" libidinal narratives of the modernist period—he is only interested in nineteenth-century fiction insofar as it anticipates a particular kind of modernist aesthetic (33; 35). While his study offers valuable insight into the narrative economy of post-Freudian experimental literature, Boone's own silences imply support for a chronology which consigns the literature of the 1880s and 90s to the much noted interregnum between the (apparently austere) literature of the Victorian period and the (libidinally-charged) literature of modernism.

In similar ways, Kathryn Simpson's more recent *Gifts, Markets and Economies of Desire in Virginia Woolf* (2008) aligns the "experimental modernist forms and aesthetics of Woolf's writing" with the characteristics of "fluidity" and "indeterminacy" that Hélène Cixous, in her feminist analysis of the gift, attributes to female acts of non-monetary exchange (6). For Simpson, gift-giving is a constitutive feature of the "libidinal economy" of Woolf's writing, the purpose of which is to circumvent the "heteropatriarchal social order that capitalism seems to keep in place" (2). Like Boone, Simpson describes a fictive "economy of desire" that, if it does not precisely draw on early twentieth-century psychosexual discourses, certainly reflects (stylistically) the kind of volatile libidinal current described in them. But perceived similarities between the libidinal impulse and modernist stylistics are not the sole means through which "economies of desire" have been keyed to the early twentieth-century cultural moment. Describing Woolf's exposure to an "increasingly impersonal and rigid economy," Simpson situates her writing's "dynamic interconnection" between economy and desire in the context of the financial instability (and "fiscal ... retrenchment") of the 1920s (4–5). Woolf's construction of a gift-orientated "feminine libidinal economy" is read as a response not only to anxieties about the stability of monetary value but, more generally, the "(all-pervasive) ethos of capitalism," the "impersonality of commodity culture" and the heteropatriarchal motors of capitalistic exchange (2; 4; 5).

At the *fin de siècle* people were already expressing resistance to the development of modern consumer culture, the banking crises of the 1890s raised fears about financial stability, and the ensuing market centralisation led people to remark on the "impersonality" of financial institutions and corporations.[1] The conditions that, as far as Simpson is concerned, opened the door to Woolf's narrative "interconnection [between] the social, the economic and representations of desire" could already be said to exist, albeit in an earlier form, at the end of the nineteenth-century (4). Why, then, do we not talk about a late Victorian economy of desire in the same way that we talk about the libidinal economies of modernism?

In his analysis of *Villette* (1853), Boone claims that Brontë's novel enters a "libidinal terrain rarely trespassed in Victorian fiction" (40). Perhaps, like others keen to lend coherence to the periodisation of the era, Boone does not include the literature of the 1880s and 90s in his definition of "Victorian fiction."[2] In fact, evidence of the "libidinal terrain" traversed by writers and thinkers of the *fin de siècle* is plentiful. For decades scholars have commented on late nineteenth-century representations of male same-sex desire (and scrutinised the "enforced hiatus" of homosexual literature following Oscar Wilde's 1895 conviction for acts of gross indecency (Gagnier 1987, 162)); they have debated how the pornographic literature of the *fin de siècle* relates and responds to dominant cultural discourses and they have described the ways in which anxieties about threatening female sexuality have been transposed into grotesque images of feminine evil.[3]

That there is no well-established critical discourse surrounding the idea of a *fin-de-siècle* (literary) economy of desire could, then, be due to the fact that unlike literary modernism, the writing of the *fin de siècle* does not have a coherent set of aesthetic or stylistic characteristics to anchor such a discussion. So, for example, while Brontë's *Villette* cannot seriously be said to access a libidinal territory unknown to nineteenth-century writers, in its commitment to the representation of interior states, it *does* provide a stylistic/structural foothold (Boone calls it "proto-modernist") for later, specifically Freudian, conceptualisations of libidinal energy/economy. Although existing studies of the *fin de siècle* have tried to move away from "end-stopped, tragic readings of the period"—nuancing remarks, such as Raymond Williams's, that characterise it as a "working-out … of unfinished lines"—the sheer range and diversity of the period's literature make this process difficult (Marshall 2007, 3; Williams 1963, 165). The critical consensus is that, while it is productive to organise *fin-de-siècle* literature around such general themes as "cultural and political conflict," or "socio-cultural fragmentation," the "issue of definition" remains, to use Gail Marshall's words, "impossibly muddied" (Ledger and McCracken 1995, 4; Marshall 2007, 3).

This is not to say that existing criticism entirely ignores the interplay between ideas of economy and desire at the *fin de siècle*. Particularly profitable strands of enquiry are those studies, like Regenia Gagnier's *The Insatiability of Human Wants: Economics and Aesthetics in Market Society* (2000), which focus on *aesthetic* philosophy and its relationship to the economy. Examining a "plurality" of nineteenth-century aesthetic agendas, Gagnier suggests that "[i]f economics … defined itself as the domain for the provision for the needs and desires of the people, aesthetics was in its most inclusive sense the apprehension and expression of the people's needs and desires at the level of sense, feeling and emotion" (145). In Gagnier's study, the physical bodies of the artist and perceiving subject become bearers of economic meaning. In the "political economy of art"—Ruskin's phrase for the movement which concerned itself with the conditions of aesthetic production—labour theories of value shaped a philosophy of creative production which similarly centred on the physical body (of the artist).[4] But later, at the *fin de siècle*, "physiological aesthetics"—the title of an 1877 treatise by Grant Allen and term for the study of the psychological/ biological foundations of aesthetic taste—focused on the "pleasured body" of the perceiving subject, that is to say the "man of taste" or the "critic" (Gagnier 2000, 135; 145). Calculating the maximum pleasure to be derived from the perception of beautiful things (resonant of Walter Pater's famous dictum to "get as many pulsations as possible into the given time"), physiological aesthetics rejected the political economists of arts' "concern for its producers" in favour of non-productive ethos of artistic consumption (Pater 1998, 153; Gagnier 2000, 135).

Gagnier's work not only maps parallel developments within nineteenth-century aesthetics and economics; pertinent to our own purposes, it demonstrates how sex and sexuality are implicated in theories of aesthetic production and consumption. Gagnier, for example, demonstrates how decadent writers recoiled from bourgeois notions of "purposive" or reproductive sexuality (the same "broadly heterosexual" productivism that underlies the applied aesthetics of Ruskin and William Morris) (Gagnier 2000, 128). The *fin de siècle*, she argues, witnessed the "cultural dialectic" between a "heterosexual aesthetic" and a "perverse" non-(re)productive aesthetic as seen, for instance, in decadence (139). The question of how homosexual writers of the *fin de siècle* positioned themselves in relation to biological and sexological thinking is one that has, and continues to be, of importance to literary critics. Martha Vicinus has similarly argued that, at the *fin de siècle*, homosexual writers pursued a productive imperative that did not, as such, challenge the heterogenital hegemony of contemporary sexological discourses. She points out that "[m]en and women whose sexual lives were in opposition to biological reproduction did not defy its hegemony but, rather, insisted upon a superior option—art. Physical reproduction was replaced with metaphysical and artistic generation" (Vicinus 1994, 94).

Building on the valuable insights of Gagnier, Vicinus and others this collection brings together a selection of original essays to suggest a way of reading the *fin-de-siècle* cultural moment which renders the themes of economy and desire—and their meeting point in the period's literature— more salient. The collection has been organised into three key sections: Articulating Desire, which focuses on how the libidinal economy is expressed in language; Human Currencies, which considers the body's imbrication in economic exchange; and Queer Performativities, which examines sexual economies of difference with an emphasis on the subversive erotics of parody and role play. In practice, there is much dialogue between these themes but the libidinal economy / economy of desire / sexual economy is as slippery as this ranging nomenclature suggests: a lack of definition that is, perhaps, reinforced through the libidinal economy's association with the qualities of "indirection, incompleteness and self-reflex[ivity]" that define experimental modernist narrative (Boone 1998, 5). It has, therefore, been

useful to think about language, the body, and (linguistic / bodily) performance as the principal crossways of economics, sexuality and desire in the
late nineteenth century.

Articulating Desire

In her seminal study, *Desire: Love Stories in Western Culture* (1994),
Catherine Belsey reflects on previous writing about desire: "It has, of course,
been done before – by poets, dramatists, novelists … But something seems
to remain unsaid. And it is primarily this that motivates still more writing.
Desire eludes final definition, with the result that its character, its nature,
its meaning, becomes itself an object of desire for the writer" (1994, 3;
qtd. in Harvey and Shalom 1997, 1–2). As Belsey indicates, the linguistic
signification—the nameability, classification, and characterisation of desire
is politically charged.[5] In particular, it is through the politics of sexuality that
Belsey suggests "Western culture's … understanding of desire is the location
of norms, proprieties and taxonomies, which constitute a form of constraint"
(1994, 4). In such figurations, desire inevitably emerges as a site of dangerous potentiality and transgressive (sexual) excess, generating anxieties about
circulation, articulation, and control. In attempting to organise and control
questions of sexuality and potentially non-normative formulations of desire,
Michel Foucault notes that "sex became an issue, and a public issue no less;
a whole web of discourses, special knowledge's, analyses, and injunctions
settled upon it" (1991, 309; Belsey 1994, 4). Yet, as Foucault tacitly suggests,
when the "rational discourse of sex" operates as an instrument of state-
power, "the things one declines to say" can become a legitimate tool in the
language of resistance (1991, 309). Indeed, taking up Foucault's remarks,
recent advances in queer theory have witnessed an increasing degree of critical attention paid to the varying levels of silence, utterances, half-formed
articulations and multiple voices. In *Victorian Sexual Dissidence* (1999),
Richard Dellamora for example, cites Eve Kosofsky Sedgwick's conceptualisation of sexual "closetedness," which Sedgwick conceives of as "a performance initiated by the speech act of silence alone" (qtd. in Dellamora
1999, 4). But whereas such silence could be indicative of sexual or personal
oppression, more recently, silence, has been considered to have affirmative
significance. In "The Voice of Silence: Interrogating the Sound of Queerness/
Raciality" (2008) for example, Esperanza Miyake proposes "that silence can
be a means to hear a pin drop, a tool to make us listen to the sounds that are
made *in* silence" (qtd. in Kuntsman 2009, 239). By scrutinising that which
is not articulated, or that which appears textually absent or unutterable, it
is possible to pay a greater degree of attention to otherwise marginalised,
indistinct, excessive or non-normative formulations of desire.

    In an essay on *fin-de-siècle* fiction, Nicholas Ruddick suggests that
"A desire might be culturally 'unspeakable' as a result of social taboos; but it
can still be articulated in fiction via symbolic motifs" (2007, 190). Similarly,

in *Sex Scandal: The Private Parts of Victorian Fiction* (1996), William A. Cohen claims that, in nineteenth-century literature, sexual or erotic content is often encoded. He suggests that:

> sexual unspeakability does not function simply as a collection of prohi-bitions for Victorian writers. Rather, it affords them abundant oppor-tunities to develop an elaborate discourse—richly ambiguous, subtly coded, prolix and polyvalent—that we now recognize and designate by the very term *literary*. Like other restrictions upon expression, the conventions of sexual unspeakability serve writers as a produc-tive constraint, contributing to a certain historical formation of the literary. (1996b, 3)

Such literary formulations of unspeakable or unutterable desire gesture towards the (libidinal) economies of linguistic expression. Building on this work, the three chapters in this section variously explore the ways in which language and text fail to adequately capture or express non-normative or excessive desire, which is expressed instead through an eroticisation of eco-nomic discourse, strict self-curtailment, or explorations of the immaterial associations of memory.

In the first chapter, "Always Leave Them Wanting More: Oscar Wilde's *Salome* and the Failed Circulations of Desire," Ruth Robbins considers the multiple, queer formulations of competing and painfully unreciprocated forbidden desires in Wilde's play. Noting that these emerge as homosexual, incestuous, cross-class, or necrophilic, Robbins demonstrates the disruptive, fatally destructive forces that they contain. Taking up Jean-François Lyotard's proposition that "desire cannot be assumed, accepted, understood, and locked up in names," (2004, 19) Robbins points to the insufficiency of language to communicate or express particularly intense or perverse configurations of sexual desire, radically re-presenting the biblical retelling of *Salome* as also a "story about what cannot be spoken" (Robbins, 23). Instead, illicit desire circulates through indirect, connotative moments of elaborate euphemism or through indirect intertextual reference. Indeed, it is through a careful read-ing of the cross-textual allusions (in nineteenth-century visual and literary culture) that the sexually voracious and "exotic—only a letter away from erotic" *femme fatale* figure of Salome silently comes into view (25). Robbins shows how Wilde's version of Salome, who is conventionally subjected to a libidinous male gaze in contemporary art and literature, is paradoxically 'exposed' for scrutiny in Wilde's play by the strategic *removal* and *omis-sion* of stage direction and textual detail—that which is not said. We are invited instead to recognise allusions to artistic and literary depictions of her performance, to fill in textual gaps with the mind's eye. Such recognitions implicate the (silently) watching audience in the transgressive potentialities of the play. Moreover, as Robbins argues, such lacunae and reversals gener-ate tension: it is once Wilde renders Salome (a traditional object of desire) a sexually self-aware subject who *"looks back"* and articulates desire that "all hell breaks loose" (29). For Robbins, intense formulations of sexual desire that can neither be defined nor consummated in *Salome* can only be perversely articulated (or spent) as violence (and with fatal consequences). A play that "takes a serious view of desire," this is Wilde's most paradoxical statement about the economy of desire: an economy which, at the same time it quickens desire, denies its performative expression (25).

Unspeakable libidinal energy is similarly denied an explicit outlet in A. E. Housman's *A Shropshire Lad* (1896), the focus of Veronica Alfano's chapter. Building upon a body of scholarship that considers Housman's homosexual proclivities, Alfano offers a highly nuanced queer reading of his first volume of published verse which sought to commemorate, mourn, and praise young male soldiers and athletes. But these short poems, which, as Alfano notes, often feature an admiring and momentarily lingering homoerotic male gaze, nevertheless stop short of engaging in that elaborate or detailed descriptions of "too-attractive boys" (Alfano, 47). Such constraint is imposed by the ballads' "discontinuous, repetitive, ... restrained, ... iterative and monosyllabic diction," a poetic curtailment that Alfano importantly terms a "ballad economy" (35). It is on this abridged, "form-based [and linguistic] economy," that Alfano centres her argument, viewing the multifarious opportunities through which speakers can simultaneously disclose desire without disclosing too much, or experience moments of self-censoring restraint, interruption or "understated self-expression," which in turn intimate at an intensity of illicit feeling (39). But beyond this, memory and nostalgia also make up a significant part of the queer formulation in the "ballad economy" utilised by Housman. For it is through the initial deployment and blending of the familiar (and therefore easily confused) notes of intertextual reference, that a conservative impulse to obscure and shield dissident desire from recognition is mobilised (in contrast to the sexually subversive deployment of intertextuality that Robbins observes in *Salome*). "Intertextual echoes" in *A Shropshire Lad* instead solidify similitude between the reader and speaker to reduce but also embed "the strange, shameful, or illicit qualities of his speakers' fears and desires" (38). Housman's use of "[r]egular rhythms, orthodox rhymes, [and] frequent alliteration," forge memorable lines that, when coupled with the nostalgic pastoral themes of the ballad tradition, materialise the past; earlier moments of homoerotic desire are temporarily brought into relief, while safely distanced in the intangible past. Adjusting Nicholas Dames's interpretation of "nostalgic forgetting," however, Alfano shows that the moments of forgetfulness that do take place in Housman's ballads act as a strategic tool to conceal homoeroticism. Reading "memory's failure's ... through the lens of homoerotic desire" (39; 38), Alfano discreetly speaks in accord with Judith Halberstam's recent work in *The Queer Art of Failure* (2011), in which forgetfulness is seen "to produce an alternative mode of knowing, one that resists the positivitism of memory projects," while rendering memory's failure instead a "useful tool for jamming the smooth operations of the normal and the ordinary" (2011, 69; 70).

Memory is likewise central to the associative, illicitly alternative and immaterial desire in Jane Desmarais's chapter "Perfume Clouds: Olfaction, Memory, and Desire in Arthur Symons's *London Nights* (1895)." Tracing the material commodification of perfume through advertisements, Desmarais begins by demonstrating the distinctly eroticised female aura with which it was associated in nineteenth-century visual culture. Symons, she argues, disperses his texts with "popular scents" not to reinforce these initial market associations (as tacitly suggested by Catherine Maxwell), but to explore perfume's more intangibly associated libidinous configurations of desire as they emerge through memory (Desmarais, 66). It is this indistinctly figured, vaguely articulated connotative relationship between memory and the vaporised, dispersed fragrance which indirectly "triggers images, memories, and yet at the same time resists clear possession," that evades fixed expression (69). In contrast to Housman's deployment of memory as identified by Alfano, Desmarais indicates that Symons "cleverly sidestep[s]" the "distancing and standardising effects of triggered memory" through the invocation of "the sense of smell, which enables him to keep closer contact with the feeling of the actual experience (yearning, desire, loss)" (70). And yet Desmarais suggests that "there is a quality of attention to language and form that suggests the simultaneity of recollection's vibrancy and limitations" (75). Through a sustained analysis of "White Heliotrope," for example, Desmarais illustrates the ways in which the perfumed scent becomes associated with the recollection of a post-coital post-coital encounter and "the ephemerality of human experience" (73). But it is the communication of the "*effect* of memory" and suggested "indistinctness" which is more firmly articulated through irregular rhythm and form, rather than the figurations of emotions or desires (72). In this way, Desmarais provides a convincing account of Symons's fixation on literary impressionism and the linguistic, immaterial formulations of libidinous desire in memory.

Human Currencies

Expressed in strikingly figurative terms, Marx's critique of the commodity value of labour-power has been critical in the construction of the human body as currency. In his polemic on the working day, Marx famously described how the worker is forced to sell his labour-power, remarking that the "vampire [of capital] will not lose its hold on him 'so long as there is a muscle, a nerve, a drop of blood to be exploited'" (Marx 1977, 224). In terms that emphasise the somatic foundations of alienated labour, Marx points out that through his indenture to the vampire capitalist, the worker can expect only diminishing returns from his enervated body-commodity. Feminist thinkers have expanded Marx's critique of labour-power as commodity to include the subordination of women. In her 1977 essay, "Women on the Market," Luce Irigaray presents a Marxist critique of the "use, consumption and circulation" of women's bodies within patriarchal societies (1985, 171). For Irigaray the imposition of the social roles of mother (re-producer), virgin (object of sexual exchange) and prostitute (sex object for hire), are involved in an alienation of women's pleasure which is structurally akin to the alienation of the proletarian's labour-power. She points out that "all the social regimes of 'History' are based upon the exploitation of one 'class' of producers, namely, women. Whose productive use value (reproductive of children and of the labour force) and whose constitution of exchange value underwrite the symbolic order as such, without any compensation in kind going to them for that 'work'" (1985, 173).

The three chapters in this section consider how female writers of the late nineteenth and early twentieth centuries represent human bodies as objects of exchange within (hetero-patriarchal) capitalist society. The first two, by Sarah Parker and Jane Ford, draw on the discourse of visual power relations and dwell on the various ways in which women's economic subordination is rendered by the male gaze. Among nineteenth-century critiques of the way the female subject is commodified within a male-dominated scopic economy, Christina Rossetti's sonnet "In an Artist's Studio," (composed 1856) as well as passages of Elizabeth Barrett Browning's *Aurora Leigh* (1856), are popularly cited. Relatively recent recovery work on writers such as Michael Field (the authorial pseudonym of Katharine Harris Bradley, 1846–1914 and her niece and ward Edith Emma Cooper, 1862–1913), further demonstrates that female homoerotic desire could be a powerful tool in subverting what Irigaray terms the "ho(m)mo-sexual monopoly" (that is, a masculine economy trading in female bodies) (171). In her analysis of Field's *Sight and Song* (1892)—a sequence of ekphrastic lyrics which describe Renaissance artworks—Krista Lysack, for instance, argues that Field circumvent the "acquisitive male-gaze" by investing typically silenced subjects with autonomous desire. Lysack argues that by celebrating a poetic discourse of "women's shared homoerotic pleasures" Michael Field anticipate "Irigaray's vision of commodity exchange as the realization of juissance or absolute desire" (2008, 131).

In her enterprising comparison of the British *fin-de-siècle* writer, Amy Levy (1861–1889), and the American modernist, Djuna Barnes (1892–1982), in chapter 4 of our collection, Sarah Parker adds nuance to existing critical readings of the visual economy of artist-subject relationships. By focusing on what she terms the "dead-woman muse," Parker demonstrates that Levy's and Barnes's poetry—composed on different sides of the 1900 divide (and indeed, different sides of the Atlantic)—offer strikingly similar critiques of how masculine writing idealises the female corpse. In their own verse, Levy and Barnes satirise the male writing-tradition which imagines the deceased body of the muse as an aesthetic and/or erotic commodity. At the same time as Barnes and Levy expose the misogyny implicit within the dead woman trope, Parker demonstrates that they invest it with more progressive possibilities through the inscription of female homoerotic desire. Terry Castle's 1993 theory of the "the apparitional lesbian"—which argues that "ghostly tropes" have simultaneously facilitated the expression of female homoerotic desire and "dematerialise[d] the threat posed by [it]" (Parker, 95)—is a key theoretical pillar of Parker's chapter. Through the pairing of Levy (writing in the 1880s and 90s) and Barnes (writing in the 1910s and 20s), Parker is able to break down "persistent demarcations between the Victorian and the Modern" to reveal an adjustment in the way homoerotic desire is inscribed on the corpse-muse (83). Unlike Levy, whose verse deploys the kind of "spectralising" techniques described by Castle, Barnes's poetry reflects an aspiration to "'re-flesh' the lesbian body"; as Parker remarks "Barnes's dead women pulse with life: their lustrous hair continues to grow, their corpses sprout flowers and weeds, they move and jerk about beneath the earth" (95). If the fleshliness of Barnes's corpse-muse is not explicitly a repudiation of the necessity to spectralise lesbian desire, it certainly encourages a more fully-embodied lesbian aesthetic. Moreover conflating images of vitality and decay within the perverse body of the flowering corpse, Barnes "evades [offering] fixed representation": a move which disrupts the visual economy of the male gaze (100).

In similar ways Jane Ford's chapter, "Greek Gift and 'Given Being': The Libidinal Economies of Vernon Lee's Supernatural Tales," demonstrates how essayist and writer of fiction, Vernon Lee (1856–1935) provided a corrective to the notion that hetero-patriarchal structures of desire immobilise female agency. Reading the short stories "A Wedding Chest" (1888) and "Dionea" (1890) through the critical lens of gift theory and informed by Luce Irigaray's figuration of women as "value-invested idealities," Ford finds in Lee a pattern of representing women as both subject and objects of desire, vulnerable to the nexus of exchange in a patriarchal matrix energised by an erotic, libidinal impetus (Irigaray 1985, 181). Taking up Lee's "mistrust of the practice of gift-giving," Ford considers her treatment of two gift events: devotional Christological giving and the mythic "Greek Gift" (Ford, 160). The reciprocity of the gift is vitally figured through the circulatory exchange of blood—as blood money—"a de facto somatic currency" devoured with vampiric-like energy (109).

Just as Parker reveals the ways in which Djuna Barnes "re-fleshes" the female corpse, commoditising the body into a material reality that both empowers and disempowers sexual otherness, Ford illustrates that the asymmetrical power dynamics enacted at the heart of a gift exchange in "Dionea" (which is mediated through homoerotic attraction) renders the eponymous protagonist as a "living corpse"—an apparently subjugated, slavish "given" "thing" to be objectified and possessed (Kojève 1980, 16). Indeed, developing Robbins's earlier proposition that the Lyotardian libidinous economy risks "mix[ing] up" and reformulating a desire which views "people as things" (Robbins, 22), Ford underlines how Lee emphasises the very "thingness" of woman in a hetero-patriarchal gift economy. But it is strikingly through a "gift economy," according to Kathryn Simpson, that it is possible to "realise a subversive economy of desire" that "prioritise[s] a different set of values" (2009, 2). "Dionea" radically explores this potentiality, disrupting and resisting patriarchal narratives of control, ownership and knowability, which as in Robbins's essay, instead become desires of fatally consumptive, self-destructive libidinal excess. Ford astutely reveals Lee's alternative figuration of the gift: a gift that can invert and transpose supremacy to the female "given being," enabling a liberating realisation of an autonomous self.

The vexed status of the gift also underpins Catherine Delyfer's account of Lucas Malet's *The Far Horizon* (1906). Delyfer shows how Malet is aware of the implicit self-interest in much gift-giving, but nevertheless wishes to reclaim the act as part of a "spiritual economy" which would stand in critical contrast to the dominant fictional structures of the period. Delyfer notes how contemporaries of Malet, like Gissing and Oliphant, were, "quick to appropriate economic themes for fictional treatment, mining contemporary financial events for characters and plots" (Delyfer, 132). Malet's work must therefore be seen in the context of a common literary gamble of the period, a bet that contemporary economic habits and institutions would provide an artistic pay-off. Malet takes this gamble further by projecting her own literary investment and its associated uncertainty of reward on to the ascetic saintliness of her main protagonist, Dominic Iglesias. As Delyfer points out, the treatment of his character, "literalises a transfer of value, or more exactly a displacement of creditworthiness. ... his trajectory in the novel is conceived as a monetary curve charting the fluctuations of a currency whose ups and down the reader is asked to follow" (134). Like the Wordsworthian attempt to create the taste by which a writer is enjoyed, *The Far Horizon*, in this account, gestures towards the set of not-yet-existing conditions necessary to appreciate its existence. It gambles on there being, in Emerson's words, "A higher work for Art than the arts" (Emerson 1869, 328). *The Far Horizon* is itself conceived as a gift which attempts to acknowledge self-interest (including its own) while looking beyond to it to an ideal of reception which is (perhaps endlessly) deferred.

Just as *The Far Horizon* is decisively bound up with temporal remoteness, it also responds to influences which are physically distant, especially in the context of colonial projects which often had their basis in the waxing and waning of particular financial speculations. As in Corvo's *Desire and Pursuit of the Whole* and Huysmans's *À Rebours*, Malet's version of exceptionalism is linked to sexual repression: "... at the end of the novel, when Malet has her protagonist die a sexually unspent man, and an un-repaid, un-thanked creditor to all those he has help materially and morally, she is in fact confirming Iglesias's capacity for indefinite deferral of gratification, thus multiplying his value through eternity" (135). The diversion of libidinal currents is therefore seen as a crucial prerequisite to overcoming the conditions of the "machine man," the economic monad. Delyfer reveals how the thinking of the period—the efforts of Bagehot and others—encouraged writers to blur the lines between the literary and financial sphere, to see the literary work as a type of financial speculation, to see financial speculation as a species of imaginative (poetic) act.

Queer Performativity

In the sixteen years since Richard Dellamora asserted in *Victorian Sexual Dissidence* (1999) that the "gaying" of criticism of the late-Victorian period had at the time been "underway now for more than a decade" the practice, has continued unabated (1). In the last three chapters of this collection, Matthew Bradley, Kristen Mahoney, and Jill R. Ehnenn show that there are still queer lives and texts to rediscover and re-read, and new ways to explore queer identities that have become increasingly familiar to contemporary critics of decadent literature. Identity politics, as we know, are at the heart of queer studies and have been since the late nineteenth century when the word "homosexual" became a demarcation. Whereas prior to sexological definitions sodomy had been considered "a temporary aberration," the homosexual was now a category, "a species" (Foucault 1980, 43). The criminalisation of homosexuality implicit in the Labouchère Amendment of 1885 concretised homosexual identity even as it drove it underground, and the Wilde trials of 1895 spotlighted the sexual economy—literal, metaphorical, and textual—that operated between gay men of the period.

In contrast, the lesbian has often remained hidden from public view. Terry Castle has discussed her "apparitional" status in cultural discourse and production; lesbian contributions to culture, she claims, "have been routinely suppressed or ignored, lesbian-themed works of art censored and destroyed, and would-be apologists ... silenced and dismissed" (1993, 5). Moreover, unlike male homosexuality, in England lesbianism has been largely disregarded by the law albeit not because of the House of Lords's "indifference" but perhaps, as Castle suggests, due to its reluctance to call attention to it, fearing its proliferation (1993, 6). Martha Vicinus has also commented extensively on the "historical denial" of lesbianism. At the *fin de siècle*, she contends, lesbian eroticism was obscured by "the Victorian image of romantic friendships" which "lacked a conceptual framework to envision their relations as sexual ones" (Vicinus 1996, 219).[6] In her 1996 introduction to *Lesbian Subjects: A Feminist Reader* she argues that faced with heteronormative assumptions that located desire in men, countered only by the asexuality offered by the romantic friendship, the early twentieth-century lesbian had little option but to embrace sexological definitions of sexual inversion and, in Butlerian terms, perform masculinity (Vicinus 1996, 219).[7] However, as Ehnenn demonstrates in chapter 9 of our collection, in the creative and collaborative *fin-de-siècle* partnership, Michael Field, such stringent demarcations of gender did not always apply. As Ehnenn shows, in their libidinal lives they adopted positional variations as desiring subjects and the objects of their affections encompassed both men and women.

Complicating perceptions of the writers' "lesbian" sexuality, in her chapter Ehnenn examines Michael Field through the critical lens of José Esteban Muñoz's concept of "disidentification." For Muñoz, both social constructivist and essentialist models of subjectivity have been "exhausted" and he argues against their efficacy believing that "neither story is complete" (5–6). It is this incompleteness that Ehnenn exploits, reading Michael Field's literary and autobiographical texts as "textual performances with queer implications" that theorise nineteenth-century representations of joint authorship, same-sex love, and cross-gender identification (Ehnenn, 180). Queering Michael Field's texts, yet challenging the tropes of sameness, coalescence, and connubial unity that have characterised much critical analysis of their writings and private lives, she highlights the complex nature of their sexual and authorial role playing, marking the shifts and breaks in Michael Field's collective production and noting the centrality of their affinity with Dionysian concepts of flux, change, and rebirth that they later translated into Catholic devotion.

In contrast to Michael Field who, thanks to recent scholarship,[8] are of increasing interest to critics and students alike, the figures Bradley and Mahoney discuss in chapters 7 and 8 respectively, have not been similarly reclaimed. The comparatively forgotten figure Eric Stanislaus, Count Stenbock (1860–1895), who is the subject of Bradley's chapter, is often considered derivative, a poor man's Oscar Wilde or real-life version of Joris-Karl Huysmans' degenerate protagonist, Des Esseintes, in *À Rebours* (1884); one whose works aspired to, but never reached the heights attained by his admired contemporaries. "The True Story of a Vampire" (1894), perhaps his best-known story, shares an Eastern European aristocrat with Bram Stoker's *Dracula* (1897), an exertion of mesmeric power that mirrors George du Maurier's *Trilby* (1894), and a vampiric depletion enacted via musical aesthetics which recalls that staged in Vernon Lee's "A Wicked Voice" (1889), but despite its engagement with many of the recognisable tropes of late-Victorian fiction, it has failed to attract significant critical interest. The common assumption is that Stenbock is a poor writer and Bradley makes no apology for his literary merits, but he asks the pertinent question: "don't bad writers have a right to perform themselves and their sexuality too?" (Bradley, 151). In doing so, he raises an important point and one that is explored in detail in his essay. According to Bradley, posterity's treatment of Stenbock and his work underlines the value systems inherent in literary decadence. Labelling Stenbock "a parody too far" in a libidinal and artistic economy that itself relied to a considerable degree on "strategies of parody and parodic subversion," Bradley shows that both the writers and, subsequently, the literary critics of decadence have made value-judgements regarding what are "acceptable and unacceptable forms of perversity and performativity" (149). Astutely, Bradley identifies Stenbock and his work as bathetic. Whereas parody can be "energising," he argues that bathos is "de-energising" and "corrosive to the performed perversity of decadent sexuality" (155). For Bradley, Stenbock has been judged a failure both as writer and decadent aesthete at least in part because he presents us with an "'unredeemed' performance of perverse identity, a failed seriousness which misses even the aim of converting itself into camp subversion" (157).

The subversiveness of camp is also at the core of Mahoney's essay on Baron Corvo (Frederick Rolfe, 1860–1913). In her chapter Mahoney asks how it was possible, in the homosexual panic that followed the Wilde trials, for writings by Corvo featuring a sexualised power dynamic between an older Englishman and young Italian youths to appear in the *Yellow Book* between 1895 and 1896. Mahoney notes that, although risqué in content, these works, later collected in *Stories Toto Told Me* (1898) and revived and extended in *In His Own Image* (1901), were "warmly received" (Mahoney, 162). Corvo's stories centre on the libidinal value of the Italian adolescent male, "Toto," whose body, reproduced in sketches and photographs, circulates desire poised precariously on the line between art and pornography. Composed of saints' lives and Italian folklore, Toto's tales reinforce the conservatism implicit in what Mahoney calls the "erotics of inequality" (162), and this may have in part contributed to their acceptance. But the Arcadian photography practised by Corvo in life and in the stories by Corvo's avatar "Don Friderico," points to the sexual undercurrent that runs so close to their surface. As Stefano Evangelista writes, in the late nineteenth century, the homosexual writer and critic John Addington Symonds collected similar images produced by photographic studios in Italy that "specialised in the male nude," and circulated "hundreds of photographs from them" among friends at home whose access to English versions of such pornography had been curtailed by the zealous watchfulness of the National Vigilance Association (2010, 93). By 1890 Symonds was purchasing photographs taken by Wilhelm von Gloeden who, like Don Friderico, "took pictures of young men and boys, often in classical attitudes or classical settings" (Evangelista 2010, 94). While the class difference between Don Friderico and Toto appears to reinforce Regenia Gagnier's negative assessment of Corvo as one invested in and supportive of exploitative social hierarchies (Gagnier 2000, 150), Mahoney challenges this reading. Focusing on the camp performativity of such hierarchies in the Toto stories, Mahoney contends that Corvo, who had himself experienced periods of abject poverty, exaggerates Don Friderico's abuses of power to tacitly critique them. "Read as camp" she argues, "the stories emerge as thoughtful and playful responses to the experience of hardship, oppression, and invisibility" (174).

As desiring subjects, the writers discussed in these essays—Michael Field, Count Stenbock, and Baron Corvo—are consumers in Ayesha's mart, that storehouse of worldly pleasures mentioned at the beginning of this introduction, and as producers of art informed by their sexuality, contribute to the libidinal economy of the *fin de siècle*. In their literature and their lives, they demonstrate the variegated nature of late-Victorian queer sensibilities, the parameters of which are constantly in expansion.

Notes

1. See Gail Turley Houston's chapter "Bankerization panic and the corporate personality in Dracula" 2005, 112–31.
2. For instance in *The Victorians* Philip Davis concludes his analysis in 1880, the year of George Eliot's death and a time when, as Davis puts it, the "high moral seriousness" of the realist project gave way to a "late Victorian aesthetic" (2004, 6).
3. For a detailed analysis of (late) nineteenth-century pornographic literature see Marcus 1966; Cohen 1996a, 107–11. Bram Dijkstra's *Idols of Perversity: Fantasies of Feminine Evil in Fin-de-Siècle Culture* (1986) is a foundational study of the literature and iconography of late nineteenth-century misogyny.
4. Gagnier explains that the labour theory of value theorised "that the cost of a commodity was the value of the labourer's wear and tear in production, plus the value of the labourers subsistence" (2000, 129).

5. Keith Harvey and Celia Shalom similarly cite this quote from Belsey in *Language and Desire* (1997) and likewise suggest that "Naming it [desire], renaming it, finding a verbal image for it, revealing it, recounting it … these are the verbal acts constantly repeated and refashioned by the desiring speaking subject" (2).

6. Much work has been done in the last twenty years, not least by Vicinus herself, to rediscover and reclaim the eroticism of these couplings. See for example Vicinus 2004, Newman 2005, Ehnenn 2008.

7. Here, Vicinus alludes to the theory of gender performativity developed by Judith Butler. See Butler, 1990.

8. See in particular Thain 2007, and Vadillo and Thain 2008.

Works Cited

Barthes, Roland. 2002. *A Lover's Discourse*, translated by Richard Howard. London: Vintage.

Belsey, Catherine. 1994. *Desire: Love Stories in Western Culture*. Oxford: Blackwell Publishers.

Birken, Lawrence. 1988. *Consuming Desire: Sexual Science and the Emergence of a Culture of Abundance, 1871–1914*. New York: Cornell University Press.

Boone, Joseph Allen. 1998. *Libidinal Currents: Sexuality and the Shaping of Modernism*. Chicago: Chicago University Press.

Butler, Judith. 1990. *Gender Trouble: Feminism and the Subversion of Identity*. New York: Routledge.

Castle, Terry. 1993. *The Apparitional Lesbian: Female Homosexuality and Modern Culture*. New York: Columbia University Press.

Cohen, Ed. 1996a. "Writing Gone Wilde: Homoerotic Desire in the Closet of Representation." *Reading Fin de Siècle Fictions*, edited by Lyn Pykett, 103–26. London: Longman.

Cohen, William A. 1996b. *Sex Scandal: The Private Parts of Victorian Fiction*. London: Duke University Press.

Davis, Philip. 2004. *The Victorians: 1830–1880*. Oxford: Oxford University Press.

Dellamora, Richard. 1999. *Victorian Sexual Dissidence*. Chicago: Chicago University Press.

Dijkstra, Bram. 1986. *Idols of Perversity: Fantasies of Feminine Evil in Fin-de-Siècle Culture*. Oxford: Oxford University Press.

Ehnenn, Jill R. 2008. *Women's Literary Collaboration, Queerness, and Late-Victorian Culture*. Burlington: Ashgate Press.

Emerson, R. W. 1869. *Essays: First Series*. Boston: Fields, Osgood & Co.

Evangelista, Stefano. 2010. "Aesthetic Encounters: the Erotic Visions of John Addington Symonds and Wilhelm Von Gloeden." In *Illustrations, Optics and Objects in Nineteenth-Century Literary and Visual Cultures*, edited by Luisa Calè and Patrizia Di Bello, 87–106. Basingstoke: Palgrave Macmillan.

Foucault, Michel. 1980. *The Will to Knowledge: The History of Sexuality*, Vol. 1 (3 vols). London: Penguin.

—— 1991. "The Repressive Hypothesis." In *The Foucault Reader*. Edited by Paul Rabinow, 301–30. London: Penguin.

Gagnier, Regenia. 1987. *Idylls of the Marketplace: Oscar Wilde and the Victorian Public*. Aldershot: Scolar Press.

—— 2000. *The Insatiability of Human Wants: Economics and Aesthetics in Market Society*. Chicago: University of Chicago Press.

Haggard, H. Rider. 1998. *She*. Edited by Daniel Karlin. Oxford: Oxford University Press.

Halberstam, Judith. 2011. *The Queer Art of Failure*. Durham and London: Duke University Press.

Harvey, Keith and Celia Shalom, eds. 1997. Introduction. *Language and Desire: Encoding Sex, Romance and Intimacy*, 1–20. London and New York: Routledge.

Irigaray, Luce. 1985. *This Sex Which is Not One*, translated by Catherine Porter with Carolyn Burke. New York: Cornell University Press.

Kojève, Alexandre. 1980. *Introduction to the Reading of Hegel: Lectures on the Phenomenology of Spirit*. Edited by Allan Bloom. Translated by James H. Nichols, Jr. Ithaca: Cornell University Press.

Kuntsman, Adi. 2009. *Figurations of Violence and Belonging: Queerness, Migranthood and Nationalism in Cyberspace and Beyond*. Peter Lang.

Ledger, Sally, and Scott McCracken, eds. 1995. *Cultural Politics at the Fin de Siècle*. Cambridge: Cambridge University Press.

Lyotard, Jean-François. 2004. *Libidinal Economy*, translated by Iain Hamilton-Grant. London: Continuum.

Lysack, Krista. 2008. *Come Buy, Come Buy: Shopping and the Culture of Consumption in Victorian Women's Writing*. Athens: Ohio University Press.

Marcus, Steven. 1964. *The Other Victorians: a Study of Sexuality and Pornography in Mid-Nineteenth-Century England*. New York: Basic Books.

Marshall, Gail., ed. 2007. Introduction to *The Cambridge Companion to the Fin de Siècle*, 1–12. Cambridge: Cambridge University Press.

Marx, Karl. 1977. *Capital: A Critique of Political Economy*. Vol I. Translated from the third German edition by Samuel Moore and Edward Aveling, edited by Frederick Engels. London: Lawrence & Wishart.

Muñoz, José Esteban. 1999. *Disidentifications: Queer of Color and the Performance of Politics*. Minneapolis: University Minnesota Press.

Newman, Sally. 2005. "The Archival Traces of Desire: Vernon Lee's Failed Sexuality and the Interpretation of Letters in Lesbian History." *Journal of the History of Sexuality* 14 (1–2): 51–75.

Pater, Walter. 1998. *The Renaissance: Studies in Art and Poetry*. Oxford: Oxford University Press.

Ruddick, Nicholas. 2007. "The fantastic fiction of the fin de siècle." In *The Cambridge Companion to the Fin de Siècle*, edited by Gail Marshall. 189–206. Cambridge: Cambridge University Press.

Simpson, Kathryn. 2008. *Gifts, Markets and Economies of Desire in Virginia Woolf*. Basingstoke: Palgrave Macmillan.

Thain, Marian. 2007. *Michael Field: Poetry, Aestheticism and the Fin de Siècle*. London: Cambridge University Press.

Turley Houston, Gail. 2005. *From Dickens to Dracula: Gothic, Economics, and Victorian Fiction*. Cambridge: Cambridge University Press.

Vadillo, Ana Parejo, and Thain, Marion., eds. 2009. *Michael Field: the Poet*. Ontario: Broadview Press.

Vicinus, Martha. 1994. "The Adolescent Boy: Fin de Siècle Femme Fatale?" *Journal of the History of Sexuality* 5 (1): 90–114.

——— 2004. *Intimate Friends: Women Who Loved Women, 1778–1928*. Chicago: Chicago University Press.

——— ed. 1996. Introduction. *Lesbian Studies: A Feminist Reader*, 1–14. Bloomington: Indiana University Press.

Williams, Raymond. 1963. *Culture and Society*. Harmondsworth: Penguin.

Part I
Articulating Desire

1   Always Leave Them Wanting More

Oscar Wilde's *Salome* and the Failed Circulations of Desire

Ruth Robbins

A cigarette is the perfect type of a perfect pleasure. It is exquisite, and it leaves one unsatisfied. What more can one want?

(Oscar Wilde, *The Picture of Dorian Gray*, 1891)

That desire is always fatal—or at least very dangerous—in Wilde's works, is signalled in part by the epigraph to this chapter. Of course we know now that the cigarette is a particularly dangerous pleasure, which gets its effect from the fact that it does indeed always leave one wanting more, causing increasing damage as it exerts its pernicious pull. The Victorians might not have known this precisely, but a certain kind of commentator certainly disapproved of smoking.[1] This was part of its pleasure for Wilde, for it allowed him to flout conventions in a variety of contexts. The joke about the "perfect pleasure" of cigarette-smoking was repeated with variations in several of his works, suggesting that Wilde always knew that you can't have too much of a good thing. In *The Importance of Being Earnest* (1895) the formidable Lady Bracknell comments, against the grain of normal expectation, that she regards smoking as a suitable "occupation" for an eligible bachelor (Wilde 1994, 368). The bachelor characters in "The Decay of Lying" (1889) smoke as a matter of course, as they discourse on art and morality (Wilde 1994, 1071). Wilde himself appeared on the stage after the premiere of *Lady Windermere's Fan* (1892) wearing a green carnation and smoking a cigarette as he congratulated his audience for their excellent taste in approving of his play (Ellmann 1988, 346). This act shocked some of his audience in part because the so-called New Woman's key marker of emancipation, along with her bicycle, was her twenty-a-day habit. But it is not the cigarette *per se* that matters here, despite its over-determined *fin-de-siècle* exoticism; it's the fact that the cigarette is defined as a *perfect* pleasure, and that perfection is itself defined by its refusal of a satisfied sigh of fulfilment, precisely because fulfilment is always unobtainable.

Although sometimes a cigarette is just a cigarette, it is also, among other things, a metaphor, which, with its wreaths of smoke, its *louche* associations and its fatality, stands for the dangerous allure of forbidden pleasures of many kinds. It has no place in the text of Wilde's biblical play, *Salome* (1891; English translation, 1893), in which it would obviously be anachronistic, and nor does it appear in any of the drawings that Aubrey Beardsley supplied for its English publication in 1893. But it is very strongly associated with Wilde as one of the planks of the new consumerism on which the naughty nineties were founded, and with which Wilde was associated following his American tour in 1882. As Michèle Mendelssohn has pointed out, Wilde's image was appropriated to "endorse products ranging from hosiery and corsets to stoves and sewing machines" (Mendelssohn 2007, 3), establishing, probably against Wilde's inclination a connection between the aesthetic creed of "Art for Art's sake" and the capitalist imperative of art for money's sake. The idea of desire and consumption does find its way into Wilde's play. Because it provokes desire but does not ever fully permit its fulfilment, the cigarette stands for the circulation of desire which cannot be met, with a clear relationship to a late nineteenth-century capitalist economy which requires insatiable desire. The late-nineteenth-century economist, William Stanley Jevons pointed out in his *The Theory of Political Economy* (1871; 3rd edition 1888), an essential distinction between 'utility' (the production of goods based on need) and consumption (the production of commodities that afford their buyers pleasure):

> it is surely obvious that Economics does rest upon the laws of human enjoyment; and that, if those laws are developed by no other science, they must be developed by economists. We labour to produce with the sole object of consuming, and the kinds and amounts of goods produced must be determined with regard to what we want to consume. Every manufacturer knows and feels how closely he must anticipate the tastes and needs of his customers: his whole success depends upon it.
>
> (Jevons 1888, Ch. 3, paragraph 5)

The fact that the cigarette was also one of the new consumer products of the period (in Wilde's case, quite deliberately and self-consciously a luxury item associated with exoticism and expense—he smoked gold-tipped Egyptian cigarettes for preference) brings together in a single image the combination of "romance and finance," which Regenia Gagnier has identified as central to Wilde's sexual practices, his relationships, and his works (Gagnier 1986, 179).

This is also a central tenet of Jean-François Lyotard's *Libidinal Economy* (1974), which is in part the pre-text for this chapter. Lyotard's title and the book it names combine the necessary desires of capitalism—we must desire *things* to make the financial world go round—and the biological desires of human sexual instinct—we must desire *people* to propagate the race, but also to realise our destiny as rounded human subjects who are in part defined by those very sexual desires. The risk of that joint set of desires is that we might desire people as things and mix up the two elements in an unethical rapaciousness. (The origin of the word rape means seizure, possession by force—turning a person into a thing.) And we also know that the Victorians understood sexuality as having an economic trace. Spending, for instance, was commonly used as a metaphor for male sexual activity, and being spent as one for sexual exhaustion, so that economic and sexual potency (and, indeed, their lack) were often couched in the same language, a set of traces which *Libidinal Economy* toys with.[2] The book's central metaphor is famously the Moebius Strip, an elastic band which is folded onto itself in a figure-of-eight. This is a figure whose force is that inside and outside cannot be distinguished from each other, which Lyotard reaches by staging a fantastic and grotesque autopsy on an imagined woman's body, laying out her skin in a lingering, repellent, and fascinating series of images of abjection, a theatre of cruelty which is both surgical and spectacular.

In my view, a third element alongside sexual desire and its displacement into the desire for things is the element of language. This is a Foucauldian point deriving from *The History Sexuality*—where Foucault argues that sexuality is at once practice and discourse, and that the two are intertwined as much as the bodies that embody them and the practices they define (Foucault, 1990). And in part, it is the displacement of desire into language that Lyotard refuses, in language which is often strikingly Wildean. He writes, for instance, of a "theatricality without reference, masks revealing no face unless it is a mask in its turn" (Lyotard 2004, 18), a sentiment with which Wilde, at his most arch and anti-realist, might well have sympathised. The relationship between words and things is one that is consistently called into question by Wilde's oeuvre. In *Salome*, this is a particularly urgent issue, since the words which define the things that are meant to stand for the people we desire, are very much part of a story about what cannot be spoken. Or as Lyotard puts it: "desire cannot be assumed, accepted, understood, and locked up in names = nomenclatured, because these intensities we desire horrify us, because we flee them, because we forget them" (Lyotard 2004, 19). We should also note the happy historical accident that intercourse means conversational exchange among other things: and that adultery was defined by the Victorian law courts as "criminal conversation," a rather neat periphrasis or euphemism—those speech habits that disguise that which should not be spoken, imagined, or dreamed. Lyotard begins his book with a naming of parts: an obscene version of the blazon in which the beloved's attributes are lovingly listed in sixteenth-century sonnets. Salome in Wilde's play also speaks of body parts, in turn attracted and, when he rejects her, repelled, by Jokanaan's attributes, until her acts eventually turn him into a corpse. She is by turn "amorous of [his] body" (Wilde 1994, 589ff), his hair, mouth; and by turns disgusted by each of them. The dismemberment of his body in speech becomes a literal decapitation. Love and hate cannot be contained in words. All this, by way of preamble. And so to begin.

§

It is a commonplace of critical commentary on *Salome* that it is very different from Wilde's other works. In the words of one of his more recent commentators, Michael Y. Bennett: "How is it possible that the same writer who made a name for himself through writing comedies of manners like *The Importance of Being Earnest* also wrote a play like *Salome*?" (Bennett 2011, vii). As Bennett points out, the anomaly of *Salome* is all the more remarkable because its composition and fraught publication history, as well as its censorship at the hands of the Lord Chamberlain, all took place absolutely simultaneously with the composition of the four major comedies of manners, *Lady Windermere's Fan* (1892), *A Woman of No Importance* (1893), *An Ideal Husband* (1895), and *The Importance of Being Earnest* (1895). Those other plays are resolutely set in the contemporary world; they all focus on a more or less realistic portrayal of the contemporary (albeit highly artificial) social world. They are utterly commercial productions with huge commercial audiences during their own time and beyond. (Neither of these things is true of *Salome*, which has never been a commercial proposition, by the way.) The comedies share a decor, a set of stock characters and situations, and they function in the realms of epigrammatic wit. Portentous people are always mocked in the comedies: they are all, as in *Earnest*'s subtitle, *Trivial Comedies for Serious People*.

In *Salome* by way of contrast we find ourselves instead in the biblical world of Herod Antipas, in Israel at the time of Christ and John the Baptist. Instead of focusing on a clearly defined genre—the comedy of manners—we are in a world marked by experiment: this play appears to have little on the surface that is typically "Wildean." Having said that, I have argued elsewhere following some of the insights of Josephine Guy and Ian Small, that Wilde was strongly concerned with self-conscious manipulations of genre and the horizons of expectation that genre enlists in the constructions of effect and affect (see Robbins 2011; Small and Guy 2000). One possible way of understanding *Salome* is to see it as a tragedy with a keen sense of the ridiculous. It is to some extent a *fin-de-siècle* trait to produce work which embodies generic instability and incongruity, a trait which is perhaps explicable in that the *fin de siècle* was also one of the first periods of mass literacy where popular genres increasingly mattered in the monetisation of literary production. Wilde was not alone in his very careful, though also highly subversive, distortions of genre. In performance, *Salome* is tragedy—she dies at the end; but it is also very funny, at least potentially (the Steven Berkoff production of 1989, for instance, brought out the comic potential of its overblown rhetoric), and a great deal of its force comes from the fact that the situation of a bedroom farce has been transported to biblical Israel and treated with high-blown seriousness. The play dramatises the farcical situation in which an apparently powerful man, Herod, is actually henpecked by his monstrous wife (Herodias), and turns out to be hysterical and weak, not omnipotent at all. Added to this, he is in lust with his stepdaughter (Salome). We also have a situation where one young man's (the Page of Herodias) longing for another (The Young Syrian) is deliberately misread by the second boy, who in turn fancies the pretty ingénue princess (who might not be quite that ingénue, I admit, but who has that role in part). In turn, she loves the pure young man, the prophet who abnegates and sublimates all desire in his all-consuming religious fervour. The fact that this particular bedroom farce is played as tragedy not comedy doesn't undo its farcical nature. In the words of Mario Praz, "[It is] a parody of the whole of the material used by the Decadents and of the stammering mannerisms of Maeterlinck's drama—and, as parody, *Salomé* comes very close to being a masterpiece" (Praz 1954, 298). More recent commentary has been a bit less kind. For Andrew Russ, "The sheer proliferation of colour, musicality, dance, spectacle and smell of language, character and form ... is certainly a heady brew. But it borders on the ridiculous" (Russ 2011, 48). It does. It *is* ridiculous. At the same time, though, it also takes a serious view of desire, which may itself be ridiculous when you come to think of it too much. In his comedies Wilde offered a corrective vision to punitive Victorianism. The sexual and financial peccadilloes of his plaster saints (romance and finance again) are forgiven rather than punished. But in *Salome*'s more primitive world, all desire is fatal. A king loses his authority to it; a young girl is killed for her desires; and even purity won't save you—Jokanaan dies too despite his utter refusal to participate in the various erotic exchanges that make up the play. The biblical decor is for Wilde the location for tragedy; to an unnamed correspondent in 1893, Wilde wrote: "Whether a comedy should deal with modern life, whether its subject should be society or middle-class existence, these are questions purely to the artist's own choice. Personally I like comedy to be intensely modern, and like my tragedy to walk in purple and to be remote: but these are whims merely" (qtd. in Ellmann 1988, 321).

This expresses the view I suppose that Wilde's position on the "earnestness" of the nineteenth century is that it is, in fact, very funny. It allows him to mock what some would have regarded as serious in the comedies. It is also a commentary that implies tragedy is impossible at the end of Victoria's reign unless it is displaced to the long-ago and far away.

As any brief glance at late nineteenth-century European culture will attest, Salome was a ubiquitous figure in the period.[3] The biblical account of her story was expanded to speak to the period's own concerns with orientalist fantasies, sexual immorality and impropriety, and the decadent assault on the sacred cows of organised religion. She was a repeated image in the art of the period, and, as Bram Djikstra has shown, the focus was on a voyeuristic vision of the sexualised female body shown as powerful and erotic, images which certainly do owe much to the view of the orient as the exotic other, primitive space, contrasted to European women who, buttoned up and covered up, flaunted clothes not bodies in their displays of conspicuous consumption. As Djikstra argues, she is *the* figure of the *femme fatale* for the period, a fruitful image because she combined the dubious sexual reputation of the dancing girl with a fatality which directly attacked institutional religion. She was also nicely exotic—only a letter away from erotic. As such, she combined a powerful (and therefore unfeminine) voracious sexuality with an exotic artistic potential. "In the turn of the century imagination," writes Djikstra, "the figure of Salome epitomized the inherent perversity of women: their eternal circularity and their ability to destroy the male's soul even while they remained nominally chaste in body" (Djikstra 1989, 384). Artists were repeatedly attracted to the image of Salome as a sexualised female body, licensed as an object of display because she is a dancer, and because she is not a contemporary woman, and because she is not a European woman.

Alongside the pictorial images that proliferated of Salome's fatal charms, there are also the multiple literary rewritings of eight biblical verses in Mark Chapter 6,[4] the most famous of which is Flaubert's short story "Herodias" from his *Trois Contes* [*Three Tales*] (1877) in which those few biblical lines are expanded into an exotic spectacle, which represents both desire and inflames it in the eyes of the beholders:

> Under a bluish veil that concealed her head and breasts, one could just make out the arch of her eyes, the chalcedonies in her ears, and the whiteness of her skin. A square of dove-coloured silk covered her shoulders and was fastened to her loins by a jeweled girdle. Her black trousers were spangled with mandrakes, and she moved with indolent ease, her little slippers of hummingbirds' down tapping on the floor.
>
> Going up to the dais, she removed her veil. *It was Herodias as she used to be in her youth.* Then she began to dance.
>
> Her feet flashed to and fro, to the music of the flute and a pair of castanets. Her rounded arms seemed to be beckoning someone who was forever fleeing from her. She ran after him, lighter than a butterfly, like an inquisitive Psyche or a wandering soul, always apparently on the point of fluttering away.
>
> The castanets gave way to the funereal sound of the pipes: hope was followed by despondency. Her poses now suggested sighs, and her whole body was so languid that *one could not tell whether she was mourning for a god or expiring in his embrace.* ...
>
> Next the girl depicted the frenzy of love that demands satisfaction. She danced like the priestesses of the Indies, like the Nubian girls of the cataracts, like the bacchantes of Lydia. ... And the nomads inured to abstinence, the Roman soldiers skilled in debauchery, the avaricious publicans, and the old priests soured by controversy all sat there with their nostrils distended with desire.
>
> (Flaubert 1965, 120–21, emphasis added)

Much might be made of those nostrils. But the two italicised phrases also speak to Wilde's version of the story with its emphasis on the fatality of desire and the tragedy of Salome (which is, in part, that she has become *like* her mother, which is every woman's tragedy, as Algernon Moncrieff says in *The Importance of Being Earnest*). But it is also worth noting that the dance as Flaubert depicts it offers no fulfilment of the desire that the dance both dramatises and provokes. Wilde certainly knew Flaubert's story—among the many comments that were made about his play, there were several reviewers who noted that his *Salome* owed much to a series of French masters including *the* French master. The unsigned review in the *Pall Mall Gazette* for 27 February 1893 noted:

> *Salomé* is a mosaic. Mr. Wilde has many masters, and the influence of each master asserts itself in his pages as stripes of different colours assert themselves in stuffs from the East. The reader of *Salomé* seems to stand in the Island of Voices and to hear around him … the utterances of friends, the whisperings of demigods. Now it is the voice of Gautier, painting pictures in words of princesses and jewels and flowers and unguents. Anon it is Maeterlinck who speaks … The chorus seems to be swelled by the speech like silver of Anatole France, perchance by the speech of gold of Marcel Schwob. But the voices that breathe life into *Salomé* are dominated by one voice, the voice of Flaubert. If Flaubert had not written *Salammbô*, if Flaubert had not written *La Tentation de Saint Antoine* – above all, if Flaubert had not written *Hérodias*, *Salomé* might boast an originality to which she cannot now lay claim. She is the daughter of many fathers. She is the victim of heredity. Her bones want strength, her flesh wants vitality, her blood is polluted. There is no pulse of passion in her.
>
> (Beckson, 135–36)

I have quoted this at length because it combines a range of interesting features. It is itself almost parodic of Wilde's style and the overblown rhetoric in his play, and it neatly identifies some of Wilde's key sources. Mosaic is exactly the right metaphor for a play that draws, with orientalist relish, on the artistic traditions of the Middle East. And it skewers Wilde's pretensions in a thinly veiled accusation of plagiarism combined with the fairly vicious implication that his is a degenerate art—which pretty much covers the consistent commentaries that Wilde suffered throughout his career.

While this reviewer is right to identify Flaubert as the key source, he is wrong to suggest that Wilde brings nothing new to the story. Where in Flaubert's story the dance itself is rendered in sumptuous detail as we have seen, Wilde's play notoriously reduces the stage direction to almost nothing. His description reads in its totality: "*Salome dances the dance of the seven veils*" (Wilde 1994, 600). He expected his readers and audiences to know his source in Flaubert—one does not compete with the master, and why rewrite it? Additionally, the imagination may be more important to the written version of the play, particularly because the object of desire is very much in the eye—or the mind's eye—of the beholder. But there is something new. What Wilde brings to the story that the other written versions do not is that his Salome is not herself a sexual innocent, unaware of her own attractions: he was also drawing inspiration from the pictorial art of his period as another source for his mosaic. Wilde's Salome acts from her own desires and fantasies not simply at the behest of her mother, as in Flaubert's narrative, where "There was a snapping of fingers from the balcony ..." (Flaubert 1965, 122). Herodias has called Salome to her to instruct her to ask for John the Baptist's head and so empty-headed and childish is she that she even forgets his name: Salome as Bimbo. In Wilde's version however, Salome explicitly states when challenged about her demand for John's head: "I do not heed my mother. It is for mine own pleasure that I ask the head of Jokanaan in a silver charger" (Wilde 1994, 600). Wilde's intervention transforms the story from one about the abuse of power by the older generation over the younger to one that focuses on the rapaciousness of desire for its own sake. In this play, everyone always wants more than they actually have, and there are no adequate words to define desire, which is always displaced on to objects and others. Desire can neither be satisfied nor expressed—Freud and Lacan on the one hand, Marx and Lyotard on the other. It circulates but it has no appropriate outlet and it is never, can never be, sated.

The world Wilde reimagines as the locus of John the Baptist's martyrdom is one in which the standard rules of everyday reality do not apply, whether these are rules of linguistic propriety or sexual continence/reticence. It opens with an encounter between two young men, a young Syrian and the Page of Herodias:

> Young Syrian: How beautiful is the Princess Salome tonight!
>
> Page of Herodias: Look at the moon! How strange the moon seems! She is like a woman rising from a tomb. She is like a dead woman. You would fancy she was looking for dead things.
>
> Young Syrian: She has a strange look. She is like a little princess who wears a yellow veil and whose feet are of silver. She is like a princess who has little white doves for feet. You would fancy she was dancing.
>
> Page: She is like a woman who is dead. She moves very slowly ...
>
> (Wilde 1994, 583)

There is clearly a wilful confusion of the "shes" to whom the pronoun might refer (a confusion which is even stronger in the original French in which Wilde wrote the play where there is no gender neutral "it" to replace a feminine-seeming "she"). The signified for the word "she" is in the eye of the beholder, and in a masculine libidinal economy, it is often through the eye that desire is provoked: the male gaze can be fatal. For the Page, all this looking at Salome is risky—just as nice girls shouldn't look on goblin men, nice boys should neither look nor touch when the object in question is a princess: "You must not look at her," he repeats. "Something terrible may happen." "It is dangerous to look at people in such a fashion" (584). Nothing, however, stops the Syrian from ogling, and as he looks he defines

Salome in similes that focus on her whiteness, barren symbol of her purity. These are similes on the whole that belong to a clichéd poetic repertoire, and are highly conventional: "She is like the shadow of a white rose in a mirror of silver ... Her little white hands are fluttering like doves. They are like white butterflies ... She is like a dove that has strayed ... she is like a narcissus trembling in the wind ... She is like a silver flower" (584; 585). And, of course, she is like the moon—that over-determined contradictory symbol of feminine purity (Diana the huntress), apocalypse (when the moon turns to blood), and of the less attractive feminine markers of menstruation and lunacy.

The Syrian is not alone in his obsessive looking. When Salome leaves the feast for a breath of fresh air, she asks herself: "Why does the Tetrarch look at me all the while with his mole's eyes under his shaking eyelids? It is strange that the husband of my mother looks at me like that. I know not what it means. Of a truth, I know it too well" (586). She is just beginning to understand her own sexual potency—she realises for the first time the effects *her looks* have on a certain kind of man. That power remains so long as she maintains a *noli me tangere* attitude. The king can look when he commands then begs her to dance, but he can't touch. So long as she is the object of desires rather than desiring subject, all is so very normal, maintaining the standard set up of heteronormative values where feminine sexuality is figured as object. When, however, Salome *looks back*, in a very different exchange of glances, and becomes herself a desiring subject, all hell breaks loose.

And when the Tetrarch leaves the feast, he too by implication makes the connection between the moon and his stepdaughter. It is a compelling image of her less as virginal and pure and considerably closer to the femme fatale:

> The moon has a strange look tonight. Has she not a strange look? She is like a mad woman, a mad woman who is seeking everywhere for lovers. She is naked too. She is quite naked ... She shows herself naked in the sky. She reels through the clouds like a drunken woman. Does she not reel like a drunken woman? She is like a mad woman, is she not?

Herodias's response to this rhetorical question is telling. She is mindful of the common-sense world of reality and retorts: "No. The moon is like the moon, that is all" (Wilde 1994, 592). Even Salome herself is moonstruck. When she enters the scene she implicitly also makes the connection between her own selfhood and the moon through her repetitious echoes of the metaphors that have already been used by others.

> How good to see the moon! She is like a little piece of money, a little silver flower. She is cold and chaste. I am sure she is a virgin. She has the beauty of the virgin. Yes, she is a virgin. She has never defiled herself. She has never abandoned herself to men, like the other goddesses. (586)

The most interesting simile here, though, is the one that has not been spoken before: that the moon is like a silver coin because in this context it speaks rather precisely to both libido and economy. Salome has come to realise that the attractiveness that lures others to her charms has economic value, as Herod puts it, "even unto half of my kingdom" (599). In the end she will reject all that he can offer her of value—whether it is jewellery, land, or an item of religious significance like the veil from the temple, for desire is the excess which capitalism cannot contain, even as it also tries to subsume it into its own systems of exchange value. It appears to be a childish simile, but its acquisitiveness speaks of the desire to possess and a perverse sexual economy in which possession is all.

There are several points to be made about this series of interpretations of the moon. In a play that disrupts any notion of a fixed point of view from which intelligent judgement can be made, no single person is able to interpret the world. The moon becomes a solipsistic signifier, representing what each person sees in it, which is a measure of their personality and their own desires: "The highest, as the lowest, form of criticism is a mode of autobiography," as the Preface to *Dorian Gray* puts it (Wilde 1994, 17), and in defence of that novel, he argued that if readers saw evidence of perversity in his text, it was because they themselves were perverse. The young Syrian associates the moon with an idealised vision of Salome for whom he had an unrequited passion—so he sees the moon as a beautiful and virginal young woman. The Page, whose own love for the Syrian is threatened by this interpretation, sees the moon as a fatal or dead woman, a *femme fatale* whose significance is deadly. Salome sees the moon as cold, virginal, and chaste, a goddess whose sexual powers have not yet been awakened—but in the very moment of noting the moon's purity she also signals that this is not a state that will persist. Herod, the dissolute and incestuous monarch, sees a drunken naked woman in the moon—the sign of his own depraved sexuality and symptom of his impotent guilt. Only Herodias, the great survivor, sees just the moon. Each of them is locked into his or her own subjectivity. Even the richest of language cannot communicate because no one is really listening.

I have argued elsewhere that one typically Wildean trait, which reaches its apotheosis in *Earnest*, is language's intransitivity: its inability to define the world and to have an effect on it. Only the most naive characters in Wilde's works believe in linguistic potency. Thus Jack Worthing is the only character in *Earnest* to obey the various commands that come his way. He is the one who stops eating muffins on command, and does as he is told. This is a sign not of his decency but of his stupidity. In *Salome*, by the same token, commands produce no action. Salome herself has to use her wiles to get someone to obey her in bringing Jokanaan to her. In turn she is profoundly disobedient to her king, refusing wine, fruit, and the pleasure of the dance until it suits her whim. His demands of her are perverse and incestuous. She mirrors that perversion in her demand of him—that she be brought the head of the prophet on a silver charger. The perversion of the communicative functions of language mirrors the perversions of other forms of human behaviour in the play. For instance, it mirrors the reduction of religion to a series of pointless arguments about the existence or otherwise of angels, rather than acting as a code for ethical action. Most significant of all, though, human sexuality is itself rendered utterly perverse through desires that have no outlet. No relationship is fulfilling, leaving everyone wanting something and always wanting more.

There is, for instance, only one consummated heterosexual relationship in the play, and that is in itself perverse, for it is both sterile (Herod and Herodias have no children, which is a point of contention between them) and it is incestuous, since Herodias was the wife of Herod's brother before she married the Tetrarch. The Page of Herodias loves the Syrian soldier, and thus breaks the heteronormative code. The Syrian loves the princess, in defiance of his lowly status. Herod lusts (again incestuously) after his step-daughter; and Salome desires Jokanaan, despite his refusal of her charms and multiple declarations of purity and sexual disgust. Salome achieves her consummation only through necrophilia when she kisses Jokanaan's decapitated head. This is a world of polymorphous perversity in which desire is always for that which is forbidden, and in which desire is also displaced into a largely useless non-functional language which has aesthetic force but not real force. ("All art is quite useless," Wilde writes in the Preface to *Dorian Gray* [Wilde 1994, 19].) And because it has no possible outlet into consummation, *Salome* articulates desire as violence. The Syrian's desire for Salome becomes his own death wish; he sees her desire for another and kills himself. Salome's desire for Jokanaan is a will towards possession, and turns him into an object that cannot resist her rather than a subject who can. This in turn is mirrored by Herod's desire for Salome which becomes his chilling final command in the play: "Kill that woman!" when he sees her kissing the dead mouth of the prophet. Her status as a desiring subject simply has to be stopped.

Wilde was never one for calling a spade a spade. "The man who does so should be condemned to use one," he wrote in a letter to a local council official (Ellmann 347). And *Earnest* has a rather good joke on the same theme in the hostile exchanges between Gwendolen and Cicely over a very fraught tea-table.[5] There is very obvious comedy to be had from the failure of language to function. The elegant periphrases of the drawing room comedies have their counterpoint in the overblown rhetoric of Wilde's exotic play. Words and things, and words and people, don't exactly match up. Blasphemously perhaps, even Jokanaan, born to bring the Word of God, is depicted speaking a language that many of his hearers claim not to understand, though this could be a tactful refusal on their part, since the prophet speaks of the Tetrarch, his wife and his stepdaughter in frankly unflattering terms, and Salome at least recognises when "it is my mother of whom he speaks" (Wilde 1994, 588). Her own language when she comes to speak of her desire for the prophet veers—just as Cecily's and Gwendolen's does—between attraction and outright hostility, as Jokanaan rejects in turn each of her approaches.

Salome can only achieve her ends—her "Climax" as Beardsley titled it in one of his illustrations—when the object of her desire has literally become an object. At the end of the play she expresses her triumph that Jokanaan, now dead, can no longer reject her advances: "Thou wouldst not suffer me to kiss thy mouth Jokanaan! Well! I kiss it now. I will bite with my teeth as one bites a ripe fruit" (604). Her desire is rapacious and even cannibalistic— savage, not civilised. But as she continues to address the severed head, the full horror of her position becomes clearer, even to her. Her existence has been constructed through the looks of others; the way she looks and the looks she forces from others confirm her power. Jokanaan, being dead, cannot recip- rocate the look, and so she learns that in the end her triumph is empty, her climax is fake, her desire unrequited: "Ah, wherefore didst thou not look at me, Jokanaan? If thou hadst looked at me thou hadst loved me" (604).

In the end the play does dramatise a typical Wildean perspective—that desire is always dangerous. There is no adequate language to express it, so that to some extent all loves are the loves that dare not speak their name, especially in cultures which veer between decadent licentiousness and an exaggerated respect for chastity, like the biblical world, but like the Victorian world, too. Desire exists but does not circulate, for the way that it is conceived is based on a capitalist version of the libidinal economy where possession and ownership are its proxies. These are cultures which, Wilde implies, have not yet imagined desire as the complex negotiation between equal subjectivities.

Notes

1. Disapproval was not based on health concerns so much as on moral ones. Tobacco meant self-indulgence, and occasionally also bad manners. In advice and conduct books of the later nineteenth century smoking is often noted as a particularly bad habit for women to get into. One example comes from J. H. Kellogg's *The Ladies' Guide* (1891), selected as an example because it is almost exactly contemporary with Wilde's play. Kellogg's views on tea, coffee and tobacco were that a person who used any of these products as a stimulant "was as bad a man from the point of view of temperance as one who drank to excess or who took narcotics" (Kellogg 1891, 218).

2. This point is explored in detail in Lawrence Birkin (1989) *Consuming Desire: Sexual Science and the Emergence of a Culture of Abundance, 1871–1914*. It is also investigated via the exploration of nineteenth-century pornographic cul- tures by Ronald Pearsall (1969) *The Worm in the Bud: The World of Victorian Sexuality*. In pornography the connection between people and objects (the pro- cess of mistaking the one for the other) is particularly forceful and uncomfort- able, and is especially focused on the cash nexus. The circulation of desire in this context is contingent on the circulation of money.

3. In literature, Flaubert's story "Hérodias" (*Trois Contes*, 1877; translated as *Three Tales*) is one of the origins of the late nineteenth-century's fascination with the figure of Salome. In his story, the dancing girl is a cipher who merely obeys her mother's orders as she dances for an excited audience of men at the court of Herod Antipas.

The theme was later picked up in Stéphane Mallarmé's poem "Hérodiade" (1887, in *Poésies*). Flaubert's narrative is almost certainly the inspiration for one of the more astonishing passages of George Egerton's short fiction. In her story "A Cross Line" (*Keynotes*, 1893) the protagonist has a fantasy in which she plays the role of Salome before an enthralled audience of men. It is, however, in the visual arts that Salome had most impact, as Djikstra's *Idols of Perversity* documents. There were paintings by Gustave Moreau (*Salome and the Apparition of John the Baptist's Head*, 1870; *Salome Carrying the Head of John the Baptist*, 1876); by Henri Régnault (*Salome*, 1870); by Pierre Bonneaud (*Salome*, c. 1900); by Jean Benner (*Salome* 1899); by Franz von Struck (*Salome*, 1906); Leon Herbo (*Salome*, 1889); by Alphonse Mucha (*Salome*, 1897); by Gustav Klimt (*Salome*, 1909). The list goes on.

4. The biblical version of this story makes no reference at all to the specifics of Salome's dance:

> Herod on his birthday made a supper to his lords ... and when the daughter of the said Herodias came in, and danced, and pleased Herod and them that sat with him, the king said unto the damsel, Ask of me whatsoever thou wilt, I will give it to thee, unto the half of my kingdom. And she went forth, and said unto her mother, What shall I ask? And she said, The head of John the Baptist. And she came in straightway with haste unto the king, and asked, saying, I will that thou give me by and by in a charger the head of John the Baptist. And the king was exceeding sorry; yet for his oath's sake, and for their sakes which sat with him, he would not reject her. And immediately the king sent an executioner, and commanded his head to be brought: and he went and beheaded him in the prison, and brought his head in a charger, and gave it to the damsel: and the damsel gave it to her mother.
>
> (Mark 6, 21–8)

5. Provoked by Gwendolen over their rivalry for the affections of the entirely ficti-tious Ernest, Cecily is betrayed into straight talking: "When I see a spade I call it a spade" she declares, earning Gwendolen's magisterial rebuke: "I am quite glad to say that I have never seen a spade. It is obvious that our social spheres have been widely different" (Wilde 1994, 399).

Works Cited

Beckson, Karl, ed. 1971, *Oscar Wilde: The Critical Heritage*. London and New York: RKP.

Bennett, Michael Y. 2011. *Refiguring Oscar Wilde's Salome*. Amsterdam, Rodopi.

Birkin, Lawrence. 1989. *Consuming Desire: Sexual Science and the Emergence of a Culture of Abundance, 1871–1914*. Ithaca: Cornell University Press.

Djikstra, Bram. 1989. *Idols of Perversity: Fantasies of Feminine Evil in Fin-de-Siècle Culture*. New York: Oxford University Press.

Ellmann, Richard. 1988. *Oscar Wilde*. Harmondsworth: Penguin.

Flaubert, Gustave. 1877; 1965. *Three Tales*. Translated by Robert Baldick. Harmond-sworth: Penguin.

Foucault, Michel. 1990. *The History of Sexuality*. Volume I, *An Introduction*. Translated by Robert Hurley. London: Vintage.

Gagnier, Regenia. 1987. *Idylls of the Marketplace: Oscar Wilde and the Victorian Public*. Aldershot: Scolar Press.

Guy, Josephine M., and Ian Small. 2000. *Oscar Wilde's Profession: Writing and the Culture Industry in the Late Nineteenth Century.* Oxford: Oxford University Press.

Holland, Merlin, and Rupert Hart-Davies, eds. 2000. *The Complete Letters of Oscar Wilde.* London: Fourth Estate Press.

Jevons, William Stanley. 1871; 3rd Edition 1888. *The Theory of Political Economy.* London: Macmillan and Co. Internet: The Library of Economics and Liberty, available at: http://www.econlib.org/library/YPDBooks/Jevons/jvnPECover.html; accessed 11 December 2014.

Kellogg, J. H. 1891. *The Ladies' Guide in Health and Disease: Girlhood, Maidenhood, Wifehood, Motherhood,* Battle Creek, Michigan: Good Health Publishing. Reprinted in Ruth Robbins (ed.) (2009) *Medical Advice For Women, 1830–1915,* 5 volumes, Volume III, London and New York: Routledge.

Lyotard, Jean-François. 2004. *Libidinal Economy.* Translated by Iain Hamilton-Grant. London: Continuum.

Mendelsohn, Michèle. 2007. *Henry James, Oscar Wilde and Aesthetic Culture.* Edinburgh: EUP.

Pearsall, Ronald. 1969. *The Worm in the Bud: The World of Victorian Sexuality.* London: Macmillan.

Praz, Mario. 1933; 1970. *The Romantic Agony.* Translated by A. Davidson. Oxford: Oxford Paperbacks.

Robbins, Ruth. 2011. *Oscar Wilde.* London: Continuum.

Russ, Andrew R. 2011. "Wilde's *Salome*: The Chastity, Promiscuity and Monstrosity of Symbols." *Refiguring Oscar Wilde's Salome,* edited by Michael Y. Bennett, 37–54. Amsterdam: Rodopi.

Wilde, Oscar. 1994. *The Complete Works of Oscar Wilde.* Edited by Merlin Holland. Glasgow: HarperCollins.

2   A. E. Housman's Ballad Economies

Veronica Alfano

1. Ballads, Brevity, and Amnesiac Nostalgia

A. E. Housman published his first volume of verse in 1896 and his second in 1922; the former (*A Shropshire Lad*) appears at first glance to have little more than its ballad-like forms in common with the self-consciously avant-garde work of the best-known decadent poets, while the latter (*Last Poems*) does not reflect stylistic development and shows no sign of having been published in the same year as *The Waste Land*. Their author's historical individuality may therefore seem indeterminate and even immaterial, as he does not embody the aesthetics most frequently associated with high Victorianism or the *fin de siècle* or early modernism. Housman himself, a classical scholar who was largely uninterested in joining contemporary bohemian coteries, was well aware of his ambiguously ahistorical status. In a 1928 letter to his publisher Grant Richards, he declined an offer to reprint his work in *A Book of Nineties Verse*: "to include me in an anthology of the Nineties would be just as technically correct, and just as essentially inappropriate, as to include Lot in a book on Sodomites; in saying which I am not saying a word against sodomy" (qtd. in Maas 1971, 271). And he had similar feelings about being selected for *Georgian Poetry 1911–1912*, informing its editor that "I do not really belong to your 'new era'" (qtd. in Maas 1971, 125).[1] Short and discontinuous, repetitive and restrained, Housman's poems occupy a space outside both the discursive prolixity of much Victorian narrative verse and the polyvocal open-endedness of much twentieth-century poetry.

In part by consistently favouring variations on the tetrameter and/or trimeter *abcb* ballad quatrain, Housman practices what I will call "ballad economy": that is, a tendency to adhere to strict formal constraints, to use iterative and monosyllabic diction, to produce brief poems, and to derive from this laconic approach an aesthetic of meticulous understatement. I will argue that this form-based economy both generates and disguises the subtle homoeroticism of Housman's poetry, which mourns and praises athletes, soldiers, and other young men. Additionally, I will show that the way in which the small and reticent verses of *A Shropshire Lad* circulate widely as affordable pocket editions, revealing another dimension of the term "ballad economy," ironically serves to counteract the inhibiting effects of Housman's style.

The apparent impersonality and atemporality of Housman's poems is bound up with their staying power; the fact that their author's life and circumstances seem irrelevant underscores the familiar-sounding quality that helps these conventional little poems appeal to the memory. Yet *A Shropshire Lad*'s brief ballad forms (which, while extremely mnemonic, are often so similar that they are difficult to distinguish in retrospect), along with its nostalgic themes (many of Housman's speakers are irretrievably distant from that which they recall), ultimately highlight the inextricability of remembering and forgetting. Considering the role of amnesia in *A Shropshire Lad*, I ask how the poet's thwarted attempts to commemorate the dead elucidate his depictions of same-sex desire. Such desire lies behind Housman's refusal to grant either lads or ballads clearly-defined particularity, his focus on exile and bereavement and regret, his tactic of using condensed and predictable stanzas to curb his speakers' passions and confessions, and his proclivity for keeping those speakers' nostalgic yearnings profoundly nebulous.

In the late nineteenth century, homosexual identity took definition from studies such as Richard von Krafft-Ebing's *Psychopathia Sexualis* (1886), which introduced the term "sexual inversion" to describe same-sex desire. Sexual inversion was categorised as an abnormality or perversion (in fact, homosexuality was not removed from the *Diagnostic and Statistical Manual of Mental Disorders* until 1974). The Order of Chaeronea, an organisation for gay men and women that was founded in 1893 and to which Housman's brother Laurence belonged, tended to refer vaguely to "the Cause" and was of necessity a secret society. Housman himself, whose beloved college friend Moses Jackson rebuffed his romantic advances, remained closeted all his life. Housman depicts Jackson's rejection in poems such as the one beginning "Because I liked you better / Than suits a man to say" (*More Poems*, XXXI).[2] Though Housman suppressed "Because I liked you better" during his lifetime, he took steps to ensure that his sexual identity would be better understood after his death. In his will, he gave Laurence permission to publish this poem, along with other selections from his notebooks (a process that resulted in *More Poems* and *Additional Poems*); several of these lyrics are overtly concerned with homosexuality. Critical interest in Housman increased after the 1967 publication of Laurence's "A. E. Housman's 'De Amicitia,'" an essay that discusses the poet's relationship with Jackson and that had been kept sealed in the British Library for 25 years. Though quite a few scholars touch on Housman's use of repetitive ballad forms, and many of late have observed that his status as a gay writer motivates the sorrows and frustrations of his poetry, few link the two areas of inquiry.[3] This chapter, then, performs just such a synthesis through its attention to amnesiac remembrance.

From one point of view, Housman's ballad economy—the brevity and repetitiveness that stem from his frequent use of balladic stanzas—supports his penchant for self-occlusion.[4] He painstakingly curtails, conceals, and generalises his desires through the familiar forms of his poems; indeed, one significant effect of his devotion to lyrical smallness is its tendency to short-circuit emotional expression. Housman undercuts hysteria and deflates tragic fervor, even as he disallows large-scale plots and earnest confessions, by keeping most of his poems under a page in length. Anti-sentimental brevity functions as self-censorship, especially because the poet will not risk self-exposure by letting his gaze linger too long on any one lad. Instead, he repeats similarly truncated descriptions of these doomed young men. His decorous stanzas contract in self-defense as if to seal off interpretive footholds, refusing to open themselves to volubility and concluding before they lose control. There is a gently ironic anticlimax, for instance, in "Loveliest of trees, the cherry now" (*A Shropshire Lad*, II): facing his own mortality, this speaker does not sink into overwrought despair but simply resolves to look about the woodlands at "the cherry hung with snow."[5] Housman's propensity for miniaturising and universalising his poems stems in part from a compulsion to interrupt his speakers before they indulge in excessive self-revelation.

In the process, Housman forces sorrow and regret into an orderly framework, at times stylising them with archaic diction and Latinate syntactical compression ("thews that lie and cumber / Sunlit pallets never thrive" ["Reveille," IV]). Passion is carefully suppressed and half-forgotten in iterative lyrics that privilege conventional formal patterns over particularising details. "Horror and scorn and hate and fear and indignation" (XLVIII) are rattled off but not explicitly motivated, while expansive first-person speech ("Oh, when I was in love with you") mixes with sententious third-person truisms ("If young hearts were not so clever, / Oh, they would be young for ever"). The putative protagonist of *A Shropshire Lad*, Terence Hearsay, does not acquire a rounded personality—and Housman's lyric voice is in fact more choric than individual as it retreats into the generalising tone of aphorism, guarding against the jeopardies of open-hearted utterance. The opening poem of *A Shropshire Lad* sets the tone when it favours collective recollection ("Lads, *we'll* remember"; emphasis mine) over the reminiscences of a single speaker.

Many of Housman's stark, striking lines and stanzas are eminently quotable and memorisable. Regular rhythms, orthodox rhymes, frequent alliteration, and the occasional refrain function as patterned memory-aids. What's more, the pastoral themes and balladic stanzas of *A Shropshire Lad* are deeply imbued with nostalgia—and by placing his poetry within the ballad tradition, orienting it toward the broadly-conceived literary past rather than experimenting with new verse forms or directly addressing topical issues or creating idiosyncratic speakers, Housman shores up its formal and cultural memorability.[6] His poems are durable precisely because they are determinedly belated and thus highly recognisable and categorisable, in a sense already known, populated largely by stock characters and containing few extraneous details that clearly tie them to a specific period. They give the impression that they can be unmoored from the circumstances of their composition, linked to other well-known works, seen as both vaguely outdated and timeless. So Housman's iteratively predictable, compact, impersonal, unelaborated, and, therefore, memorable lyrics come to stand in for his audience's mental life. Each reader can lay claim to the sentiments and sub-jects of *A Shropshire Lad*, fitting them to their private experience.[7] It is apt, then, that the nostalgia depicted in Housman's poems is often undefined and generalised and forgetful. It is directed toward places and times that seem impossibly distant and indeterminate. In his evocations of Shropshire, the poet both recalls and deliberately fails to recall the past. "What are those blue remembered hills, / What spires, what farms are those?" (XL). He looks back on a dimly inaccessible realm that is intimately familiar yet strangely alien, "both memory and fantasy," associated with lost happiness or haunt-ing pain but never coming into focus (Scott-Kilvert 1955, 9).[8] So as this volume recollects other verses and days gone by, shoring up its mnemonic qualities in the process, it allows readers to summon a long-ago time of their own choosing. Pastoral Shropshire, with its lads and lasses, encompasses everyone's illusory desires for a simpler way of life or for a romanticised youth. It is stubbornly remote and non-particular because it never existed, uninhabitable because it never was inhabited. As a generic no-place heavily influenced by other texts, it is an ideal forum for non-confessional intimacy.

Accordingly, ballad economy further shields Housman by making his forbidden thoughts—which are frequently unattached to an identifiable time or place or speaker—part of a shared literary tradition and so already part of each reader's memory or consciousness. These poems attempt to avoid attracting excessive scrutiny or disturbing the reader's equanimity. Indeed, the introductory verse to Housman's posthumous *More Poems* positions itself within a long history of pain by speaking of "sorrow / Not mine, but man's" (Housman 2004, 113). Crucially, relying on well-worn themes and prefabricated forms and recognisable intertextual echoes diminishes the strange, shameful, or illicit qualities of his speakers' fears and desires. In the context of the poet's sexuality, the universalised and unfocused nature of his descriptions—particularly when coupled with the formal memorisability that may prompt us to misremember his decep-tively simple and easily-internalised lyrics by overlooking their erotic aspects—becomes a distortion or distraction or disguise. The intense libid-inal energy of *A Shropshire Lad*, is tamped down by the austerity of its ballad forms.[9]

The way in which readers remember and forget this volume, it seems, allows for a revaluation of the way in which its treatment of memory and of memory's failures can be read through the lens of homoerotic desire. As I have established, impersonal little lyrics are often easy to get by heart. But because techniques that aid memorability (brevity, allusiveness, repetition) also tend to prevent revelatory outpouring, one who memorises Housman's poems also internalises the experience of amnesia and the fact of forgetta-bility. She encounters many similarly unobtrusive lyrics and similarly anon-ymous speakers, and her struggles to make distinctions among them echo these speakers' estrangement both from their own emotional lives and from the half-recalled pasts that they seek to capture or crystallise in small poems.

Nicholas Dames posits that Victorian novels deliberately employ amnesia, forgetting some aspects of the past in order to lend their plots a teleological trajectory; I adapt this theory of "nostalgic forgetting" for Victorian poetry.[10] A lyric's strategic failures to recall do not necessarily produce cohesive narrative temporality or locate an individualised speaker in a stable and specific context. Its amnesia may remain determinedly non-cumulative, leaving both past and present shadowy and cryptic. With its penchant for obsessively recalling disparate or nebulous images in symmetrical stanzas, it will not always privilege crucial details over peripheral ones. Its brevity and its inertial repetitive patterns may fragment and distort what it apparently tries to safeguard or commemorate, yielding disorienting lacunae. Both Housman's ballad economy and his speakers' vague nostalgia demonstrate that impercipient recollection threatens to undermine the elegiac project of *A Shropshire Lad*, which sinks into forgetfulness despite its efforts to remember the longed-for past and the beloved dead. Housman's poems, fixating on individuals who quickly fade into typicality, are unable to differentiate those whom they memorialise; this amnesiac nostalgia applies not only to specific people and to days gone by but also to particular poems. A host of fatalistic little ballads, like a multitude of short-lived lads, resists our endeavors to distinguish single verses or single lives. Declining to function as personal plaints or to honour identifiable men, these ballads attempt to minimise their libidinal content.

Yet *A Shropshire Lad* also authorises and discloses the very urges that it strives to conceal.[11] Why would a taciturn 37-year-old don choose to publish a book of plaintive poems about young men if his aim was only to censor himself? In writing verse that hides shameful thoughts, he is also revealing those thoughts – and making them more shameful in so doing. The over-affectionate speaker of "Because I liked you better / Than suits a man to say" agrees to "throw the thought away" after his companion demands "forget me" (*More Poems*, XXXI). But the fact that he continues to dwell on the incident shows that he cannot blot that thought from his mind, and Housman's posthumously-published poem guarantees that it lives on in the minds of others as well. (As I point out later in this chapter, there are erotic overtones to publishing and circulating even heavily-coded poems of same-sex love.) Housman's attempts to forget both hinder and heighten taboo desire; just so, an aesthetic of exaggerated self-withholding creates a forum for understated self-expression. Housman captures this paradox when he compares his compositional process to an involuntary "morbid secretion," like an oyster forming a pearl (1933, 48).[12] Though this focus on unwilled instinctiveness is likely meant to guard against psychological scrutiny of his work, the metaphor he chooses is perhaps more apt than he would have liked to admit. *A Shropshire Lad* consists of small, symmetrical, polished lyrics closed tightly around—and thus simultaneously relying on and concealing, simultaneously burying and preserving—a wound or flaw or unease. And Housman's description of unwilled secretion hints that this unease is sexual in nature.

"Because I liked you better" shows that the strategic *forgetting* of individual lads (along with other amnesiac omissions or refusals of specificity) can function for Housman like the *repression* of dangerous yearnings. And this being the case, his thwarted but incessant efforts to commemorate those lads and the insistently mnemonic nature of his echoic lyrics hint at the partial return of repressed feelings, which flicker in and out of focus like dim but persistent memories. He can, in the act of muting them, give voice to desires that might otherwise be unspeakable. Not so different from his late-century coevals in this regard after all, he appropriates familiar forms for transgressively nonconformist purposes. Highly recognisable tetrameter and trimeter quatrains provide a protective framework of formal restraint and conventionality within which Housman can express attenuated versions of unorthodox longings. His economical ballad forms, then, both impede and enable his self-fashioning.

Mnemonic allusiveness, which makes the personal into the commonplace, can cloak or discipline raw emotion. Again, because Housman's nostalgic lyrics often echo other poems both inside and outside *A Shropshire Lad* (examples of the latter include Shakespeare's songs and sonnets and the Border Ballads), they present themselves as half-forgotten recollections that dwell in a kind of collective literary unconscious rather than the utterances of a particular speaker. But Housman's special fondness for classical allusions—which underlies his pastoral nostalgia, his epigrammatic brevity (tellingly, this brevity echoes that of Sappho, whose work Housman knew well), and his elegiac tactic of broadening personal sadness over the loss of friends into sorrow over human mutability—encapsulates the manner in which his poetry both obscures and produces homoerotic content. When he praises a runner's strength and beauty in "To an Athlete Dying Young" (XIX), Housman may seem merely to be echoing Pindaric odes in his role as a student of the classics. A poet paying homage to distinguished forebears and honouring the literary past seems only natural and admirable; there appears to be nothing intimate or confessional about such learned references to the ancients. But even if one does not know that Moses Jackson was an accomplished athlete who excelled at rowing and running, the Hellenistic roots of Housman's poem also amplify its sexual implications by providing a durable historical precedent for socially-sanctioned love between men. Recalling Oxford Hellenism, aligning the late-Victorian world with that of Greek pastoral (Housman was at Oxford not long after the scandal that accompanied the publication of Walter Pater's *The Renaissance*, and his residence briefly overlapped with that of Oscar Wilde), these references give a carefully-coded local habitation and a name to their volume's vaguely wistful orientation toward the long-ago. Brian Reade captures both the belated classicism and the evasiveness of *A Shropshire Lad* when he compares it to "a beautiful ruin built over an invisible framework" (Reade 1970, 48). And as Archie Burnett puts it, allusion offers Housman "a way of breaking silence, a veil for disclosure, at once catering to reticence and facilitating expression"; because it "discreetly los[es] the particular present in the universal," it simultaneously dissociates

Housman from his poetic speakers and creates sympathetic links to other like-minded men (Burnett 2003, 151–53).[13] "Loitering with a vacant eye" (LI) illustrates this phenomenon by describing a displaced rustic and a Greek statue who are united in their troubled estrangement from their surroundings. I have observed that, in contrast to Dames's novelistic forgetting, Victorian lyric's imperfect or selective remembrance of the past does not necessarily illuminate a present self. Yet Housman's memory-based methods of withholding his personality in verse both suppress and divulge that personality.

Housman's accounts of the genesis of *A Shropshire Lad* reflect this same ambiguity. He defensively insists that Terence Hearsay is "an imaginary figure, with something of my temper and view of life. Very little in the book is biographical." And in a 1933 letter to Maurice Pollet, he claims that his pessimism (or, as he calls it, "pejorism") is due to "observation of the world, not to personal circumstances." He adds that "I did not begin to write poetry in earnest until the really emotional part of my life was over" (qtd. in Maas 1971, 328–29). Yet this emphasis on impersonal detachment contradicts Housman's earlier association of the book with overwhelming emotion. He wrote *A Shropshire Lad* in 1895, the same year as the Wilde trials; this historical connection may explain why, as he says in the preface to *Last Poems*, the volume was composed in a state of "continuous excitement." Housman also informs Jackson, in a 1922 letter, that "You are largely responsible for my writing poetry" (qtd. in Watson 1957, 211). Behind *A Shropshire Lad*'s ubiquitous anguish lies the memory of an impossible love affair, nostalgically recalled and frustratingly distant, replayed in verse that harps on gloomy themes and that makes romance synonymous with disappointment or death. Its doomed lads evoke the absent and inaccessible Jackson, who is symbolically lost or banished again and again—though these obsessive annihilations only highlight his unforgettable nature.[14] There is a sadomasochistic side to poems that seem to relish both recounting and enacting trauma. Unable to portray fulfilled desire, claims Peter Howarth, Housman takes a perversely compensatory pleasure in iterating unjust prohibition and punishment in exquisitely-crafted lines—a "grim enjoyment of painful endurance" that itself becomes a source of eroticised shame (Howarth 2009, 765; 772).[15] His art can never quite break free of social strictures to achieve a decadent state of self-justification. Yet in the very act of never speaking his heart, of underscoring his volume's socially-enforced omissions and renunciations, Housman proves his devotion to a hopeless cause.

In the preface to *Lyrical Ballads*, Wordsworth argues that metre is a double-edged sword. While "tempering and restraining the passion" like Tennyson's dull narcotics, it can also imbue even the simplest expressions with deeply-felt associations, and so "heighten and improve the pleasure" a reader takes in verse (Coleridge and Wordsworth 2008, 181; 180). Housman straddles this divide, using the economy of balladic form both to curb and to accentuate emotion. *A Shropshire Lad*, then, creates not only a closeted aesthetic but also a queer aesthetic.

2. We Cannot Stop to Tell: Ballad Economy in Action

This equivocal self-censorship is especially noticeable in poems of male affection and communion.

> Look not in my eyes, for fear
> They mirror true the sight I see,
> And there you find your face too clear
> And love it and be lost like me.
> One the long nights through must lie
> Spent in star-defeated sighs,
> But why should you as well as I
> Perish? gaze not in my eyes.
>
> A Grecian lad, as I hear tell,
> One that many loved in vain,
> Looked into a forest well
> And never looked away again.
> There, when the turf in springtime flowers,
> With downward eye and gazes sad,
> Stands amid the glancing showers
> A jonquil, not a Grecian lad.
> (*A Shropshire Lad*, XV)

"Look not in my eyes, for fear" avoids clarifying the connection between the genderless beloved addressed in its first eight lines and the "Grecian lad" described in its last eight lines; stanzaic division scrupulously separates these two entities and blocks erotic fulfillment. In fact, the lyric negates itself as it turns away from Hellenic beauty, converting "A Grecian lad" into the closing phrase "not a Grecian lad." An obtrusive enjambment ("why should you as well as I / Perish?") draws attention to Housman's use of ballad economy and shows the poem straining against the formal limitations its tetrameter imposes. It deceptively yet tantalisingly implies that this poem would say more in each line—that it would explain precisely why this love can never be, and what it has to do with Narcissus—if it could slip into a more-expansive pentameter. As it stands, it makes do with vague melancholy that recalls any number of star-crossed lovers with its "star-defeated sighs." And Housman further camouflages any hints of erotic self-revelation by ensuring that "Look not in my eyes, for fear" echoes comparable poems portraying the smitten gazes of heterosexual lovers.[16]

Likewise, "The street sounds to the soldiers' tread" (XXII) employs economical form to emphasise self-silencing.

> The street sounds to the soldiers' tread,
> And out we troop to see:
> A single redcoat turns his head,
> He turns and looks at me.

My man, from sky to sky's so far,
We never crossed before;
Such leagues apart the world's ends are,
We're like to meet no more;

What thoughts at heart have you and I
We cannot stop to tell;
But dead or living, drunk or dry,
Soldier, I wish you well.

A soldier and a spectator lock eyes and wonder about one another's "thoughts at heart," but partly because they have reached the final stanza of a small poem, they "cannot stop to tell." Housman keeps these men apart by having them run out of time on the page. Vaguely-sketched characters cannot be permitted to interact at length, as the lyric insists on turning an individual encounter into a generalised meditation on the occlusion of identity and the vastness of the world ("Such leagues apart the world's ends are / We're like to meet no more"). A moment of imagined connection may be preserved in the mind—but this memory encodes ineluctable separation and incognisance.

"Others, I am not the first" (XXX) encapsulates Housman's resolutely non-confessional style and explicitly demands that the speaking "I" be forgotten. When the poem is read in isolation, its reasons for doing so are not particularly clear. But juxtaposing it with the other texts considered in this chapter begins to elucidate the nature of its fears and desires.

Others, I am not the first,
Have willed more mischief than they durst:
If in the breathless night I too
Shiver now, 'tis nothing new.

More than I, if truth were told,
Have stood and sweated hot and cold,
And through their reins in ice and fire
Fear contended with desire.

Agued once like me were they,
But I like them shall win my way
Lastly to the bed of mould
Where there's neither heat nor cold.

But from my grave across my brow
Plays no wind of healing now,
And fire and ice within me fight
Beneath the suffocating night.

The second stanza's well-worn metaphor subsumes this speaker's physical sensations and restless anxieties to those of countless poets whose loves are like to ice, and they to fire. As the speaker dwells on mortality in an attempt to escape his own libidinal energies, assuring that the only bed he will occupy is a "bed of mould," so Housman uses textual memories to render private angst public and universal.[17] The ballad's formal dexterity—its elegantly clichéd iterations of "hot and cold," "ice and fire," "heat nor cold," "fire and ice"— is easier to remember than the undefined causes of this speaker's freezing, burning dread and longing. Individuals die while humanity marches on, just as particular verses blur together while their themes endure (this poem, for instance, bears a resemblance to "When I watch the living meet" [XII] and "We for a certainty are not the first" [*Last Poems,* IX]).

Despite the impression of straightforward lucidity that his neat little verses often convey, then, lyric's intimate impersonality allows Housman to dull and distance his sentiments. As "When I was one-and-twenty" (*A Shropshire Lad*, XIII) advises, he does not give his heart away. This need for self-protection helps explain why, even after a generation and a world war, he neither adjusts his style nor produces more substantial forms. But discursive pentameter, in spite of what "Look not in my eyes" hints, is not the only path to poetic self-figuring. The constrained austerity and prominent lacunae of these and other *Shropshire Lad* poems inevitably prompt readers to wonder what drives their emotional states and what details they are leaving out. In *Biographia Literaria*, Coleridge links poetry to a "more than usual state of emotion, with more than usual order" (2010, 807); indeed, as Housman uses formal control to hold his speakers in check and shun self-exposure, the very excess of his restraint hints at the intensity of his taboo feelings.

"Shot? so quick, so clean an ending?" (XLIV), for instance, addresses a young man who has killed himself in order to avoid committing an unnamed transgression:

> Shot? so quick, so clean an ending?
> Oh that was right, lad, that was brave:
> Yours was not an ill for mending,
> 'Twas best to take it to the grave.
>
> Oh you had forethought, you could reason,
> And saw your road and where it led,
> And early wise and brave in season
> Put the pistol to your head.
>
> Oh soon, and better so than later
> After long disgrace and scorn,
> You shot dead the household traitor,
> The soul that should not have been born.
>
> Right you guessed the rising morrow
> And scorned to tread the mire you must:
> Dust's your wages, son of sorrow,
> But men may come to worse than dust.

Souls undone, undoing others,
Long time since the tale began.
You would not live to wrong your brothers:
Oh lad, you died as fits a man.

Now to your grave shall friend and stranger
With ruth and some with envy come:
Undishonoured, clear of danger,
Clean of guilt, pass hence and home.

Turn safe to rest, no dreams, no waking;
And here, man, here's the wreath I've made:
'Tis not a gift that's worth the taking,
But wear it and it will not fade.

A Shropshire Lad admires speedy actions, decisive finality, hasty terminations that produce short and unsullied existences: "Shot? so quick, so clean an ending?" echoes "Quick then, while your day's at prime" (XXIV); "Take my hand quick and tell me" (XXXII); "play the man, stand up and end you" (XLV); "take the bullet in your brain" (LVI). Housman treasures a flower that "has not long to stay" ("The Lent Lily" [XXIX]) and proposes that the soldier who dies first is grieved for longest ("The Day of Battle" [LVI]). "In Shot?," he seems to hint that both the self-slain lad and the mnemonic verse commemorating him will become immortal ("here's the wreath I've made … wear it and it will not fade"). But being whole and sound saves neither short-lived lad nor short lyric. "[I]t will not fade," the poem's last phrase, undercuts its own gnomic confidence by fading into silence. And the young man's only individuating act, after all, is to snuff out his selfhood. Housman memorialises the suicide while omitting particularising details. His unfocused elegy is easily confused with similar lyrics elsewhere in *A Shropshire Lad*; in fact, with its seven quatrains and its wreath imagery, it resembles "To an Athlete Dying Young."[18]

But "Shot? so quick, so clean an ending?" has a very specific and deeply-felt motive behind its conspicuous turn away from individual commemoration. This poem was inspired by an August 1895 newspaper article about the suicide of Henry Clarkson Maclean, a cadet at the Royal Military Academy. Housman deduced that this young man, who killed himself in the same year as the Wilde trials, was gay. Ironically, it is only by maintaining a sufficiently calm and detached tone that the poet can safely offer an intimate apostrophe to Maclean, quietly implying that he understands the young man well. Thus the fervent staccato of the opening line is balanced by the studied decorum of chiasmus ("early wise and brave in season"), of alliteration ("pass hence and home"), and of allusions to the Bible and to *Cymbeline* ("Dust's your wages, son of sorrow"). The poem is an emblem of raw material disguised and refined via ballad economy; its conventional stanzas and learned references draw attention away from that newspaper article, which Housman saved and which is the work's most important intertext. Portraying suicide, this concise poem terminates itself early in order to purge away not only troubling desires but also confessional tendencies. Yet at the same time, Housman's decision to mourn Maclean with a nod to Shakespeare—whose sonnets famously admire the beauty of a young man—is, like the classical allusions mentioned above, telling. Furthermore, this lyric is understatedly dissident in its insistence that the cadet has become a paragon of virtuous masculinity, that he has died "as fits a man." Housman tacitly makes homosexuality compatible with heroic virility. The poet's praise of Maclean's suicide ("Oh that was right, lad") can be read as a bitter indictment of Victorian bigotry or as a self-hating internalisation of it; perhaps it is both, an ambivalence reflected in the knotty double negation of "undishonoured."[19] Several other meditations on suicide in *A Shropshire Lad* ("the lover / That hanged himself for love" [XVI]), along with several depictions of ill-fated men who are unambiguously in love with women, intersect with and obscure the cadet's memorial. This ensures that neither the lad nor his ballad is overly conspicuous. Hiding this subtly transgressive poem among many similar ones, allowing his verses to be haunted by older elegies and by one another, Housman takes advantage of the fact that his mnemonic techniques of compression and repetition can also make individual poems forgettable.

"The lads in their hundreds to Ludlow come in for the fair" (XXIII) confirms that the faltering of memory in this volume, its apparent inability to recapture the past or preserve the integrity of discrete poems and specific people, is driven in part by the author's attempts to conceal—and in so doing, to explore and express—his ineffable desires:

> The lads in their hundreds to Ludlow come in for the fair,
> There's men from the barn and the forge and the mill and the fold,
> The lads for the girls and the lads for the liquor are there,
> And there with the rest are the lads that will never be old.
>
> There's chaps from the town and the field and the till and the cart,
> And many to count are the stalwart, and many the brave,
> And many the handsome of face and the handsome of heart,
> And few that will carry their looks or their truth to the grave.
>
> I wish one could know them, I wish there were tokens to tell
> The fortunate fellows that now you can never discern;
> And then one could talk with them friendly and wish them farewell
> And watch them depart on the way that they will not return.
>
> But now you may stare as you like and there's nothing to scan;
> And brushing your elbow unguessed-at and not to be told
> They carry back bright to the coiner the mintage of man,
> The lads that will die in their glory and never be old.

On its surface, this poem praises the "lads that will never be old," those fortunate few who will achieve the culminating perfection of an early death.

These boys again implicitly converge with transitory verses, as Housman's speaker attempts to "scan" them. Yet even as he extols the distinctiveness provided by brevity, this speaker is overwhelmed by manyness—reflected in his use of an unusually expansive and capacious modified-anapestic pentameter. Exaggerated anaphora ("There's men from the barn and the forge and the mill and the fold") signals this lyric's predicament: as we make fleeting contact with so many (bal)lads, how are we to remember any particular one? "And" is a conjunction that both joins and separates, simultaneously drawing distinctions and creating a droning monosyllabic catalogue in which all distinctions are flattened out. Certain lads, in dying young, will "carry back bright to the coiner the mintage of man." But coins, while valuable, are also virtually identical. In the somatic economy of *A Shropshire Lad*, bodies and coins alike proliferate, circulate, and are ultimately interchangeable. "[Y]ou can never discern" or recognise the lucky youths, and you cannot promise to recall select individuals or specific poems within an echoic collection.

Particularly when juxtaposed with "Shot?," "The lads in their hundreds" seems sexually charged. Its speaker relishes gazing at and cataloguing and touching these men ("many the handsome of face … brushing your elbow unguessed-at"), and is sorry that he must remain at a remove from them ("I wish one could know them"). As this line shows, the lyric often self-protectively substitutes "one" and "you" for "I." Warren H. Kelly detects further homoerotic hints in this speaker's urge to uncover the lads' hidden "truth," and in his assertion that only some boys are there "for the girls" (Kelly 2001, 98–103). As in "Shot?," the poem's brevity (despite its uncharacteristically long five-beat lines) draws attention to the way in which it cuts itself off before it says too much. Especially when read in isolation, it can be remembered without being fully understood. Housman must refrain from lingering on or individuating either too-attractive boys or too-detailed poems in which he might divulge his state of mind in an overly direct fashion. Cuing his audience to (at least partially) misapprehend a lyric like "The lads in their hundreds," Housman can himself resemble a memorised *Shropshire Lad* poem in remaining both known and unknown.

The instants of brief communion that appear in "The street sounds to the soldiers' tread" and in "The lads in their hundreds" shed light on one of Housman's most opaque ballads, "From far, from eve and morning" (XXXII)—which depicts a mysterious speaker who has coalesced from the "stuff of life," and who may dissolve again at any moment. Crucially, it also portrays obstructed expression and a yen for physical connection that becomes more intense as it is thwarted.

> From far, from eve and morning
> And yon twelve-winded sky,
> The stuff of life to knit me
> Blew hither: here am I.

Now—for a breath I tarry
Nor yet disperse apart—
Take my hand quick and tell me,
What have you in your heart.

Speak now, and I will answer;
How shall I help you, say;
Ere to the wind's twelve quarters
I take my endless way.

"Now—for a breath I tarry / Nor yet disperse apart" turns an exaggerated version of life's transience into a muted *carpe diem* appeal. Too hurried even to use a polysyllabic adverb to modify his urgent imperatives ("Take my hand quick ... Speak"), this speaker seems eager to make a confession to the anonymous addressee. But that confession never comes. Abridged form, which creates the potential for intimate disclosures that do not give too much away, also curtails these disclosures.[20] Housman frustrates his speaker's longing for bodily contact, allowing him to lose his contours entirely ("to the wind's twelve quarters / I take my endless way"). Those "twelve quarters," as well as the "twelve-winded sky," map onto the twelve lines of the ballad and the twelve beats of each trimeter quatrain; like its dissipating speaker, this brief poem exists only for an instant. Yet it wants to be known, to access the heart of its interlocutor ("What have you in your heart"), which is the symbolic seat of memory. Like many economical *Shropshire Lad* verses, it balances between passionate revelation and concealment, between mnemonic self-containment and fragile forgettability— and between autonomy and allusive nostalgia. With its wind-of-life imagery, it echoes "Into my heart an air that kills" (XL) and "The winds out of the west land blow" (XXXVIII). It is absorbed into the self-referential texture of Housman's collection; its memorable ephemerality does not protect its integrity.

In a similar vein, "To an Athlete Dying Young" seems to promise that early death will preserve a runner in his glorious prime. Forever enshrined as a champion, frozen in time, he will not sink into middle-aged mediocrity:

The time you won your town the race
We chaired you through the market-place;
Man and boy stood cheering by,
And home we brought you shoulder-high.

Today, the road all runners come,
Shoulder-high we bring you home,
And set you at your threshold down,
Townsman of a stiller town.

Smart lad, to slip betimes away
From fields where glory does not stay,

And early though the laurel grows
It withers quicker than the rose.

Eyes the shady night has shut
Cannot see the record cut,
And silence sounds no worse than cheers
After earth has stopped the ears:

Now you will not swell the rout
Of lads that wore their honours out,
Runners whom renown outran
And the name died before the man.

So set, before its echoes fade,
The fleet foot on the sill of shade,
And hold to the low lintel up
The still-defended challenge-cup.

And round that early-laurelled head
Will flock to gaze the strengthless dead,
And find unwithered on its curls
The garland briefer than a girl's.

Again, the speaker elevates memorable brevity as an ideal. He describes a laurel that withers quickly, a brief commemorative garland, a man who perishes so that his name will not. He touts a short life as the path to immortality. Moreover, laurel belongs to both athletes and poets, which allows the runner's "fleet foot" to take on metrical overtones; lucky lad and little lyric run swiftly and conclude hurriedly, laying claim to perfection in their attenuation, and so appeal to the remembrance. Ending early, embracing circumscription, paradoxically appears to prevent both poems and people from vanishing.

As I have shown, however, this is a false hope. Words and phrases of negation or delay, such as "before its echoes fade" and "unwithered," inevitably raise the possibility of fading and withering. Even "fields where glory does not stay," which overtly refers to the waning of physical abilities over time, also hints that this runner's fame will dwindle after his demise. The athlete travels "the road *all* runners come" and joins a throng of the feebly undifferentiated "strengthless dead." His particular narrative is assimilated to a pre-known archetype of universal mortality and forgettability. After all, the athlete's death is echoed in the similar fates of many young men, and *A Shropshire Lad* contains a plethora of similar epitaphs describing them. Neither a youthful corpse nor a mnemonic form, then, is guaranteed a secure place in the world's remembrance.

In forgetting the runner's individuality, "To an Athlete" also forgets his too-enticing physical charms—which call to mind the athletic Jackson. Closing this man's eyes, contemplating his corporeal decay, and denying his body parts personal pronouns ("*the* fleet foot," "*the* ears," "*that* early-laurelled head," "*its* curls"), Housman's speaker curbs and deadens the persistent eroticism of his descriptions.[21] By shunning specificity and allowing dim recollection to eclipse keen immediacy, Housman can safely admire male bodies. The short life and the economical ballad are forms of containment that do not guarantee immortality—but that can make dangerous beauty available to the gaze as long as it remains far-off, disembodied, and unattainable. Once an athlete is dead, he can be spoken to affectionately. Soldiers marching off to battle, who often resemble ancient Greek warriors as much as nineteenth-century ones, will soon exist only in the past—and so they can be closely scrutinised and addressed in heartfelt tones ("Soldier, I wish you well" [XXII]). Housman can praise and mourn them without arousing suspicion if he nostalgically consigns them to a land of faint memories.

In this context, even the apparently impersonal and near-objectless nostalgia of "Into my heart an air that kills" begins to sound like an unquiet longing for what is both tempting and forbidden.

> Into my heart an air that kills
> From yon far country blows:
> What are those blue remembered hills,
> What spires, what farms are those?
>
> That is the land of lost content,
> I see it shining plain,
> The happy highways where I went
> And cannot come again.

Keith Jebb points out a pivotal pun in the phrase "land of lost *content*": this word connotes "idea" or "substance" or "meaning" as well as "satisfaction" (Jebb 2000).[22] The lost content is the love that dare not speak its name. Just as the speaker never truly inhabited those retrospectively-idealised blue hills and therefore cannot return to them, so a homosexual community never existed for Housman and therefore cannot truly be recalled (except, perhaps, via references to classical texts). A timeless and universal remembrance that nonetheless rarely embodies a comforting or stable memorial realm, Shropshire can also become a microcosm of Housman's repressive society in ensuring that the hills of lost content remain inaccessible and that certain urges remain unspeakable.

Forgetful remembrance is both an aesthetic strategy and a recurrent theme for Housman. His volume is fixated on death, separation, exile, mourning, and regret, subjecting even present happiness to anticipatory nostalgia ("And take from seventy springs a score, / It only leaves me fifty more" [II]). Poem after poem recalls those who are gone ("Now Dick lies long in the churchyard, / And Ned lies long in jail" [LVIII]), remembers vanished joy ("Oh tarnish late on Wenlock Edge / Gold that I never see" [XXXIX]), or dwells on lost love ("Is my girl happy, / That I thought hard to leave?" [XXVII]). It has become clear that the haziness of many of these memories functions as a defense mechanism, permitting Housman's speakers to avoid directly interacting with the objects of their remembrance. But just as his allusive reticence becomes a means of disclosure, so this amnesiac distancing also allows the poet to counteract his themes of isolation and self-conceal-ment. Their very forgettability unites various lonely Housman men:

> When I watch the living meet,
> And the moving pageant file
> Warm and breathing through the street
> Where I lodge a little while,
>
> If the heats of hate and lust
> In the house of flesh are strong,
> Let me mind the house of dust
> Where my sojourn shall be long.
>
> In the nation that is not
> Nothing stands that stood before;
> There revenges are forgot,
> And the hater hates no more;
>
> Lovers lying two and two
> Ask not whom they sleep beside,
> And the bridegroom all night through
> Never turns him to the bride. (XII)

This proleptically-deceased speaker disengages from the world by turning it into a fading memory, prompting himself to contemplate the impercipient grave: "Let me mind the house of dust / Where my sojourn shall be long." Death is a land of static oblivion—"There revenges are forgot" seems to signal not sweet forgiveness but utter blankness—in which individuality evaporates. Accordingly, the speaker's unmotivated "hate and lust" defensively broaden to encompass the plight of humanity in general as his first-person pronouns disappear. Despite the narrative gesture of its opening lines, "When I watch the living meet" presents only the familiar non-plot of mortality. Neglecting to offer even the hesitant assurances of "To an Athlete," this poem does not suggest that those who die in their prime will be forever preserved. The grave obliterates defining features: a self-muting repetition asserts that "the hater hates no more," lovers are loveless, and a bridegroom ignores his bride. Alliterative echoes of negation ("not," "nothing," "no," "never") resound throughout the text, which apparently underscores only amnesiac emptiness.

All the same, its description of "the nation that is not" captures this poem's key ambiguity. On the one hand, the fact that this line features a phantom enjambment ("that is not" *what?*) encodes its emphasis on cryptic deficiency and lack. But on the other hand, Housman describes this non-nation as a recognisable and cohesive entity. It signifies a lasting fellowship of the solitary, joined together by forgettable tenuousness. *A Shropshire Lad,* with its undifferentiated characters and iterative lyrical units, embodies this fellowship. Given his volume's tacit equation of short-lived lads and brief ballads, along with its relative paucity of women, Housman forms a community based not only in human mortality but also in the intimate bonds that stem from the shared traumas and estrangements and enforced invisibilities of men in particular. Though he was not invited to Moses Jackson's 1889 wedding, and indeed did not learn that the marriage had taken place until after the fact, Housman imaginatively inserts himself into the wedding party in a rather somber "Epithalamium" (published in *Last Poems*): "So the groomsman quits your side / And the bridegroom seeks the bride: / Friend and comrade yield you o'er / To her that hardly loves you more." But "When I watch the living meet" prevents such painful separation. It muses that after death, "the bridegroom all night through / Never turns him to the bride" (XXIV). Perhaps this as-yet-uninhabited nation where men do not seek the affections of women, hatred vanishes, "lust" is no longer troublesome, and lovers need not worry about "whom they sleep beside" is more an enticing alternate reality than a terrifyingly meaningless void. The description of the bridegroom begins to sound more like deliberate erotic refusal than deanimated stasis—a postmortem continuation of libido that persists despite the dampening effects of Housman's forms, and that obtrudes itself on the attention because of these mnemonic forms and their striking effects.

3. The Nation that is Not: Homoerotic Bonds and the Literary Marketplace

The last poem in *A Shropshire Lad*, "I hoed and trenched and weeded" (LXIII), depicts a slightly different version of this disguised male community.

> I hoed and trenched and weeded,
> And took the flowers to fair:
> I brought them home unheeded;
> The hue was not the wear.
>
> So up and down I sow them
> For lads like me to find,
> When I shall lie below them,
> A dead man out of mind.
>
> Some seed the birds devour,
> And some the season mars,
> But here and there will flower
> The solitary stars,
>
> And fields will yearly bear them
> As light-leaved spring comes on,
> And luckless lads will wear them
> When I am dead and gone.

Comparing verses to flowers, the poem hopes that Housman's works will continue to interest certain ill-fated men even after he himself has been forgotten ("luckless lads will wear them / When I am dead and gone"). Tellingly, these posies are marks of unacceptable difference: "The hue was not the wear." Housman's notebook poem, "Oh who is that young sinner with the handcuffs on his wrists?," which shows Wilde being dragged off to prison "for the colour of his hair," confirms the metaphorical implications of those strangely-colored blooms (*Additional Poems*, XVIII). "I hoed and trenched and weeded" continues using allusive techniques to universalise its sentiments and guard against self-revelation, as the phrase "dead man out of mind" is taken from Psalms 31.12. But it simultaneously offers an alternative and more paradoxically personal way of generalising the individual voice—not only through self-repression or references to everymen, but also through the creation of a concealed homoerotic fellowship. The nation that is not, the land of lost content, harbors those unfortunate and alienated few whose sexual identities are (as "Oh who is that young sinner" puts it) as "nameless and abominable" as the shade of Wilde's hair. Despite its best efforts, Victorian society cannot render this hidden nation non-existent.

Indeed, an understated openness emerges in this poem. Some seeds will never blossom, but "here and there will flower / The solitary stars": emboldened by its status as one relatively inconspicuous ballad among many, "I hoed and trenched and weeded" concludes by allowing for the possibility of future self-disclosure. Its mention of "light-*leaved* spring" connects its late-blooming flowers to the pages of Housman's volume. Perhaps same-sex love precludes physical reproduction. But Housman brings forth textual children that are immortal *en masse* if not as discrete works, and that he hopes will whisper his secrets to attentive ears: "So up and down I sow them / For lads like me to find."[23] And lads like Housman did find his verses, expanding the homoerotic fellowship. When Wilde was serving his prison sentence, his friend Robert Ross would learn Housman's poems by heart and recite them to the inmate, who also memorised them.[24] Their mnemonic nature, which further manifests itself in the clear influence of *A Shropshire Lad* on the 1898 *Ballad of Reading Gaol*, allows Housman's suggestive lyrics to establish themselves in the thoughts of perceptive readers.

Lyrics are consistently feminised in the Victorian period; by taking up an apparently womanly stance, writing what Tom Burns Haber calls "unmanly" verses of "feminine faintheartedness," Housman can attach wistful sentiment to young men's lives and deaths (1954, 316). Despite his use of economical form to diminish and disguise his verse's libidinal energies, Housman also makes the most of the link between gender and genre that lends his lines a faintly romantic tone (while at the same time defensively joining them to well-established conventions). Lyrical feminisation notwithstanding, however, the anonymity of the ballad form in particular encodes the socially-enforced anonymity of same-sex desire. In fact, *A Shropshire Lad* was originally to be called "Poems by Terence Hearsay" and to omit its true author's name (as Wilde would elect to do with *The Ballad of Reading Gaol*), a depersonalising impulse reflected in the indefinite article of the volume's title. So the fact that Housman ultimately chooses to write under his own name is significant, especially given that publishing even coded poems of unorthodox affection represents a quasi-sexual communion with the reader; with his memorable work, Housman can appeal to male bodies and hearts. There is a flirtatious play in his studied ambiguities, his decision to speak but not to say too much, his tendency almost (but not quite) to violate taboos—patterns that both produce and inhibit dangerous desire. As he says in a 1908 letter to Witter Bynner, "My chief object in publishing my verses was to give pleasure to a few young men here and there" (qtd. in Maas 1971, 65). Lending a new resonance to the seemingly-timeless nature of his poetry, Housman joins himself to a silent and marginalised trans-historical community of unlucky lads past, present, and future, all united by solitude and despondent self-erasure. This nation is ready to be discovered or created by readers who know which poems to juxtapose and which speakers to compare.

Ironically enough, the formal economy of these unassuming verses augments their influence as it shapes their role in the literary marketplace. *A Shropshire Lad* is an unusually slim volume, and Housman preferred that it be published in cheap pocket editions rather than in more substantial and costly versions. Though this preference might seem to signal the same reticence or self-suppression reflected in the poet's use of traditional ballad stanzas, inexpensive editions in fact ensure that Housman's collection remains accessible to many, small and portable, able to circulate widely and to become widely known. In 1936, for instance, one writer recalls purchasing *A Shropshire Lad* because it was "such an attractive-looking little book," "only three or four inches tall and costing only sixpence" (Richards 1942, 345). When translated to the marketplace, then, the phrase "ballad economy" takes on a very different meaning; along with its apparent conventionality, the poet uses his collection's affordability—which stems in part from its commitment to brevity—to expand his sphere of sympathy and counteract his estrangement. He can commodify his desires, reproducing them in print and in minds. Housman's "The lads in their hundreds" compares the circulating proliferation of coins to that of young men's bodies (a metaphor that derives additional force, perhaps, from the sexual connotation of the verb "to spend"). And the material circulation of the book itself, driven by literal rather than figurative currency, has a similar erotic charge ("to give pleasure to a few young men here and there," qtd. in Maas 1971, 65). Ballad economy is the vehicle that smuggles heterodox content from society's margins to its centre.

Indeed, despite his disputed status among literary scholars—starting in the 1930s, his work fell into critical disfavour for several decades—for many readers Housman earns a lasting place in the cultural memory. *A Shropshire Lad* was frequently reprinted throughout the twentieth century, having gone through over 90 editions by 1986. It remains popular on both sides of the Atlantic, and in fact has never been out of print. Its short and iterative lyrics have often been selected for inclusion in anthologies (275 of them by 1953) and for compulsory classroom memorisation. In 1996, Jeremy Bourne nostalgically recalled how as a schoolboy he was often "set as homework the learning of 'something by Housman'"; John Masefield narrates of meeting a tramp who carried a battered copy of *A Shropshire Lad* and could quote it from memory (Bourne 1996, 13; Hoagwood 1995, viii).[25] This volume's veiled references to unorthodox sexuality, its tone of weary enervation, and its interest in beauty and death align it more with Housman's decadent coevals than he would have admitted.[26] But unlike most of these writers, Housman can exploit both aspects of ballad economy to slip his homoerotic yet unobtrusive poems not only into breast pockets but also into the cultural mainstream via schoolbooks and anthologies; as a telling example, the 1963 *Penguin Book of Religious Verse* includes two selections from *A Shropshire Lad*. Housman's subversive commercial and canonical roles thus illuminate a less self-effacing aspect of his tendency to use succinct forms that prevent emotional overflow and serve as mnemonic aids. Everyone who purchases and reads *A Shropshire Lad* shares its author's sorrows and fears in the process, even if the sources of those emotions are not always clear. In this way, as I have shown, Housman uses memorably concise stanzas and familiar diction to insinuate his libidinal drives into the reader's mind, tempering those drives' illicit nature. Short poems may express guilt at their failures to immortalise the individual lads they describe, but they do propagate those lads' nameless longings.

Given *A Shropshire Lad*'s commitment to forming communities of doomed men across time and space, it is appropriate that World War I cements its reputation. In the years immediately following the war, England strove both to memorialise her innumerable dead and to forget a national trauma—a paradoxical state of affairs echoed in Housman's collection, which not only struggles to recall or commemorate young men (while implicitly effacing them by acknowledging their interchangeable nature) but also attempts to repress, depersonalise, disavow, and forget the very desires it produces and preserves. Small wonder that *A Shropshire Lad*'s popularity soared both during and after the war. About 16,000 copies sold in 1918 alone, and special editions were printed for soldiers in the trenches. In a 1916 letter to Grant Richards, Housman fancifully envisions a soldier having a bullet "turned aside from his heart by a copy of *A Shropshire Lad* which he is carrying there" (qtd. in Maas 1971, 149). Only a relatively little book would be convenient for a soldier to carry at his breast, and so this literal version of a laying-to-heart reflects Housman's penchant for convenient pocket editions. Nevile Watts confirms that in addition to being "carried in the tunic-pocket by soldiers," *A Shropshire Lad* was continually "chanted or crooned by undergraduates," and so became "part and parcel of the daily lives of thousands" (qtd. in Gardner 1992, 353). "Everyone read Housman" at this time, adds Paul Fussell; his compact little volume was in everyone's hands partly because it engaged with "the theme of beautiful suffering lads, for which the war sanctioned an expression more overt than ever before" (Fussell 1975, 161; 164). With its focus on life's transience and on elegiac pastoral nostalgia, *A Shropshire Lad* captures wartime readers' longing for simpler and more peaceful days, and becomes more topical than Housman ever intended it to be. One suspects that the rather apolitical poet favours depictions of war in part because they encapsulate senseless suffering, and in part because they provide an opportunity to gaze wistfully on departing lads. And the volume's role as a widely-circulating cultural artifact, a source of anthology pieces and of selections for pedagogical memorisation, will cue many readers to unmoor Housman from historical temporality. Yet despite and because of their insistent amnesia, despite and because of the non-specificity that authorises a forgetfully nostalgic reader to make them part of her own mental life, his poems also come to serve as memorials for a particular Lost Generation—and his choric voice as the voice of a grieving nation. The apparent timelessness of Housman's work, in conjunction with its ballad economy, here serves to re-historicise it. In this wartime context, *A Shropshire Lad*'s understated yet deeply-felt eroticism becomes one of its most prominent features, and its influence on war poets Wilfred Owen and Siegfried Sassoon marks them as members of the nation that is not.[27]

Relatedly, it has become clear that the controlled reticence of Housman's ballads represents both an escape from and an expression of personality. The two accounts of the composition of *A Shropshire Lad*, one describing detached restraint and one describing continuous excitement, can be reconciled. Though the familiarity of Housman's verse conceals and inhibits its passionate sincerity, that same commonplace quality can also make it exceptionally moving; grief and disillusionment are as ineluctable in his work as the march of regular meter or the conclusion of a brief stanza, as predictable as well-established rhymes. This poetry's poignancy derives from its conspicuous socially-imposed curtailments, from its recognisable and highly regulated sentiments, from the impression it gives of longing to speak its whole heart but always fading into the general or impersonal. These repetitive little ballads, which both highlight and camouflage libidinal content, simultaneously appeal to the memory and disguise their desire to be known.

A Shropshire Lad's derivative nature also assures that it endures the passage of time, that it can be internalised and reclaimed by many readers. The titles of (for instance) Storm Jameson's *The Happy Highways* (1920) and E. L. Woodward's *The Twelve-Winded Sky* (1930) confirm that phrases from Housman's volume become part of the early twentieth century's cultural unconscious, even if an average reader could not reliably identify their source. And even when they are not being selectively recontextualised, because their styles and topics are conventional and familiar—because they point away from themselves, prompting readers to recall sentiments and poems they already know—Housman's lyrics are, like the pastoral world he describes or like his young men and their sorrows, both remembered and forgotten. This writer's enduring forms have quietly influenced artists from William Faulkner to Joyce Kilmer to Ralph Vaughn Williams. This is a fitting fate for his work. If *A Shropshire Lad* offers a hesitant solution to human transience and alienation, it is in the existence of shared thoughts and emotions that outlive their individual incarnations—as reflected in the compelling resonances among unobtrusive yet erotic ballads, and in the tacit links among luckless lads.

Notes

1. Housman also hesitates to align himself with mid-century predecessors; though he admires Tennyson, the Laureate's cautious Christian optimism contrasts sharply with his atheistic pessimism. Housman once summarised the moral of *In Memoriam* as "things must come right in the end, because it would be so very unpleasant if they did not" (Chambers 1939, 371).
2. Unless otherwise stated, citations from *A Shropshire Lad, More Poems* and *Additional Poems* are taken from A.E. Housman. 2010. *A Shropshire Lad and Other Poems*, edited by Nick Laird. London: Penguin and will be cited by number parenthetically in the text.
3. For perspectives on Housman's sexuality, see: Burnett 2000; Bristow 2013; Efrati 2002; Robbins 1995; Howarth 2009.
4. A 1933 lecture, "The Name and Nature of Poetry," is the only substantial public statement Housman made about his compositional methods. Verse, he writes, is distinguished from prose in "the superior terseness which usually goes along with it" (Housman, 1933, 9). Miniature lyrics ("tiny gems of purer ray") epitomise poetry (Housman, 1933, 29).
5. To give another example, a murderer's confession ends with laments for the loss not of life but of hot food: "Long for me the rick will wait ... And dinner will be cold" ("Farewell to barn and stack and tree" [VIII]). Another poem regretfully concludes "And I am two-and-twenty, / And oh, 'tis true, 'tis true" (XIII). This anticlimactic lyric is so short that the speaker—who thinks back to the time when he was one-and-twenty—does not have time to become a wise old man, and can only become a slightly-less-callow young man. Insistent truncations that cut off sentimental overflow and self-revelation also emphasise the brevity of life and the transience of beauty. "The True Lover" (LIII) illustrates this focus with the quadruple redundancy "When I *from hence away* am *past.*"
6. For the purposes of this chapter, I consider nearly all *A Shropshire Lad* poems—with their three- and four-beat quatrains and their impersonal tone—to be ballads (though because I believe that the category of "lyric" essentially comprises short poems, I will also be referring to them as lyrics). Some of Housman's verses do employ traditional ballad techniques. "Farewell to barn and stack and tree" matter-of-factly recounts a violent tale, for instance, while "Is my team ploughing" (XXVII) offers formulaic dialogue. It is true that the eighteenth and nineteenth centuries saw a renewed interest in balladry; there is the appearance of *Lyrical Ballads*, the flowering of street ballads and urban broadside ballads (and, for that matter, music hall songs), as well as the publication of Francis Gummere's *The Popular Ballad* (1907). So this genre is not necessarily backward-looking.

But because Housman tends to resist narrating events that are explicitly topical or autobiographical (as Wilde does in *The Ballad of Reading Gaol*), because he avoids modern slang and, as a rule, overt political commentary (unlike Kipling), and because he does not allow ballad stanzas to accrue into lengthy works that engage with the dramatic monologue genre (as D. G. Rossetti does in *Sister Helen*), his verses do sound strikingly nostalgic. They seem especially steeped in the past, and especially similar to one another, because their forms and themes are so determinedly conventional. Even *More Poems* and *Additional Poems*, assembled from Housman's notebooks and published after his death, sound very much like *A Shropshire Lad*. See Hughes 2010, 40–88.

7. As John W. Stevenson puts it, this verse "is remembered and endures the passage of time" because it speaks in "the language [a reader] remembered when he thought of poetry" (1986, 613–15; 618–19).

8. As John Bayley says, "Shropshire is the myth, the view remembered" (1992, 3). Housman was in fact a Worcestershire lad; Shropshire, visible on the horizon from his childhood home, was a well-known sight that remained hazy and far-off. "Mount Pisgah," Housman's name for the hill that gave him a view of the county, emphasises this region's mythic quality.

9. In Kenneth Millard's phrase, Housman's work is "disabled by the limitations of [its] chosen medium" (1991, 91–2). See also Burnett's "A. E. Housman's 'Level Tones'" for a discussion of emotion suppressed by decorous form; as Burnett says, "The poem is the means of achieving composure" (2000, 12). Of course, none of this is to imply that Housman's work is damaged or undermined or made less effective by its ballad medium, or that he would have poured forth openly homoerotic confessions if he had chosen to write a seven-book epic.

10. Dames *passim* (2001, 16). For instance, Dames argues that many of David Copperfield's recollections (such as his account of Dora's death) function as simplified and condensed "acts of leavetaking" rather than "acts of recovery" (2001, 142).

11. Bristow remarks on Housman's use of a "not entirely evasive lyric voice to speak of same-sex desires that were almost impossible to address publicly" (2013, 34); Craft makes a similar point about *In Memoriam* when he associates it with "a problematization not merely of desire between men, but also of the desire (very urgent in the elegy) to speak it" (1994, 47). And as Adam Parkes says in his discussion of Arthur Symons and Walter Pater, the "discourses of ambiguity and ambivalence that constituted new forms of male desire in turn-of-the-century Britain" ensure that "the very act of withdrawing or concealing the self may indirectly publicize it" (2011, 71; 65). On this topic, I am also indebted to Yopie Prins, David Kurnick, and Erik Gray for their insightful responses to a version of this chapter presented at the 2012 Northeast Victorian Studies Association conference.

12. Housman, "The Name and Nature of Poetry" (1933, 48). It is intriguing to consider the Sapphic suggestiveness of these pearls and oysters, though this is a line of argumentation that I do not have space to pursue here.

13. For a related perspective on Housman's classicism, see: Bishop 1940, 151.

14. Northrop Frye confirms that composition re-enacts past trauma, observing that a poem "often takes off from something that blocks normal activity, something a poet has to write poetry about instead of carrying on with ordinary experience. This block has traditionally been frustrated love" (1985, 32). From another

point of view, Housman guiltily kills off rejected versions of himself in these lyrics, taking on the guise of a condemned criminal or an ill-fated conscript or a suffering exile.

15. At the same time, one could argue that Housman mocks these prohibitions by exaggerating his self-suppression.

16. See, for example, Ben Jonson's "Song: To Celia" ("Drink to me only with thine eyes / And I will pledge with mine") (1996, 106) and Thomas Moore's "Did Not" ("We saw it in each other's eye ... She felt my lips' impassioned touch") (1823, 165).

17. Efrati points out that the word "reins" means both "seat of the passions" and "means of control," highlighting the hesitation between self-expression and self-stifling in "Others, I am not the first" (2002, 269–72).

18. I owe this comparison to John Whitehead (1995, 143).

19. Martha Vicinus (1994, 89) and Bristow (2013, 36–7) both offer related analyses of this poem.

20. Millard (1991, 87) makes a comparable point about this lyric.

21. Erik Gray points out that "*the* name died before the man" gives the impression that Housman's speaker is "beautifully ignor[ing] the runners of the previous line" (136).

22. As Howarth notices, the phrase "shining plain" appears in both "Into my heart" and Alfred Douglas's "Two Loves" (Howarth 2009, 772).

23. Vicinus shows that, for many nineteenth-century homosexuals, "[p]hysical reproduction was replaced with metaphysical and artistic generation" (1994, 94).

24. Housman himself sent Wilde a copy of *A Shropshire Lad* on his release from prison. Robbins argues compellingly that Ross used the Housman verses to teach Wilde strategies of poetic ambiguity and control (1995, 147); she also points out the ability of Housman's subversive poems to circulate widely, which I note below. For a related reading of impersonality in *The Ballad of Reading Gaol*, see: Page, 1994.

25. For a tally of Housman poems in collections, see William White's "A. E. Housman Anthologized" (*Bulletin of Bibliography* XXI, 1953). Laurence Housman confirms the memorisability of his brother's work: when *A Shropshire Lad* first appeared, he recounts, "Before the end of the day I knew a dozen of the poems by heart, and before the end of a week nearly all of them" (1938, 80).

26. Bristow makes a similar point about Housman's understated decadence (2013, 28–9).

27. Meredith Martin points out that both Owen and Sassoon would have been required to memorise poetry in a pedagogical context; during wartime, she proposes, their ability to remember "traditional poetic forms" took on a heightened "disciplinary and therapeutic" function (Martin 2012, 150). See also Robson (2012, 217) on the role of well-known verses in postwar commemoration.

Works Cited

Bayley, John. 1992. *Housman's Poems*. Oxford: Clarendon Press.

Bishop, John Peale. 1940. "The Poetry of A. E. Housman." *Poetry*, no. 56, 144–53.

Bourne, Jeremy. 1996. *The Westerly Wanderer: A Brief Portrait of A. E. Housman*. Bromsgrove: The Housman Society.

Bristow, Joseph. 2013. "How Decadent Poems Die." In *Decadent Poetics: Literature and Form at the British Fin de Siècle*, edited by Jason David Hall and Alex Murray, 26–42. Houndmills: Palgrave Macmillan.

Burnett, Archie. 2000. "A. E. Housman's 'Level Tones.'" In *A. E. Housman: A Reassessment*, edited by Alan W. Holden and J. Roy Birch. Houndmills: Macmillan Press.

———. 2003. "Silence and Allusion in Housman." *Essays in Criticism* 53 (2): 151–73.

Chambers, R. W. 1939. *Man's Unconquerable Mind*. London: Jonathan Cape.

Coleridge, Samuel Taylor. 2010. *Biographia Literaria; or Biographical Sketches of My Literary Life and Opinions*. In *The Broadview Anthology of Literature of the Revolutionary Period, 1770–1832*, edited by D.L. Macdonald and Anne McWhir, 798–819. London: Boadview Press.

Coleridge, Samuel Taylor, and William Wordsworth. 2008. *Lyrical Ballads, 1798 and 1800*, edited by Michael Gamer and Dahlia Porter. London: Broadview Press.

Craft, Christopher. 1994. *Another Kind of Love: Male Homosexual Desire in English Discourse, 1850–1920*. Berkeley: University of California Press.

Dames, Nicholas. 2001. *Amnesiac Selves: Nostalgia, Forgetting, and British Fiction, 1810–1870*. New York: Oxford University Press.

Efrati, Carol. 2002. *The Road of Danger, Guilt, and Shame: The Lonely Way of A. E. Housman*. Madison: Farleigh Dickinson University Press.

Frye, Northrop. 1985. "Approaching the Lyric." In *Lyric Poetry: Beyond New Criticism*, edited by Chaviva Hošek and Patricia Parker, 31–7. Ithaca: Cornell University Press.

Fussell, Paul.1975. *The Great War and Modern Memory*. Oxford: Oxford University Press.

Gardner, Philip, ed. 1992. *A. E. Housman: The Critical Heritage*. London: Routledge.

Gray, Erik. 2000. *The Poetry of Indifference: From the Romantics to the Rubáiyát*. Amherst: University of Massachusetts Press.

Haber, Tom Burns. 1954. "A. E. Housman's Downward Eye." *The Journal of English and Germanic Philology* 53 (3): 306–18.

Hoagwood, Terence Allan. 1995. *A. E. Housman Revisited*. New York: Twayne Publishers.

Holden, Alan W., and J. Roy Birch, eds. 2000. *A. E. Housman: A Reassessment*. Houndmills: Macmillan.

Housman, A. E. 2010. *A Shropshire Lad and Other Poems*, edited by Nick Laird. London: Penguin.

Housman, A. E. 1933. "The Name and Nature of Poetry." The Leslie Stephen Lecture Delivered at Cambridge. May 9. Accessed May 15, 2015. http://www.bu.edu/clarion/guides/The-Name-and-Nature-of-Poetry-by-Housman.pdf

Housman, A. E. 2004. "They Say My Verse Is Sad: No Wonder." In *The Poems of A.E. Housman*, edited by Archie Burnett, 113. Oxford: Oxford University Press.

Housman, Laurence. 1938. *My Brother, A. E. Housman*. New York: Charles Scribner's Sons.

Howarth, Peter. 2009. "Housman's Dirty Postcards: Poetry, Modernism, and Masochism." *PMLA* 124 (3): 764–81.

Hughes, Linda. 2010. "Victorian Dialogues with Poetic Tradition." In *The Cambridge Introduction to Victorian Poetry*, 40–88. Cambridge: Cambridge University Press.

Jebb, Keith. 2000. "The Land of Lost Content." In *A. E. Housman: A Reassessment*, edited by Alan W. Holden and J. Roy Birch, 37–51. Houndmills: Macmillan.

Jonson, Ben. 1996. "IX Song. To Celia," *The Forest* in *Ben Jonson: The Complete Poems*, edited by George Parfitt, 106. London: Penguin Classics.

Kelly, Warren H. 2001. "The Mechanics of Metaphor in *A Shropshire Lad.*" *Housman Society Journal*, no. 27, 93–103.

Maas, Henry, ed. 1971. *The Letters of A. E. Housman*. Cambridge: Harvard University Press.

Martin, Meredith. 2012. *The Rise and Fall of Meter: Poetry and English National Culture, 1860–1930*. Princeton: Princeton University Press.

Millard, Kenneth. 1991. *Edwardian Poetry*. Oxford: Clarendon Press.

Moore, Thomas. 1823. *The Works of Thomas Moore: Comprehending All His Melodies, Ballads, Vol. 5*. Paris: A. and W. Galignani.

Page, Norman. 1994. "Decoding *The Ballad of Reading Gaol.*" In *Rediscovering Oscar Wilde*, edited by C. George Sandulescu. Gerrards Cross, Buckinghamshire: Colin Smythe.

Parkes, Adam. 2011. *A Sense of Shock: The Impact of Impressionism on Modern British and Irish Writing*. Oxford: Oxford University Press.

Reade, Brian, ed. 1970. *Sexual Heretics: Male Homosexuality in English Literature from 1850 to 1900*. New York: Coward-McCann.

Richards, Grant. 1942. *Housman: 1897–1936*. New York: Oxford University Press.

Ricks, Christopher, ed. 1968. *A. E. Housman: A Collection of Critical Essays*. Englewood Cliffs, N.J.: Prentice-Hall.

Robbins, Ruth. 1995. "'A very curious construction': Masculinity and the Poetry of A. E. Housman and Oscar Wilde." In *Cultural Politics at the Fin de Siècle*, edited by Sally Ledger and Scott McCracken, 137–60. Cambridge: Cambridge University Press.

Robson, Catherine. 2012. *Heart Beats: Everyday Life and the Memorized Poem*. Princeton: Princeton University Press.

Rosenthal, M. L., and Sally M. Gall. 1983. *The Modern Poetic Sequence: The Genius of Modern Poetry*. New York: Oxford University Press.

Scott-Kilvert, Ian. 1955. *A. E. Housman*. London: Longmans, Green & Co. Ltd.

Stevenson, John W. 1986. "The Durability of Housman's Poetry." *The Sewanee Review* 94 (4): 613–19.

Vicinus, Martha. 1994. "The Adolescent Boy: Fin de Siècle Femme Fatale?" *Journal of the History of Sexuality* 5 (1): 90–114.

Watson, George L. 1957. *A. E. Housman: A Divided Life*. London: Rupert Hart-Davis.

Whitehead, John. 1995. *Hardy to Larkin: Seven English Poets*. Munslow: Hearthstone Publications.

3   Perfume Clouds

Olfaction, Memory, and Desire in Arthur Symons's *London Nights* (1895)

Jane Desmarais

Draw the curtains, kindle a joss-stick in a dark corner, settle down on a sofa by the fire, light an Egyptian cigarette and sip a brandy and soda, as you think yourself back. … Another sip of brandy and another Egyptian cigarette; a whiff of opium perhaps and we can see the mood of the time.
[original emphasis]
(Betjeman 1948, xii–xiii)

Curling cigarette smoke and clouds of exotic perfume infuse decadent art and fiction at the *fin de siècle*. They suggest timeless indulgence, profusion, and erotic excess, but they also articulate a sophisticated urban aesthetic and a bourgeois hankering for the Orient. The passively over-consuming male aesthete, a version of Baudelaire's *flâneur*, was a symbol of new economic circumstances in the late-nineteenth century. He stood in contrast to the bourgeois and eschewed the demands of the marketplace and the exigencies of middle-class consumer culture. He stood at a well-judged distance, preoccupied with beauty and constantly in search of new sensations.

At the *fin de siècle*, the decadent tropes of cigarette smoke and perfume clouds displace earlier connotations of smoke with industry. The iconic billowings of smoke from the funnel of a steam train become the elegant wisps of an Egyptian cigarette and the lingering fragrance of lilac and patchouli. Between aestheticism and 1890s English decadence there is a shift away from the material commodifiable culture of the Beautiful Object to the immaterial realms of desire and the imagination. In the early erotic verse of Arthur Symons, and *London Nights* (1895; revised 1897) in particular, we encounter English decadence in transition, moving away from the economic dimensions to the immaterial traces of desire, a shift that evolves with Symons's growing interest in a symbolist and modernist aesthetic.

§

When Baudelaire, living in the Hôtel Pimodan in the Quartier Latin of Paris, obscured the lower panes of his attic apartment to concentrate on passing clouds ("les merveilleuses constructions de l'impalpable"—"those marvellous, intangible constructions"), he was looking up and away from the life on the street, the hoardings and advertisements, the commercial bustle of Haussmann's new boulevards (Baudelaire 1988, 67).[1] He was celebrating the resistance of nature to commodification and human control. This dreamy sentiment is found throughout his work. In his prose poem, "L'Etranger," in response to the question "Eh! qu'aimes-tu donc ...?" ("So what do you love?"), the stranger replies, "J'aime les nuages ... les nuages qui passent ... là-bas ... là-bas ... les merveilleux nuages!" ("I love the clouds ... the clouds that pass overhead ... yonder ... yonder ... the marvellous clouds!") (Baudelaire 1989, 28). And in the "tableaux parisiens" section of *Les fleurs du mal* (1857) we repeatedly encounter new urban development obscured by rolling fogs, mists, and steam, while more intimate spaces are hazed with opium, eastern perfumes and the animal scent of woman. By the 1880s and 1890s, perfume clouds and trailing cigarette smoke are parodied in the conservative press as the accessories of a languid aestheticism. As Lord Henry remarks in *The Picture of Dorian Gray* (1891): "A cigarette is the perfect type of a perfect pleasure. It is exquisite, and it leaves one unsatisfied. What more can one want?" (Wilde 2006, 69). Commercial culture in both England and the United States at the *fin de siècle* was keen to appropriate the material insatiability of aestheticism. The aesthete represented both a target market, and a marketable commodity. When Wilde embarked on his lecture tour of the United States and Canada in 1882, he became a symbol of exclusive aesthetic taste, and although he signed no contract, his name was used to endorse a range of products on trade cards: "the cards insidiously implied that he was a part of this commercial enterprise and that consumerism was an integral part of being 'truly aesthetic'" (Mendelssohn 2007, 3).

Decadence clearly bears the hallmarks of an earlier aestheticist materialism, but in the 1890s it moves away from this to embrace a symbolist aesthetic. While the olfactory aesthetic in decadent writing signifies the close relationship between aestheticism and consumerist culture and advertising,[2] and reflects the decadent obsession with collecting and material culture, it also suggests feminine, emotive, and imaginative realms that resist possession and classification. Perfume is a recurring motif. It is an expression of material desire, but it is also a metaphor for a conversely immaterial and uncommodifiable libidinal desire. If the precise meaning of perfume as metaphor is sometimes difficult to establish, that is the point. In decadent writing, perfume is less about the product than about its power of suggestiveness; it leads us away from the economic and material dimensions of desire towards a signification of desire more resistant, more dilute, and in symbolist terms, more *idéative*.

In material terms, perfume was an expanding and lucrative business at the *fin de siècle*, dominated by French perfume houses like Guerlain and Rimmel, and in French advertisements and posters it was associated with a brand of glamorous cupidity. In the late-nineteenth century, perfume becomes synonymous with seduction and women at their toilette, and this seductive potential of perfume—"olfactionism" as Havelock Ellis refers to it in *Studies in the Psychology of Sex*[3]—is underlined by representations of "sexual chemistry" between men and women. In an 1889 poster for the Exposition Universelle Paris advertising Gellé Frères's perfume *Régina*, two bourgeois men sit comfortably in the dressing-room of a smiling scantily-clad actress in the process of powdering her face and neck. On her dressing-table we see a mirror, a light and a perfume atomiser stand. On another table in the foreground, there are hairbrushes, a plate filled with calling cards, a red box of "Brisas de Palermo" (Palermo Breezes) and three different-sized bottles of Gellé Frères's perfume. In his book, *Perfume: A Cultural History of Fragrance from 1750 to the Present*, Richard Stamelman notes the influence of Manet's painting, *Nana* (1877) on Gellé Frères's poster, and goes on to comment: "Clearly the narrative of seduction expressed by the scene—it was acceptable for upper-class fin de siècle men to visit the dressing-rooms of the dancers and actresses (even if the latter were changing their clothes) who would become their mistresses—is meant to enhance the erotic aura of the advertised perfume" (Stamelman 2006, 159).

The associations between decadence, desire and the over-consumption of decorative superfluities are clearly gendered. To yearn for and to be seduced by fripperies, to have one's appetite weakened by tempting treats and beautiful accessories, was to surrender to a feminine mode of expression, and we can trace the articulation of this idea to the French critic, Désiré Nisard, and his ponderous *Studies in Manners* (*Etudes de mœurs et de critique sur les poètes latins de la décadence*), published in 1834 (see Nisard and Baldick, ed. 2012, 75–78). Nisard's *Studies in Manners* were to a large extent a corrective response to the poetic experimentation of Victor Hugo and the generation of 1830, whose handling of alexandrine verse was viewed by the French Academy as subversive. Nisard regarded Hugo's violations of rhetorical rules as enfeebling, and argued that decadent manners (*mœurs*) were responsible for the modern preoccupation with individual eccentricity, recondite subject matter and description for its own sake. In much the same way that an appetite can be weakened by the consumption of sweets and trifles, Nisard argued, so the writer's creative talent is impoverished (and made effeminate and decadent) by over-attention to description, detail, and literary flourishes.

Nisard provides the first useful definition of decadent literary style in the late-Romantic period, but by the *fin de siècle*, literary affectations in the form of flourishes and a dandified personal aesthetic are self-consciously amalgamated by leading decadent celebrities. In England, *Punch* was on their trail, creating Jellaby Postlethwaite, an aesthetic poet, and Maudle, an aesthetic painter: two figures intended as caricatures of Oscar Wilde and his association with the limp and languid gestures of the aesthetic movement. The floral trademarks of decadents—lilies, orchids, and synthetic fragrances of French perfume—reflected a regard for heightened sensory perception. Male decadent writers were *olfactifs*; they were Dandy connoisseurs of smell, and were familiar with fashions in women's perfume and perfume houses. Joris-Karl Huysmans's fiction is impregnated with a variety of smells, from rose water and frangipani to whiffs of ether and ptomaine (essential oils extracted from corpses). In his short story, "Le gousset" ("The Armpit"), he details the range of odours found in women's "boîtes à épices" ("spice-boxes"): "l'odeur du gousset pourrait se diviser à l'infini; nul arome n'a plus de nuances; c'est une gamme parcourant tout le clavier de l'odorat" ("the odour of the armpit could be analysed ad infinitum; no aroma has more nuances, its range traverses the whole keyboard of the sense of smell") (Huysmans 2004, 128). One of the most knowledgeable scholars in the odiferous field was Robert de Montesquiou, Proust's "professor of beauty" and decadent and aesthete *ne plus ultra*. In *Le Chef des odeurs suaves* (1907), he celebrates the fragrance of flowers, their variety and their suggestiveness, claiming that they "speak to the five senses which become one" (Montesquiou 1907, 277). In other poetic works and essays, he waxes lyrical on the capacity of perfume to take us on a journey to "l'au delà," or "the Beyond." His symbolist rhetoric in the essays he published between 1897 and 1908, and his association of perfume with nebulous, immeasurable desire, comes principally from Baudelaire's *Les fleurs du mal*. Several of Baudelaire's poems in this collection give us a sense of the provocative and vertiginous expansiveness of scent. This is the third stanza from "Le Flacon":

> Mille pensers dormaient, chrysalides funèbres,
> Frémissant doucement dans les lourdes ténèbres,
> Qui dégagent leur aile et prennent leur essor,
> Teintés d'azur, glacés de rose, lames d'or.

> (A thousand thoughts, tombed chrysalises, slept here
> Quietly quivering in the heavy shade
> Who now, shaking their wings, take to the air
> Azure-tinted, rose-glazed, gold-inlaid.)[4]

In much decadent writing, there is a preoccupation with intersensoriality and synaesthesia.[5] We are led by our senses, enticed to smell atmospheres, moods and states of mind. When Wilde envisaged the performance of his drama, *Salome* (1893), he imagined all the actors dressed in yellow and the orchestra to be replaced by braziers of perfume: "Think," he said, "the scented clouds rising and partly veiling the stage from time to time … a new perfume for each emotion" (Ellmann 1988, 351). In decadent writing, sounds, scents and tastes are orchestrated, arranged and juxtaposed to create special aesthetic effects. The opening paragraphs of Wilde's *The Picture of Dorian Gray*, for example, wilfully confuse the natural and the artificial and we, like the feminine and aestheticised Dorian, are meant to appreciate the scene as "a kind of momentary Japanese effect" (Wilde 2006, 5). In an unnatural synthesis of the visual, olfactory and aural, Wilde endows language with the sensuality of paint on canvas. Our attention is directed by a series of natural scents and artificial perfumes from the garden exterior, with its "rich odour of roses," "the heavy scent of the lilac" and "the more delicate perfume of the pink-flowering thorn," to the interior of the studio and the perfume of Lord Wotton's "innumerable cigarettes" (Wilde 2006, 5).[6] In Aubrey Beardsley's drawing *L'Abbé*, published to accompany his romance "Under the Hill" in the *Savoy* in 1896, the Abbé Fanfreluche dominates the natural setting, frowning at the rose on his muff. In this drawing, leaves curl in surrender and large petals droop, revealing full seed pods and erect pistils, and Beardsley depicts nature as overripe, "heavy with perfume, dripping with odours" (Wilde 2006, 5).[7]

Scholarly research into olfaction, or "smell studies," as Clare Brant has described, has been developing since the late 1980s, when Alain Corbin published his influential book, *The Foul and the Fragrant: Odour and the Social Imagination* (1986) (Brant 2004, 441). This was followed by a number of cultural-historical studies on smell, including Constance Classen, David Howes and Anthony Synnott, *Aroma: The Cultural History of Smell* (1994), and works on olfaction in literature and the visual arts: Hans Rindisbacher, *The Smell of Books* (1992) and Janice Carlisle, *Common Scents: Comparative Encounters in High-Victorian Fiction* (2004).[8] More recently, Catherine Maxwell has been exploring the relationship between olfactionism and aesthetic writing. In her essay "Scents and Sensibility: The Fragrance of Decadence," she suggests that a "poetics of perfume" directs our attention to the "strongly symbolic or figurative dimension" of relatively unodiferous English decadent writing, "providing a powerful set of connections between the material and immaterial, the body and the spirit" (Maxwell 2013, 202; 222). Maxwell focuses on the work of Wilde and two poems by Arthur Symons, "White Heliotrope" and "Peau d'Espagne," which evoke past erotic encounters through fragrances that were popular in the late-Victorian period. Drawing attention to the poems' modernity in two important ways, Maxwell argues that the visual impressionism of the poems shares some techniques of modern advertising copy (blurring, layering, close-ups, fade-outs), and she concludes that in both poems we find pre-Proustian associations between perfume and memory.

These pre-Proustian associations define a turning point in the literary culture of the 1890s, away from the materialist fixations of aestheticism towards a more symbolist preoccupation with olfaction and memory. The visual impressionism of Symons is modern, as Maxwell suggests, but Symons's subtle evocations of the way fragrance creates new spheres of imagination and recollection derives from his reading of continental symbolists. In his 1895 collection, *London Nights*, in particular, the physical spectacle of London theatre-land is counterpointed by the presence of intangible and imaginary realms teeming with the poet's thoughts, desires, and memories.

Symons's evocation of certain popular scents creates a recognisable material world of stage-door pick-ups and back-alley sex, and the poems transport us to a depressive realm of urban sexual manners and popular music-hall culture.[9] As Joseph Bristow has remarked, "Countless poems in *London Nights* deepen the impression that every aspect of the poet's life, especially his art, has been adulterated through contact with boisterous popular culture" (Bristow

2005, 3). Symons might name the perfume on the odd occasion (White Heliotrope, Peau d'Espagne, Patchouli, Lily of the Valley), but "economic" or "market" desire is sublimated to libidinal desire in his writing. Perfume is not principally a straightforward signifier of French artifice, an endorsement of the more lubricious aspects of modern French marketing culture, branded by conservative critics as "tainted whiffs from across the Channel" (Armour 1896, 12).[10] Symons's preoccupation is with the uncontained perfume cloud, the vaporising moment of scent, the point at which fragrance diffuses and images refract. Unlike Wilde, who uses floral fragrances and heavy perfume to symbolic and decorative effect, Symons associates perfume in its unstoppered formlessness, with the state of longing and the intangible and limitless spheres of the imagination and memory. In *London Nights*, the more abstract realms of "life," "thought" and 'ways" are described as perfumed. Perfume functions as a powerful metaphor for what Regenia Gagnier has termed the "insatiability of human wants" and the resistant, uncommodifiable agency of memory in pursuit of desire (Gagnier 2000). In Symons's poems, perfume supports both these metaphoric functions, but not to the same degree. While they vividly evoke modern consumerist culture at the *fin de siècle*, they are to a more substantial degree concerned with representing the impossibility of capture and ownership. Symons phrases this more elegantly in "Rosa Mundi":

> Love, they say, is a pain
> Infinite as the soul,
>   Ever, a longing to be
>   Love's, to infinity,
> Ever a longing in vain
> After a vanishing goal.
>   (1897, 39)

§

In the 1890s Symons's work is heavily influenced by his travels back and forth from the Continent. Symons's initial visit to France in 1889 and his subsequent trips in the early 1890s made a deep impression on the young poet, not least because he became entranced by ballet, music-hall and the world of "wigs and tights" ("On the Stage" 1897, 15). His meetings with prominent literary figures—Paul Verlaine, Stéphane Mallarmé, Catulle Mendès, Maurice Maeterlinck, and Joris-Karl Huysmans—gave him ideas about language and form, as his encounters with the work of Whistler, Degas, and the French Impressionist painters encouraged him to experiment with visual techniques in his poetry ("Parisian Impressionism," as Yeats termed it in *Autobiographies*) (Yeats 1890, 307). The literary sketches Symons made of writers, painters, sculptors, and musicians while travelling around with Havelock Ellis were brief and suggestive. On his return to London in 1892 he became music-hall and ballet critic for the *Star*, and commented that he had "the pleasant duty of running around from flat to flat after actresses, from stage-door to grill-room club after actors" (Symons 1892, Brotherton Collection, qtd. in Roger Lhombreaud 1963, 89). Reflecting back in 1900 on his times on the Continent, he remarked: "A wheel of memory seems to turn in my head like a kaleidoscope, flashing out the pictures of my own that I keep there" (Symons 1918, 46). Symons never personally doubted his own memory. "I have an extraordinary memory," Symons declared in a letter to the American professor, Warner Taylor, "which can be as vivid as visions" (Symons 1989, 257).

Symons was not concerned so much with the moral content of decadent writing (indeed, he publicly had to defend his own work several times against the moralising critics), as with the aesthetic of decadence, the way that decadence borrows from the other arts, including painting, music and dance, to create impressions and insights that imitate direct experience of the subject itself. The writer should "convey to us the impression which he has felt in such a way that we, too, feel it, and feel it to be the revelation of the inner meaning of just that landscape" (Symons 1923, 345). We find an anticipation of Symons's ideas in Anatole Baju's *L'École décadente* (*The School of Decadence*, 1887), in which he asserts that "la pensée écrite embrasse toute une époque, en résume toutes les tendances et est la source unique de cette vie vécue, vivante, pantelante que nous aimons, et qui nous secoue jusqu'au fond de l'être par d'électriques et vibrantes commotions" ("the written thought embraces an entire epoch, summarises all of its trends, and is the unique source of this lived, living, breathless life that we love, and that shakes us to the core of our being with electric and vibrant commotion") (Desmarais and Baldick, ed. 2012, 27). Baju's attempt to cohere decadence as a school of literature might not have been successful, but his pronouncements in his journal, *Le Décadent*, were clear. He demanded writing that represents the vividness of life, and "nous secoue jusqu'au fond de l'être" ("shakes us to the core") (Baju 1887, 6). Symons essentially found these qualities in the poetry of Paul Verlaine. "Poetry is something vague, intangible, evanescent," he wrote of Verlaine's "L'Art poétique," "a winged soul in flight 'towards other skies and other lives'" ("The Decadent Movement in Literature" 1923, 103). He goes on:

> compared with Verlaine at his best, all other contemporary work in verse seems not yet disenfranchised from mere "literature." To fix the last fine shade, the quintessence of things; to fix it fleetingly; to be a disembodied voice, and yet the voice of a human soul: that is the ideal of Decadence, and it is what Paul Verlaine has achieved. (1923, 106)

The paradox at the heart of Symons's notions about decadent poetics, that poetry should "fix" "fleetingly" "the quintessence of things" is distinctively both decadent and modern and looks back to the psychological unfixities of Baudelaire's poetry and forward to the melancholy and romantic modernism of T. S. Eliot.[11] In his poems, Symons uses perfume, like music in fact, with all its associations and suggestiveness, as a central metaphor; it not only evokes images of the remembered love object,[12] but through the form of the poem (and Symons was emphatic about the fusion of substance and form) suggests (rather than imitates) the act of remembering also. Perfume performs another role too—and this distinguishes Symons as a more accomplished and experimental poet than his fellow decadents (with the exception perhaps of Ernest Dowson)—perfume both triggers images, memories, and yet at the same time resists clear possession of them, creating a distance between the poem and its personal origins. As Symons phrases it in his poem "Memory," "Fragrant memories / Come and go" (1897, 100).

In his third collection of verse, *London Nights*, the relationship between notions of erotic desire and the transience of memory is delicate and ambiguous. He creates a carefully circumscribed and thus consistent world of eroticised artifice, across which flits a troupe of dancers and "footlight fanc[ies]" ("Nora on the Pavement" 1897, 7). In their entirety the poems evoke, with some despair, "the perfumed life" ("To Muriel: At the Opera" 1897, 51). In *London Nights*, we encounter the quintessence of *fin-de-siècle* poetry: a poetry of sensation, and, arguably, Symons at his lyrical best. "My life is like a music-hall" ventures the poet in "Prologue," and in the highly reflexive lyrics that follow in this first section, he offers the impression of London theatre-land as a place of longing, a space of countless looks and glances, both desirous and arousing desire. In "To a Dancer," "The eyes of all that see / Draw to her glances, stealing fire / From her desire that leaps to my desire / Her eyes that gleam for me!" (1897, 5). Caught up in the swirling rhythms and circuitous phrasings, repetitions and refrains, we are as if grabbed from the sidelines to dance along with the speaker. Alongside him, we watch from the stalls and loiter outside stage-doors where "Faces flicker and veer" in expectant desire ("At the stage-door" 1897, 16).

In this first group of poems, memory is a contingent and layered phenomenon triggered by visual experiences. In "Nora on the Pavement," for example, the sight of young Nora dancing on the "midnight pavement" engenders "Thronging desires and longing looks recur / And memorably re-incarnate her" (1897, 7). The speaker often seems dazzled, as if he is a stranger to the world of "wigs and tights," and this intensifies the sense of a bewilderingly remote perspective. In "On the Stage," the effort to see through the "whirling mist of multi-coloured lights" is intensified by the succession of impressions that disembody the dancers: "And after, wigs and tights, / Then faces, then a glimpse of profiles, then / Eyes, and a mist again: / And rouge, and always tights, and wigs, and tights" ("On the Stage" 1897, 15). The last sequence in this first section, entitled "Décor de Théâtre," draws our attention to appearance, façade, and the emptiness of performance. In "La Mélinite: Moulin Rouge," there is a dream-like succession of circles, roses, mirrors and shadows. In the rhythm and enjambments of the poem, is a single, twirling dancer who narcissistically "dances for her own delight" (1897, 24). In this poem, which Yeats called "one of the most perfect lyrics of our time," the restless movement of the poem suggests a "dance of shadows" (Yeats 2013, 334; Symons 1897, 24). Written in 1892, the poem is reminiscent of the curious line in the first act of Wilde's play, *Salome*, where the Young Syrian declares of the pallor of the princess: "How pale the Princess is! Never have I seen her so pale. She is like the shadow of a white rose in a mirror of silver" (Wilde 1997, 719). In Symons's poem, the reflected image of the dancer is as indistinct. Lines 11–12 and 13–16 use the same language and imagery for the most part, but the differences between the two sets of lines cleverly evoke the distortion in the dancer's mirrored image. Reality and the reflection of reality, Symons implies, do not match: "Alone, apart, one dancer watches / Her mirrored, morbid grace; / Before the mirror, face to face, / Alone, she watches / Her morbid, vague, ambiguous grace" ("La Mélinite" 1897, 24).

In a number of poems from *London Nights*, Symons uses perfume to suggest both the powerful impact of remembered experience ("In the Temple") and the inherently transient quality of remembering itself ("At the Ambassadeurs"). The distancing and standardising effects of triggered memory are cleverly sidestepped by Symons as he invokes the sense of smell, which enables him to keep closer contact with the feeling of the actual experience (yearning, desire, loss) for as long as the poem lasts. Huysmans attempts to elucidate the notion of a fleeting experience in one of his *Croquis Parisiens* (*Parisian Sketches*) entitled "The Folies-Bergère in 1879":

> C'est ainsi pourtant que les lieux et les choses les plus disparates se rencontrent dans une analogie qui semble bizarre, au premier chef. On évoque dans l'endroit où l'on se trouve les plaisirs de celui où l'on ne se trouve pas. Ça fait tête-bêche, coup double. C'est la courte joie que le présent inspire, déviée à l'instant où elle lasserait et prendrait fin et renouvelée et prolongée en une autre qui, vue au travers du souvenir, devient tout à la fois plus réelle et plus douce.
>
> (It's in this way that the most disparate places and things come together, through an analogy that seems bizarre at first sight. You evoke in the place you happen to be, the pleasures of the place you are not. This topsy-turvy fact cuts both ways. Like when a fleeting pleasure inspired by the present is diverted just as it's fading and coming to an end, and is renewed and prolonged in another which, seen through the eyes of memory, becomes at one and the same time both sweeter and more real.)
>
> (Huysmans 2004, 38)

In the controversial poem "Stella Maris," for example, which was published in the *Yellow Book* in 1894 (and accompanied by Aubrey Beardsley's *Night Piece*), Symons aestheticises his encounter with a "Juliet of the night" to such an extent that the beauty of his under-aged lover supersedes the shame and guilt (not that his critics appreciated this): "And I, remembering, would declare / that joy, not shame, is ours to share" (1897, 41). The poem uses both the intermittence of the lighthouse beam and the ebb and flow of waves against shore and rocks to suggest something orgasmic about the waves of memory that come and go. The memory of the young girl returns to the poet more strongly as the poem progresses, but as she materialises through remembrance it is not clear whether this will be a safe or dangerous re-experience. Like the lighthouse beam that both attracts and warns seafarers, the processes of memory are ambiguous and overwhelm the poet. In the second section, the physical intimacy of the lovers is realised in voluptuous detail:

> I feel the perfume of your hair,
> And your soft breast that heaves and dips,
> Desiring my desirous lips,
> And that ineffable delight
> When souls turn bodies, and unite
> In the intolerable, the whole
> Rapture of the embodied soul.
>
> (1897, 41)

Yet, in spite of the powerful nature of olfactory reminiscence, the object of the reminiscence remains tangled in a complex of thoughts and the effort in the last section of the poem is concentrated on justifying the sex and on redeeming the poet and his lover.

At the heart of *London Nights* is a poem, "White Heliotrope," in which Symons correlates olfaction, memory and desire. He uses the popular perfume, White Heliotrope, to mnemonically create a fleeting impression: an impression not only of a past sexual encounter, but also one of memory's transience. Perfume is both material and immaterial; it functions as the nominal subject of the poem and its vaporising qualities are suggested in the places where regular rhythms of the poem falter. White heliotrope, or *arborecum alba*, is an old-fashioned, Victorian plant that has a vanilla-baby-powder fragrance. In its synthetic state, heliotropin or piperonal is used as an ingredient in many perfumes, along with lily, rose, and musk. The scent *White Linen* by Estée Lauder, for example, contains late-Victorian base notes of white cedarwood, patchouli, and white heliotrope. In this poem, Symons exploits the sweet fragrance of the perfume to suggest what he calls in his poem "Paris" (1897, 89) "the scented ways," a vague reference to illicit eroticism. "White Heliotrope" opens with the drained and drowsy atmosphere of remembered post-coitus:

> The feverish room and that white bed,
>   The tumbled skirts upon a chair,
>   The novel flung half-open, where
> Hat, hair-pins, puffs, and paints, are spread;

The mirror that has sucked your face
    Into its secret deep of deeps,
    And there mysteriously keeps
Forgotten memories of grace;

And you, half dressed and half awake,
    Your slant eyes strangely watching me,
    And I, who watch you drowsily,
With eyes that, having slept not, ache;

This (need one dread? nay, dare one hope?)
    Will rise, a ghost of memory, if
    Ever again my handkerchief
Is scented with White Heliotrope.
                 (1897, 50)

The poem recalls an intimate scene, containing a woman, a bed and a "fever-ish room," which is evoked as "a ghost of memory" for the speaker "if / Ever again my handkerchief / Is scented with White Heliotrope." A woman reclines among a disarray of "Hat, hair-pins, puffs, and paints," watching the speaker, who watches her from an aesthetic distance. The speaker describes the recalled scene in quite strict iambic tetrameter in four stanzas of four lines, and yet the form of the poem yields occasionally to various irregularities of rhythm that suggest indistinctness, a ghosting of the memory. It is the *effect* of memory rather than the emotions engendered by remembering that pre-occupies the speaker, whose eyes "having slept not, ache." The atmosphere is soft and drowsy, and in the first stanza the repetition of "half"—in a "novel flung half-open," "half dressed and half awake"—suggests a soft exhalation of breath, echoed in the "white bed," the "Hat, hair-pins," "having," "hope," and "handkerchief," filling the poem with breaths and sighs.

There are two notable hesitations among the iambic tetrameter. In the first and fourteenth lines, the words "feverish" and "memory" add inconve-nient extra feet to the lines. It is less noticeable in the first line, as the reader is not yet familiar with the rhythm of the poem, but "the feverish room and that white bed" causes a stall upon "feverish," leading the reader to pause awkwardly upon the object at the centre of the scene—the bed—and also the first breath-like "h" noise of "white." In the final stanza, the second line, "Will rise, a ghost of memory, if" results in a similar hesitation, sign-posting the final lines with a forced decision over "me-mo-ry" or "mem-ry" and a caesura in the form of a comma mid-foot. Caesuras are dotted inconve-niently elsewhere; the fourth line includes an unsettling comma in the first foot: "Hat, hair-pins, puffs, and paints, are spread." This jars, as does the twelfth line: "With eyes that, having slept not, ache," a physical sensation we find articulated similarly in "Leves Amores II" ("The bed-clothes stifle me, I ache / With weariness, my eyelids prick") (1897, 46).[13] Both the hesi-tations in "White Heliotrope" cause a pause, followed by an aspirated "ha," thus causing the effect of the repeated "h" throughout the poem to stand out even further. Symons refuses to let the reader ignore these breathy sounds, which compound an atmosphere of gloaming, and the dim, yet potent, sensation of glimpsing (through the mind's eye) intimate abandon.

To return to the final stanza: the second line, and the words "Will rise" are notable for their position following the bracketed query, as they suggest a swelling of the poem to its climax and also serve as part of the sexual imagery that is strewn throughout the poem. This touch of sexuality is subtle at first, but it becomes pronounced on re-reading, as "sucked," "tumbled," "spread," "flung half-open," "secret deep of deeps," "feverish," and finally "this ... will rise" combine to impress us with the sensation of past vigorous sexual activity.

All this is evoked for the speaker by the heady scent of White Heliotrope, a "ghost of memory" rising from the perfume of his white handkerchief. Maxwell describes the speaker in the final stanza as "self-congratulatory about breaking taboos," and as "adopting a pose of insouciance" (Maxwell 2013, 216). However, I would argue that the persona of the speaker (as well as the objects in his consciousness) is not debonair and pleased with himself, but that the end of the poem in particular leaves us with a sense of his intangible sadness, full of a melancholy that acknowledges the limits of perfume and the ephemerality of human experience. Once released from its bottle, fragrance lasts only a short while, and like desire, perfume, so Symons suggests, intoxicates but then evaporates. The paradox suggested by Symons's poems is the fact that memory, like desire, is impossible to contain or "fix." The resuscitated sensation of desire for a past moment only intensifies the impossibility of being able to possess it for longer than it lasts. This is the vivid sensation at the heart of the poem. Baudelaire puts it perfectly in "Je t'adore, à l'égal ..." ("I love you as I love ... "), "Et t'aime d'autant plus, belle, que tu me fuis" ("And I love you more since you escape me") (Baudelaire 1993, 52). In "White Heliotrope," the ephemerality of the remembered experience implied by the perfume moves away from the more material or commercial allusions of the poem.

In "White Heliotrope," the sighs and breaths across the poem unify the series of refracted images, but they also soften and dim our perception, and as with "Memory," what remains is the reflexive impression or the sensation of reminiscence itself. Symons paints a vivid picture of this in "Stella Maris," in which "The glancing of the lighthouse light" suggests something potent about the searching quality of remembrance: "For, surely as I see to-night / The glancing of the lighthouse light / Against the sky, across the bay, / As, turn by turn, it falls my way, / So surely do I see your eyes / Out of the empty night arise" (1897, 40).

Symons was not only concerned with the problem of definition and the capture of the elusive romantic moment. In the fifth and final section of *London Nights*, he suggests the subtle paradoxical blocking by the processes of memory itself of the formation and retention of thoughts and memories. As *London Nights* comes to a close, the oscillating tension between physical desire and the states of confusion and loss that it engenders are visualised as wafts and "billows" of perfume.[14] In "Wine of Circe" the poet drowns in his own senses:

> Pantingly close, against your breast: the rose
> Of your lips reddens to a rose of fire,
> That sinks and wavers, odorously, nigher.
> And your breast beats upon me like a sea
> Of warmth and perfume, ah! engulphing me
> Into the softness of its waves that cover
> My drowning senses amorously over.
>
> (1897, 101)

In this section, the physical ache of sexual desire is fused with the painful sensation of remembering. "Only the aching sense of sex / Wholly controls and does perplex," Symons says in "Liber Amoris" (1897, 104). In the poem, "Memory," Symons brings together the idea of the object of reminiscence: "the thought of you remaining" with musings on the transience of memory itself, which erases the object almost as soon as it appears to the mind, so that it becomes "A hid sweetness, in my brain." (1897, 100). The poem refuses to yield its subject—the poet's loved one—to the reader; thoughts of her stay recessed in the way that perfume lingers in the folds of cloth, but although the poem is not able to recreate her (that is the point), she is *more* because "Other moments I may know / That shall waft me, in their going, / As a breath blown to and fro"(1897, 100). What we are left with is the fragrance of the memories, but not the memories themselves. What we are left with, in short, are the cloud-like formations of memory: memory as a vaporising, distancing agency that resists our attempts to possess and decipher. Jean-Bertrand Pontalis describes this well in his book *Windows* (2003). In a chapter entitled "Memory," he says:

> It could be that memories function like an obstacle to memory itself even though they claim to be what is put in it, what memory preciously preserves, protected from the erosion of time (being able to evoke at one's will a crowd of memories means having an excellent memory). However, I see the inventory of memories as almost opposed to the work of the memory in that dreams put it into play in their strange connections and analysis brings it to light. Even remembrance—the return of events sometimes insignificant, scenes, forgotten sensations that suddenly resurface and then it's more even than a reminiscence: a resuscitation—is distanced from this silent memory, from this stuff of which we are made.
>
> (Pontalis 2003, 69)

The distinction Pontalis is making here between willed memory and involuntary remembrance is pertinent to Symons's invocation of memories in

London Nights, for what Symons is creating is a world in which man is subject to the vicissitudes of the unconscious. In a later poem, "Hallucination: II" (1902), he apostrophises "Dreams are the truth: let the world fade!" As sensations intensify and longings reach a crescendo, the clarity upon which we rely for direction deserts us. Words fail, and the poet is overwhelmed by a correspondence of the senses:

> Giddy expectancy consumes
> My senses; but what breath perfumes
> The air with scents of heliotrope?
> I sicken with a wild desire,
> I drown in sweetness, till it seems
> As if the after-taste of dreams
> Came back into my mouth like fire.
>
> ("Hallucination: II" 1902, 119)

Throughout his long career Symons was preoccupied with the "interpenetration of substance and form," and the way that literature borrows from the other arts, including painting, music, and dance, to create impressions and insights that imitate direct experience of the subject itself (Symons 1904, 194).He was a poet of transition, both a decadent and a modern poet. His preoccupation with form, however, with literary impressionism and transience distinguishes him from other decadent poets. English decadent verse tended to follow the technical conservatism of its age, and with the exception of only a few experiments in free verse and prose poetry, tended to favour fixed rhyming forms in both lyric and narrative verse (especially the sonnet and ballad). Its truly distinctive features lie in subject matter and in figurative treatment. There is a determined avoidance of positive natural imagery and instead a preference for recurrent tropes of decline, decrepitude, and disease, which are often interwoven with an eroticism in which artificiality, cruelty, and sterility are emphasised. We find all this in Symons's verse, but we also find something more. As I hope to have shown, there is a quality of attention to language and form that suggests the simultaneity of recollection's vibrancy and limitations, which indicate the vital importance for Symons of acknowledging "the great suspense in which we live" (1908, 171). He articulates this in his revision of the essay, "The Decadent Movement in Literature." In the six years since its publication in *Harper's New Magazine* and its revision as *The Symbolist Movement in Literature* in 1899, Symons champions literature as the embodiment of spiritual forces, and he praises the symbolists for evading "the old bondage of rhetoric":

> Here, then, in this revolt against exteriority, against rhetoric, against a materialistic tradition; in this endeavour to disengage the ultimate essence, the soul, of whatever exists and can be realized by the consciousness; in this dutiful waiting upon every symbol by which the soul

of things can be made visible; literature, bowed down by so many bur-
dens, may at last attain liberty, and its authentic speech. (1908, 8–9)

In *London Nights*, especially in those poems that are about memory and
desire, such as "White Heliotrope," Symons experiments with the suggestive
range of poetry. For him the poem is a perfume bottle, a container of sensa-
tions, impressions and effusions, a place where fleeting reality is momentarily captured. We find the most vivid representation of this idea in modern
French verse in the second half of the nineteenth century—in Baudelaire,
Mallarmé, Verlaine, for instance—and, at the *fin de siècle*, in the writings of
Robert de Montesquiou who commented in "Pays des aromates" ("Land of
Fragrances") that a poem is "un bal des odeurs" ("a dance of fragrances")
(Montesquiou 1999, 110). But in Symons's most fragrant collection of
verse, *London Nights*, the references to perfume signal the disengagement
of English decadence with physicality and materialism and herald a more
symbolist contemplation of immateriality, of "things as shadows, through
which we have our shadowy passage" (1908, 174).

Notes

1. Unless otherwise stated, translations are my own. See also "L'Etranger." In Charles
   Baudelaire. 1989. *Baudelaire. Vol 2, The Poems in Prose with La Fanfarlo*, edited,
   introduced, and translated by Francis Scarfe, 28. London: Anvil.
2. This point is made by Regenia Gagnier in *Idylls of the Marketplace: Oscar
   Wilde and the Victorian Public* (Gagnier 1896, 14).
3. "Even in ordinary normal persons, personal odour tends to play a not inconsid-
   erable part in sexual attractions and sexual repulsions. This is sometimes termed
   'olfactionism'" (Ellis 1936, 2:75).
4. Translation by Derek Mahon for the author, August 2012.
5. See Steve Connor. 2004. "Intersensoriality." Paper presented at the Conference
   of the Senses, Thames Valley University, February 6.
6. "These opening sentences fairly reek," claims John Sutherland, and he goes on
   to state that for Anglo-Saxon literature "smells are indelicate" (Sutherland 1997,
   196; 197). In regard to the horticultural references in *Dorian Gray*, Sutherland
   underlines their unnatural coincidence: "It is not inconceivable that the flowers,
   blooms and blossoms which Wilde describes (lilac, rose, laburnum, thorn) might
   just coincide on the branch in mid-June—but not in the full odiferousness about
   which the first chapter is eloquent" (196–7).
7. See Chapter 1 of Aubrey Beardsley. 1896. "Under the Hill: A Romantic Story"
   The Savoy, no.1 (January): 151–70; 160–64. Reprinted as Aubrey Beardsley.
   1998. "The Story of Venus and Tannhäuser." *In Black and White: the Literary
   Remains of Aubrey Beardsley*, edited by Stephen Calloway and David Colvin.
   London: Cypher Press.
8. In 2006 two edited collections were published: Jim Drobnick (ed.), *The
   Smell Culture Reader* (Oxford: Berg) and Lara Feigel (ed.), *A Nosegay:
   A Literary Journey from the Fragrant to the Fetid* (London: Old Street).
   In the last few years, scholarly attention has focused on late nineteenth-
   century fiction and painting, with particular emphasis on the traditions of

aestheticism and decadence. In her doctoral thesis, Christina Bradstreet considers nineteenth-century debates surrounding the role of smell in aesthetics. See Christina Bradstreet. 2008. "Scented Visions: the Nineteenth-century Olfactory Imagination." PhD diss., Birkbeck, University of London. In her article "'Wicked with Roses': Floral Femininity and the Erotics of Scent," Bradstreet offers a detailed visual analysis of Charles Courtney Curran's painting *Scent of the Rose* (1890) and John William Waterhouse's *The Soul of the Rose* (1908). See Christina Bradstreet. 2007. "'Wicked with Roses': Floral Femininity and the Erotics of Scent." *Nineteenth-century Art Worldwide* 6 (1):1–20 http://www.19thc-artworldwide.org/index.php/spring07/144-qwicked-with-rosesq-floral-femininity-and-the-erotics-of-scent.

9. For studies of Symons's music-hall poems, see R. Van Bronswijk. 2006. "The Brilliance of Gas-Lit Eyes: Arthur Symons's Erotic Auto-Eroticism Observed." In *'And Never Know the Joy': Sex and the Erotic in English Poetry,* edited by C. C. Barfoot, 287–302. Amsterdam: Rodopi. Also Karlien Van den Beukel. 2005. "Arthur Symons's Night Life." In *Babylon or New Jerusalem? Perceptions of the City in Literature*, edited by Valeria Tinkler-Villani, 135–53. Amsterdam: Rodopi.

10. Armour refers to the "tainted whiffs from across the Channel that lodge the Gallic germs in our lungs" (12).

11. Finding the traces of Symons in Eliot is described by Maxwell in terms of the metaphor of "drydown." She explains, "Symons's decadent mnemonic perfumes do not completely fade away but become the ghosts of fragrance in one of his grudging inheritors" (Maxwell 2013, 220).

12. To borrow a useful, if dismissive, phrase from Edna O'Brien's short story "The Love Object."

13. See also Symons, Arthur. 1897. "Clair de Lune." *London Nights*, 88. 2nd ed. London: John Lane; Symons, Arthur. 1897b. "Remembrance." *Amoris Victima*, 27. London: Leonard Smithers.

14. In "Escalade," Symons refers to the "Scented billows of soft thunder" (1897, 97).

Works Cited

Armour, Margaret. "Aubrey Beardsley and the Decadents," *Magazine of Art* 20, (1896): 12.

Baju, Anatole. 1887. *L'Ecole décadente*. Paris: L. Vanier.

Baudelaire, Charles. 1988. "La soupe et les nuages." In *Twenty Prose Poems*, translated by Michael Hamburger, 67. San Francisco: City Lights Books.

———. "Le Flacon." In *The Flowers of Evil*, translated by J. McGowan, 48. Oxford: Oxford University Press.

———. 1989. "L'Etranger." In *Baudelaire. Vol 2, The Poems in Prose with La Fanfarlo*, edited, introduced and translated by Francis Scarfe, 28. London: Anvil.

———. 1993. "Je t'adore, à l'égal …," In *The Flowers of Evil*, translated by J. McGowan, 52. Oxford: Oxford University Press.

Beardsley, Aubrey. 1896. "Under the Hill: A Romantic Story" *The Savoy*, no.1 (January): 151–70; 160–64.

Betjeman, John. 1948. Introduction to *The Eighteen-Nineties: A Period Anthology in Prose and Verse*, edited by John Betjeman and Martin Secker, xi–xvi. London: Richards Press.

Bradstreet, Christina. 2007. "'Wicked with Roses': Floral Femininity and the Erotics of Scent." *Nineteenth-century Art Worldwide* 6 (1): 1–20 http://www.19thc-artworldwide.org/index.php/spring07/144-qwicked-with-rosesq-floral-femininity-and-the-erotics-of-scent.

———. 2008. "Scented Visions: the Nineteenth-century Olfactory Imagination." PhD diss., Birkbeck, University of London.

Brant, Clare. 2004. "Fume and Perfume: Some Eighteenth-Century Uses of Smell." *Journal of British Studies* 43 (4): 444–63.

Bristow, Joseph. 2005. Introduction to *The Fin-de-Siècle Poem*, 1–46. Athens, Ohio: Ohio University Press.

Connor, Steve. 2004. "Intersensoriality." Paper presented at the Conference of the Senses, Thames Valley University, February 6.

Desmarais, Jane and Chris Baldick, ed. 2012. *Decadence: An Annotated Anthology*. Manchester: Manchester University Press.

Drobnick, Jim., ed. 2006. *The Smell Culture Reader*. Oxford: Berg.

Ellis, Havelock. 1936. *Studies in the Psychology of Sex: Sexual Selection in Man*. Vol.2. New York: Random House.

Ellmann, Richard. 1988. *Oscar Wilde*. London: Penguin.

Feigel, Lara, ed. 2006. *A Nosegay: A Literary Journey from the Fragrant to the Fetid*. London: Old Street.

Gagnier, Regenia. 1986. *Idylls of the Marketplace: Oscar Wilde and the Victorian Public*. Stanford: Stanford University Press.

———. 2000. *The Insatiability of Human Wants: Economics and Aesthetics in Market Society*. Chicago: University of Chicago Press.

Huysmans, Joris-Karl. 2004. "The Armpit." In *Parisian Sketches*, translated by Brendan King, 126–28. Sawtry, Cambs.: Dedalus.

———. 2004. "The Folies-Bergère in 1879." In *Parisian Sketches*, translated by Brendan King, 29–44. Sawtry, Cambs.: Dedalus.

Maxwell, Catherine. 2013. "Scents and Sensibility: The Fragrance of Decadence." In *Decadent Poetics: Literature and Form at the British Fin de Siècle*, edited by Jason David Hall and Alex Murray, 201–25. Basingstoke: Palgrave.

Mendelssohn, Michèle. 2007. *Henry James, Oscar Wilde and Aesthetic Culture*. Edinburgh: Edinburgh University Press.

Montesquiou, Robert de. 1907. *Le Chef des odeurs suaves*. Paris: Georges Richard. Quoted in Richard Stamelman, *Perfume: Joy, Obsession, Scandal, Sin—A Cultural History of Fragrance from 1750 to the Present* (New York: Rizzoli, 2006), 147.

———. 1999. "Pays des aromates." In Robert de Montesquiou and Marcel Proust, *Professeur de beauté*, 101–10. Paris: Editions La Bibliothèque.

Pontalis, J.-B. 2003. *Windows [Fenêtres, 2000]*, translated by Anne Quinney. Lincoln and London: University of Nebraska Press.

Stamelman, Richard. 2006. *Perfume: Joy, Obsession, Scandal, Sin - A Cultural History of Fragrance from 1750 to the Present*. New York: Rizzoli.

Sutherland, John. 1997. *Is Heathcliff a Murderer? Puzzles in 19th-century Fiction*. Oxford: Oxford University Press.

Symons, Arthur. 1892. Brotherton Collection, Leeds University. Quoted in Roger Lhombreaud, *Arthur Symons: A Critical Biography* (London: Unicorn, 1963), 89.

———. 1897. "At the Stage Door." *London Nights*, 16. 2nd ed. London: John Lane

———. 1897. "Clair de Lune." *London Nights*, 88. 2nd ed. London: John Lane

———. 1897. "Escalade." *London Nights*, 97. 2nd ed. London: John Lane.

——. 1897. "La Mélinite: Moulin Rouge." *London Nights*, 24. 2nd ed. London: John Lane.

——. 1897. "Leves Amore II." *London Nights*, 46. 2nd ed. London: John Lane.

——. 1897. "Liber Amoris." *London Nights*, 104. 2nd ed. London: John Lane.

——. 1897. "Memory." *London Nights*, 100. 2nd ed. London: John Lane.

——. 1897. "Nora on the Pavement." *London Nights*, 7. 2nd ed. London: John Lane.

——. 1897. "On the Stage." *London Nights*, 15. 2nd ed. London: John Lane.

——. 1897. "Prologue." *London Nights*, 3. 2nd ed. London: John Lane.

——. 1897. "Rosa Mundi." *London Nights*, 39. 2nd ed. London: John Lane.

——. 1897. "Stella Maris" *London Nights*, 41. 2nd ed. London: John Lane.

——. 1897. "To a Dancer" *London Nights*, 5. 2nd ed. London: John Lane.

——. 1897. "To Muriel: At the Opera" *London Nights*, 51. 2nd ed. London: John Lane.

——. 1897. "White Heliotrope." *London Nights*, 50. 2nd ed. London: John Lane.

——. 1897. "Wine of Circe." *London Nights*, 101. 2nd ed. London: John Lane.

——.1897b. "Remembrance." *Amoris Victima*, 27. London: Leonard Smithers.

——. 1902. "Hallucination: II." In *Poems*, 119. London: Heinemann.

——. 1904. "What is Poetry?" In *Studies in Prose and Verse*, 194. London: J. M. Dent.

——. 1908. *The Symbolist Movement in Literature* [1899]. London: Constable.

——. 1918. "Paris and ideas." [1900] In *Colour Studies in Paris*, 43–51. New York: E. P. Dutton & Co.

——. 1923. "Impressionistic Writing." In *Dramatis Personae*, 343–50. Indianapolis: Bobbs-Merrill.

——. 1923. "The Decadent Movement in Literature." In *Dramatis Personae*, 96–117. Indianapolis: Bobbs-Merrill.

——. 1989. "Letter to Warner Taylor [late 1931?]." In *Selected Letters, 1880–1935*, edited by Karl Beckson and John M. Munro, 257. Basingstoke: Macmillan.

Van Bronswijk, R. 2006. "The Brilliance of Gas-Lit Eyes: Arthur Symons's Erotic Auto-Eroticism Observed." In *'And Never Know the Joy': Sex and the Erotic in English Poetry*, edited by C. C. Barfoot, 287–302. Amsterdam: Rodopi.

Van den Beukel, Karlien. 2005. "Arthur Symons's Night Life." In *Babylon or New Jerusalem? Perceptions of the City in Literature*, edited by Valeria Tinkler-Villani, 135–53. Amsterdam: Rodopi.

Wilde, Oscar. 1997. *Salome* [1894, original French composed 1891, published 1893]. In *The Collected Works of Oscar Wilde*, 717–42. London: Wordsworth.

Wilde, Oscar. 2006. *The Picture of Dorian Gray*, edited by Joseph Bristow. Oxford: Oxford University Press.

Yeats, W. B. 2013. *The Collected Works of W. B. Yeats*. Vol. 9, *Uncollected Articles and Reviews: Uncollected Articles and Reviews Written between 1886 and 1900*, edited by J. P. Frayne and M. Marchaterre. Basingstoke: Palgrave.

——. 1980. *Autobiographies*. London: Macmillan.

Part II
Human Currencies

4 Urban Economies and the Dead-Woman Muse in the Poetry of Amy Levy and Djuna Barnes

Sarah Parker

1. The Dead Woman as Muse

This chapter addresses, for the first time, the revealing continuities between the late Victorian poet and novelist Amy Levy (1861–1889) and the American modernist Djuna Barnes (1892–1982).[1] During the latter half of the twentieth century, both poets enjoyed a critical revival which focused on the complex portrayal of identity in their work, particularly their constructions (and deconstructions) of gender, sexuality, race, ethnicity, and religion. Thematically, their poetry exhibits striking parallels—as suggested by the kinds of critical attention that their work has tended to attract. Both Levy's and Barnes's work has frequently been read in terms of gender identity, the New Woman, diasporic and abject identities, lesbian identity, Jewish identity, urban space, and modernity.

However, persistent demarcations between the Victorian and the Modern have meant that critics have yet to fully consider the parallels between their works: parallels that reveal productive insights into gender identity, the new urban woman, and queer desire. My aim in this chapter is, therefore, to compare their poetry and simultaneously, to probe the more troubling aspects of their work by focusing particularly on Levy's and Barnes's shared portrayal of the dead woman as muse. Their poems uncover the ways in which the new urban woman was endangered by her presence in the city street, objectified by the male gaze and threatened by male violence (most notoriously, in the case of Jack the Ripper, whose murders took place at the time Levy was writing). In both poets' work, female corpses are categorised and commoditised, suggesting that women, whether living or dead, are entrapped within a system of urban consumption that denigrates the female body. In this sense, their poetry constitutes a reflection on the libidinal economies of the city space, in which the new public woman is revealed to be a victim of ruthless capitalist logic, circulating as a ghostly reminder of the price of so-called liberation.[2]

The dead-woman muse is a ghostly presence that haunts both Levy's and Barnes's bodies of work with startling persistence, as critics of both poets have noted. For instance, Rebecca Loncraine observes that Barnes is "preoccupied with images of the body, and especially the corpse. Her muse is a dead woman" (2003, 42), while Emma Francis remarks that Levy's lyric poems frequently "use death as lexicon through which the speakers seek to understand their experience" (1999, 190). However, despite these continuities, Levy's and Barnes's representations of the dead-woman muse exhibit subtle distinctions. In Amy Levy's work, particularly in her final volume *A London Plane-Tree, and Other Verse* (1889), this dead woman appears primarily as a hazy urban spectre; in the unsettling lyric entitled "In the Mile End Road," the beloved appears to walk up "the crowded street" towards the speaker (50). At the poem's close, the speaker suddenly recollects "My only love was dead" (50), revealing this to be an impossible encounter.[3] Elsewhere in the volume, this sense of the uncanny endures, since in numerous poems—particularly in a sub-section entitled "Love, Dreams, and Death"—speakers are visited by disembodied spirits that subtly permeate their dreams, such as in "Borderland":

> As the first faint dawn comes creeping
> Thro' the pane, I am aware
> Of an unseen presence hovering,
> Round, above, in the dusky air
>
> (1889, 42)

In marked contrast to such airy visitations, Barnes's dead beloved is portrayed as grotesquely corporeal. Less a ghost, more a corpse, Barnes finds inspiration in a dead woman whose material reality is unassailable. For example, in "The Flowering Corpse" (1923), a beloved woman's body nourishes the earth, causing flowers and ferns to sprout:

> Over the body and the quiet head
> Like stately ferns above an austere tomb,
> Soft hairs blow; and beneath her armpits bloom
> The drowsy passion flowers of the dead.
>
> (2005, 91)[4]

As the final poem in *The Book of Repulsive Women* (1915), Barnes presents us with "Suicide: Corpse B": "Her body shock-abbreviated / As a city cat" (2005, 55). The darkly comic edge of such poems echoes Barnes's *Vanity Fair* article (published under her pseudonym, Lydia Steptoe) entitled "What Is Good Form in Dying? In Which a Dozen Dainty Deaths Are Suggested for Daring Damsels" (1923). In this article, Barnes advises on elegant modes of suicide, unnervingly combining this with the flippant rhetorical style of a fashion magazine: advising that blondes, for example, "hang sweetly, debonairly, and perseveringly by the neck," while brunettes should drink "slow green poison" (Steptoe 1923, 73). In this sense, Barnes's corpses are shockingly commodified. Throughout her *oeuvre* she consistently points up parallels between the female corpse feeding the earth, and the woman's body as urban detritus, promiscuously circulating through the city space, eternally bound to perform the role of fashion victim and object of the gaze, even after her death. Through the dead-woman muse, Barnes articulates her critique of a modernity that holds out the promise of female liberation, while women in fact remain stuck in an economic system that constantly depreciates their value.

Of course, the dead woman is part of a tradition that reaches far beyond Levy's and Barnes's work. Elisabeth Bronfen's seminal study *Over Her Dead Body: Death, Femininity and the Aesthetic* (1992) documents the persistent presence of the dead woman throughout literary history. Taking her cue from Edgar Allan Poe's assertion that "the death of a beautiful woman is, unquestionably, the most poetical topic in the world" (Poe 1846, 165), Bronfen explores the appeal of this trope that recurs throughout art and literature, from Samuel Richardson's *Clarissa* (1748) to Vladimir Nabokov's *Lolita* (1955). Using psychoanalytical theory, Bronfen considers why death, femininity, and the image of the dead woman are consistently linked in the work of male artists and writers. She concludes that the dead woman in art serves "as a displaced signifier for masculinity, survival, preservation and continuation" (Bronfen 1992, 433), and is obsessively invoked as a way of warding off the threat of annihilation:

> The beauty of Woman and the beauty of the image both give the illusion of intactness and unity, cover the insupportable signs of lack, deficiency, transiency and promise their spectators the impossible – an obliteration of death's ubiquitous 'castrative' threat to the subject.
>
> (Bronfen 1992, 64)

However, such repression is always doomed to fail, particularly since the actual act of representation 'kills' the living feminine body—to whom it ostensibly refers—into a 'dead' image: "Beauty, however, always also includes death's inscription, because it requires the translation (be it in fantasy or in reality) of an imperfect, animate body, into a perfect, inanimate image, a dead 'figure'" (Bronfen 1992, 64).

In order to understand how Levy and Barnes manipulate this trope, it is necessary to contextualise the dead-woman muse in terms of the concept of the muse more generally. Throughout literary tradition, the muse has served as the passive signifier of the male artist's active inspiration: the vessel through which he expresses his subjectivity. This muse-poet dynamic has been gendered throughout literary history; from the earliest appearance of the nine muses in Ancient Greek mythology, to Dante's Beatrice and beyond, the muse has consistently appeared as a beautiful feminine figure. Even when the muse's image is based on that of a real, living woman, the image projected in art or poetry is composed primarily by the male artist's shaping imagination, formed from the 'raw material' that her living presence provides. To the extent that she serves as object of the poet's desire, and inspiration for his art, the muse is the poet's opus. She does not have (as far as *he* is concerned) an identity outside of his objectifying gaze. Christina Rossetti—who had modelled for her brother's paintings and witnessed his relationships with various muse-figures such as Elizabeth Siddal—explored this discrepancy between the living woman and the artist's muse in her poem "In an Artist's Studio" (written 1856):

> He feeds upon her face by day and night,
> And she with true kind eyes looks back on him,
> Fair as the moon and joyful as the light:
> Not wan with waiting, not with sorrow dim;
> Not as she is, but was when hope shone bright;
> Not as she is, but as she fills his dream.
>
> (Rossetti 2008, 49)

The dynamic described in Rossetti's poem, in which (from the male artist's perspective) the "dead" artistic representation of the model is preferable to her living reality, in part explains the popularity of the dead woman as the ultimate muse figure. As suggested by Bronfen, in performing the role of muse, a woman becomes nothing more (or less) than a dead image of perfection. This transmogrification is more easily accomplished if the living woman is no longer there. In other words, if the "real" woman is absent, her image can be reconstituted with abandon, free from the troubling alterity announced by her actual presence. In this sense, the dead woman and the concept of the muse are inextricably connected; *every* muse is in some sense a dead woman.

Thus, poetic inspiration, death, and femininity become enmeshed through centuries of art and literature, so that the image of the dead woman comes to serve as a commentary on the creation of art itself:

> Because her dying figures as an analogy to the creation of an art work, and the depicted death serves as a double of its formal condition, the 'death of a beautiful woman' marks the *mise en abyme* of a text, the moment of self-reflexivity, where the text seems to comment on itself and its own process of composition, and so decomposes itself.
>
> (Bronfen 1992, 71)

But what does the prevalence of the dead-woman muse mean for a *woman* writer? If, in the prevailing cultural *mythos*, the creation of art can only be accomplished through female destruction, how can a living woman assert her own power to create art, without falling victim to this potentially self-annihilative narrative? For in the case of women writers, the dead-woman muse comes to represent not the imagined annihilation of the other, but the female artist's own death or self-destruction. Bronfen suggests a number of strategies by which women writers may attempt to subvert this destructive dynamic. Chief among these is what she terms a "hysteric strategy": a strategy by which women writers repeat and parody the conventions of male literary tradition. This exposes such male conventions to strip them of their power and authority: "hysterical writing installs conventions such as the masculinity of the gaze, the deadness of the feminine body, only to subvert and disturb the security of these stakes in cultural self-representation" (Bronfen 1992, 406). [5]

While Bronfen, following Linda Hutcheon, identifies a hysteric strategy as one found primarily in contemporary, postmodern women's writing, I argue that we can identify the roots of such a strategy in Levy's and Barnes's various poetic representations of the dead-woman muse. In many ways, the dead woman serves as the ultimate embodiment of Levy's and Barnes's complex ideas about gender, sexuality, desire, femininity, identity, authorship, and otherness. As such, this aspect of their work, which has been largely neglected, deserves more critical attention than it has hitherto attracted. Such neglect may in part arise from the fact that the presence of the dead woman in Levy's and Barnes's poetic *oeuvre*, when it *has* been noted, has been read as highly problematic. For example, in her foundational survey of lesbian literature *Surpassing the Love of Men* (1981), Lillian Faderman laments that Barnes apparently internalised decadent male writers' negative portrayal of lesbianism (Faderman 1985, 364).[6] Levy has also been criticised for drawing connections between female homoerotic desire and death.[7] For critics, there is perhaps something embarrassing (if not dangerous) in these women poets' clinging to a trope irredeemably associated with the male-orientated poetic traditions that cast woman as a dead object, rather than an active creator. Moving on from this critical position, I will illustrate that while Levy and Barnes consistently draw on the tradition of the dead-woman muse—and draw on it in ways that are disturbing, challenging and riven with ambivalence—they also reimagine this trope for their own ends. Their verse parodies masculine conventions and imbues their portrayal of the dead woman with a sense of female subjectivity and homoerotic desire. Rather than rejecting them as politically insanitary, we can benefit from looking in detail at Levy's and Barnes's representations of the dead-woman muse.

Despite the differences in the representation of the dead-woman muse briefly mentioned above—Levy's wispy apparition; Barnes's earthy corpse—I propose that in both Levy's and Barnes's poetic *oeuvres*, the dead woman serves two purposes. The first is to reveal the ways in which women were both empowered and endangered by their increasing access to, and visibility within, urban city spaces in the late nineteenth and early twentieth century. The second is to establish how female homoerotic desire (and nascent queer identity) is subtly encoded through the trope of the apparitional lesbian: a concept theorised by Terry Castle (1993). Read together, Levy's and Barnes's depictions of the dead-woman muse, therefore, reveal much about the changing position of women and emerging constructions of homosexuality in the late nineteenth and early twentieth century, particularly in the context of the increasingly modernised urban environments that both poets inhabited.

2. Suicide in the City: The New Woman, Transportation and Dangerous Urban Economies

In her final volume, *A London Plane-Tree, and Other Verse* (1889), Levy is primarily inspired by urban scenes, portraying women as confident traversers of the city space. For example, in "Ballade of an Omnibus," the speaker is a female passenger who gleefully relates how:

> The city pageant, early and late
> Unfolds itself, rolls by, to be
> A pleasure deep and delicate.
> An omnibus suffices me.
>
> (1889, 22)

Critics such as Ana Parejo Vadillo have read this volume of Levy's poems as voicing the "new public woman" of the late nineteenth century: an increasingly visible and independent public woman emerging as a regular presence on public transport, or on foot, confidently traversing the city streets. This figure came to be linked with the many images of the "New Woman," which were circulating in art and literature at that time (such as Grant Allen's *The Woman Who Did* [1895] and New Woman fiction by Sarah Grand, George Egerton, and Mona Caird). Indeed, as Deborah Parsons notes, "urbanness" was one of the hallmarks of the New Woman: "[a]s both social figure and literary caricature, she was a specifically urban character, the result of the circumstances and qualities of a growing metropolitan society" (Parsons 2000, 82–3). Previously, the term "public woman" denoted a fallen woman or prostitute, forced to live by her wits and display herself as a commodity to the roving eye of the male *flâneur*. The increasing presence of women in the city led to a shift in the meaning of the term "public woman," and thus to a transformation of the signification of this figure in literature. As Lynda Nead notes, by the 1860s, even unaccompanied, middle-class women were publically present in the city, challenging rigid notions of the "separate spheres" (2000, 67). As growing numbers of independent women employed as shop-girls, secretaries, post office clerks, dress-makers and typists, moved around the city, the "public woman" lost her stigma and instead became associated with modernity and the hastening pace of urban life.

Amy Levy, who was born in Clapham and later moved with her family to Endsleigh Gardens, Bloomsbury, was particularly inspired by the possibilities of the urban environment opening up to women at this time: "[f]or Levy … writing the city, writing London, marked a sense of exciting newness, of poetic self-discovery and presence" (Vadillo 2005, 57). For example, the title poem in Levy's final volume *A London Plane-Tree* (1889) neatly aligns the female poet with the city-scene, observing from her garret window the plane-tree which "loves the town":

> Green is the plane-tree in the square,
>   The other trees are brown;
> They droop and pine for country air;
>   The plane-tree loves the town.

> Here from my garret-pane, I mark
>   The plane-tree bud and blow,
> Shed her recuperative bark,
>   And spread her shade below.
> ("A London Plane-Tree" 1889, 17)

Several critics have linked Levy's enthusiastic celebration of the city to her status both as a Jew and a woman; Alex Goody in particular notes that "[a]s an independent late nineteenth-century woman and a Jew, Levy has a double affinity with the urban space as the 'paven ground' for her subjectivity" (2010, 161). Indeed, with increasing numbers of Jews occupying London during the late nineteenth century, city life and Jewish identity were often linked. This was partly due to a wave of immigration from Eastern Europe in the 1880s, which proved troubling to assimilated Jews already living in London: "the new immigrant 'ghettos' were both an embarrassment and a threat, with the potential, it was believed, to undo the social and political gains made by anglicized Jews" (Endelman 2002, 171–72). Levy herself frequently expressed the view that the Jew was "quintessentially an urban creature" (Hunt Beckman 2000, 124); for example, in her essay "Jewish Children" (1886) she describes the Jewish child as the "descendant of many city-bred ancestors" (1993, 530). It is the cultural trope of the "Wandering Jew" that connects Jewish identity with a nomadic, unfixed urban existence.[8] Though such "wandering" carries connotations of exile and diasporic identity, it might also suggest the freedom of the urban traveller.

Therefore Levy's gender and Jewish identity enabled her to make the crucial move from *passante* to *flâneur*. As Parsons notes, for male writers such as Charles Baudelaire, the "urban muse was consistently the female figure of the prostitute/*passante*" (2000, 89). She was observed by the male gaze and transformed in male-authored poetry into an alluring figure that combined the ephemerality of modern life, male freedom, and (a hint of) sexual danger. Levy, in contrast, "is one of the first women writers to consistently adopt the perspective of the female writer-observer or *flâneur*" (Parsons 2000, 87). Vadillo argues that Levy achieves this by reimagining the poet as a passenger:

> for Levy, the figure of the passenger had important social and political implications because it was as passengers, she argued, that women poets could become spectators of modern life, challenging masculinist representations of women in the modern metropolis, and transgressing the incarcerating ideology of the private/public spheres. (2005, 40)

Transportation played a key role in establishing the writer-observer's *flâneur*-like inspection of urban life. In particular, the omnibus enabled women to travel on top and in the open air, looking down upon the city they were moving through. While such a highly visible mode of transportation might attract censure (depending on one's social class), crucially, the omnibus "allowed the woman of the 1880s and 1890s to move in and observe the city without threat on the streets" (Parsons 2000, 97).[9]

In "Ballade of an Omnibus," we can see how adopting this position of observation enables Levy's speaker to harness poetic identity and become one with the city:

> The 'busmen know me and my lyre,
> From Brompton to the Bull-and-Gate.
> When summer comes, I mount in state
> The topmost summit, whence I see
> Croesus look on, compassionate—
>   An omnibus suffices me.
>
> (1889, 21)

Through the prism of Greek mythology, Levy's speaker adopts a Vatic persona, depicting herself as an Orpheus-like figure, whose poetic skill raises her above "Croesus" (the name of a Lydian king famed for his wealth). Noting that "men to carriages aspire" (1889, 21), the poem makes clear that while the omnibus admits passengers of all classes, it literally and metaphorically elevates the female passenger by granting her a privileged perspective. Vadillo argues that mass transport "thus emerges in the work of Amy Levy as the key element in the reconfiguration of race, gender and class in the everyday life of the city" (2005, 72).

Despite its apparently "levelling" effect, critics such as Goody contend that "the in-between urban space, is not simply positive and enabling" (2010, 166). Levy's poems also hint at the dangers for women inhabiting the city space, by invoking the image of a female spectre: a motif that reappears in several poems throughout *A London Plane-Tree and Other Verse*. Perhaps the most famous of these is "In the Mile End Road":

> How like her! But 'tis she herself,
>   Comes up the crowded street,
> How little did I think, the morn,
>   My only love to meet!
>
> Whose else that motion and that mien?
>   Whose else that airy tread?
> For one strange moment I forgot
>   My only love was dead.
>
> (1889, 50)

The title of this poem locates this ghostly encounter specifically in London's East End, an area populated by Jewish immigrants during the late nineteenth century. It also recalls Jack the Ripper's Whitechapel murders of 1888.[10] Therefore, the woman at the heart of the poem might well be interpreted as a street-walking woman/prostitute, or conversely, as an independent New

Woman. This woman has clearly "passed on," but remains as an apparition, walking the streets. In contrast to "Ballade of an Omnibus" or "A London Plane-Tree," the speaker in this poem is not a city-dwelling woman herself, but is more closely aligned with the (traditionally) male *flâneur* who observes the "passing" woman in the street. Emma Francis even draws a link between the deceased woman of Levy's poem and Jack the Ripper's murders: "[a] poem published in 1889 which describes an erotic fixation upon the ghost of a street walking woman cannot but be read as dealing, at least in part, with the Whitechapel murders of 1888 ... Levy has produced a poem in which the voice of the lover and perhaps of the lesbian is concurrent and interchangeable with the voice of the Ripper" (1999, 200–01).

Goody suggests that the speaker of the poem is aligned with Jack the Ripper (who was believed by many to be Jewish) and asserts that "[a]t some level in this poem, the evil Jewish murderer stalks the streets and dispenses with the unsettling presence of the urban woman" (2010, 174).[11] In this sense, one could argue that the poem embodies Levy's sense of an irrevocably split identity; one "side" of her identity destroys the other. Whether we interpret the poem's speaker as linked to Jack the Ripper or not, "In the Mile End Road" certainly hints at the dangers for women occupying the "crowded street[s]." As such, the poem acts as a counterbalance to poems such as "Ballade of an Omnibus" since it implies that the urban woman's liberation could potentially be "the cause of her own destruction" (Goody 2010, 175). Removed from the protective environment of the omnibus, the female spectre here hints that the woman who traverses London's thoroughfares on foot may meet a deadly fate.

Twenty-six years after the publication of Levy's *A London Plane-Tree*, Djuna Barnes took up the role of *flâneur* in her first poetic collection, *The Book of Repulsive Women* (1915). Unlike Levy, whose verse is set in London, Barnes's poems lead the reader through a specific New York geography. Some of the poems in *The Book of Repulsive Women* are entitled after particular areas of the city ("From Fifth Avenue Up"; "From Third Avenue On"). Recalling Levy's omnibus, Barnes's poetics of movement directs the reader through the city space. This is implied by the title of one of her poems: "Seen from the 'L'" (The "L" refers to the elevated train-line which formed part of the New York City subway system, travelling between Manhattan and Brooklyn.) Barnes uses this modern form of transportation in a similar way to Levy's omnibus, utilising the "L" as a "locomotive site of spectatorship" (Hardie 2005, 129). From this vantage-point, the speaker of "Seen from the 'L'" observes a nude woman standing at her window:

> So she stands—nude—stretching dully
> Two amber combs loll through her hair
> A vague molested carpet pitches
> Down the dusty length of stair.
> She does not see, she does not care
>   It's always there.

> The frail mosaic on her window
> Facing starkly toward the street
> Is scribbled there by tipsy sparrows—
> Etched there with their rocking feet.
> Is fashioned too, by every beat
>   Of shirt and sheet.
>
>   (2005, 49)

The poem functions as a vignette, offering a brief glimpse of a down-at-heel woman languidly beginning (or ending) her day. The "L" of the title, therefore, offers the speaker—and the reader—a voyeuristic glimpse of this woman's domestic interior and her naked body. A sense of the brevity of this moment is produced by the short final line of each stanza, and the rhyming couplet which concludes it, replicating the sense of rushing onward through various urban scenes, each impression quickly tailing off into another. This sense of falling away or unravelling occurs throughout the poem—for example, in the description of the woman:

> Raveling grandly into vice
> Dropping crooked into rhyme.
> Slipping through the stitch of virtue,
>   Into crime.
>
>   (49)

Several of Barnes's poems encode the risks for women inhabiting these city spaces. In many poems, we are compelled to see that the freedom associated with the "modern girl" or "girl about town" in fact masks a sordid, exploitative reality. In these poems, Barnes implies that to prosper—or indeed to survive—in such a fast-paced urban environment, a young woman must construct herself as a commodity on the market. Either as a dancer, a singer, an office employee, or a prostitute, her livelihood depends on attracting and securing the male gaze. The effort and exhaustion of soliciting this gaze leads to a destructive, enervating cycle that is difficult to break. This trajectory is illustrated particularly well in a poem entitled "To a Cabaret Dancer." This poem portrays a carefree young woman who comes to the city in search of entertainment, and potentially fame and romance. However, she quickly becomes jaded by the limited pleasures and opportunities that the city has to offer:

> She came with laughter wide and calm;
>   And splendid grace;
> And looked between the lights and wine
>   For one fine face.
>
> And found life only passion wide
>   'Twixt mouth and wine.
> She ceased to search, and growing wise
>   Became less fine.

Alienated by the fleeting encounters and lack of intimacy that characterise urban relationships, the woman degrades into a washed-up performer in the seedy "cabaret" of the title. Since we observe her "as she groped and clung" about a man's "neck" (2005, 53), it is implied that her employment is little more than a form of prostitution. However, the speaker—who uses the first person plural throughout, as if speaking collectively on behalf of the customers who scrutinise the dancer—suggests that some mysterious element within the woman remains untarnished and inaccessible:

> Yet some wondrous thing within the mess
>   Was held in check—
> ....
> One master chord we couldn't sound
>   For lost the keys,
> Yet she hinted of it as she sang
>   Between our knees.

Eventually, the cruel "jibes" of the customers and the relentless pace of city life, lead the woman to deteriorate further, until her acquaintances no longer recognise her as they pass her in the street:

> We saw the crimson leave her cheeks
> Flame in her eyes;
> For when a woman lives in awful haste
> A woman dies.
> ....
> Barriers and heart both broken—dust
>   Beneath her feet.
> You've passed her forty times and sneered
>   Out in the street.
> A thousand jibes had driven her
>   To this at last;
> Till the ruined crimson of her lips
>   Grew vague and vast.
>   ("To a Cabaret Dancer" 2005, 53–4)

The fate of the "cabaret dancer" is deliberately ambiguous. The reference to her presence "in the street" implies that she ends up homeless and destitute, and the description of her pale cheeks and "ruined crimson" lips suggest disease. The poem functions as a warning that women will struggle to survive economically in a relentless urban system that requires their constant circulation among men, the performance of femininity, and the repeated abnegation of subjectivity in the gaze of the male other. Living in the glare of this gaze, the woman is driven to increasingly desperate acts, and the final one, it is inferred, will be suicide. The phrase, "*this* at last," (emphasis added) and the image of her mouth growing "vague and vast" gestures towards a violent, bloody end, fulfilling the poem's prophecy that "when a woman lives in awful haste / A woman dies" (2005, 53). Her speaker evidently blames the city for this fate, claiming: "A thousand lights had smitten her / Into this thing" (2005, 53).

Barnes's poem intimates that women's increased freedom and visibility within the city may lead to prostitution, rape and suicide, as women become commodities (their shelf-life ever waning) within destructive, misogynistic urban economies.[12] This trajectory is taken explicitly to its conclusion in the final poem of *The Book of Repulsive Women*, entitled "Suicide." This poem consists of two stanzas, labelled "Corpse A" and "Corpse B." Though following the exact same prosodic pattern (e.g. end rhymes, line lengths, stresses), the descriptions of the two female corpses are conspicuously different in tone; Corpse A is "brought ... in," Corpse B is given "hurried shoves this way / And that" (2005, 55). Corpse A is described using mystical, self-consciously "poetic" imagery: her "little bruisèd body like / A startled moon" (2005, 55). In contrast, Corpse B is described in strikingly bathetic terms: "She lay out listlessly like some small mug / Of beer gone flat" (2005, 55).

These descriptions of the two women, and the ironic parallels drawn between them, serve to emphasise the fact that, even in death (or, especially in death), women continue to circulate as commodities and aesthetic objects. To begin with, these women are literally commoditised in the sense that they are labelled as "Corpse A" or "B," rather than named as individuals.[13] "Corpse B" is clearly a victim of city-life. Described as "shock-abbreviated / As a city cat" (2005, 55), she is bedraggled and physically-stunted as a result of the urban struggle for survival. The comparison to a "mug of beer" figures her as the unwanted "dregs" of the city, the punch-line of a tired joke.

Though more elegiac on the surface, the description of "Corpse A" also figures the female corpse as a commodity. The phrase "all the subtle symphonies of her" (2005, 55) employs the rhetoric of a fashion magazine, recalling the tone of Barnes's *Vanity Fair* article mentioned above. The comparison of the dead woman's body to "[a] twilight rune" represents the female corpse as an esoteric symbol to be decoded by the male gaze. While "Corpse B" is an unwanted by-product of the city and "Corpse A" is a poetical fragment, both are described as objects, as less than human. It may even be that these descriptions represent different accounts of the same woman, rather than two different women, demonstrating that a woman's death can be aestheticised in different ways: romanticised as poetical and tragic, or rendered mundane and insignificant. Thus, Barnes reveals how the female body has been relentlessly aestheticised, dehumanized, and objectified. These dead women are commodities; wheeled in, assessed by the male gaze, and transformed into art, or cast aside, as mere fodder for the city.

3. The Apparitional Lesbian and the Flowering Corpse

Levy and Barnes use their dead-woman muses in various ways to encode female homoerotic desire. Indeed, "Love, Dreams, and Death," (a section of Levy's *A London Plane-Tree*) has attracted critical attention from those queer theorists interested in the apparitional beloveds that feature in these poems. These poems recount nightly visitations from airy spectres, which leave the waking speaker aching with longing. The persistent gender ambiguity of the speaker *and* the spectral visitor in these poems invites a homoerotic inter- pretation; the shared looks of desire between the speaker and the ghost, and the subtle fragrance that lingers on its departure encode these encounters as erotic, yet ultimately impossible, liaisons. This reading of Levy's poems reinforces Terry Castle's path-breaking work in *The Apparitional Lesbian* (1993), which argues that ghostly tropes have been consistently invoked in order to "ward off" and dematerialise the threat posed by lesbian desire, and conversely, to enable the writing of female homoerotic desire. This appari- tional metaphor has proved particularly effective as it enables an acknowl- edgment of homoerotic desire, whilst simultaneously disembodying that desire, rendering it less threatening:

> The spectral figure is a perfect vehicle for conveying what must be called ... that 'recognition through negation' which has taken place with regard to female homosexuality in Western culture since the Enlightenment. Over the past three hundred years ... the metaphor has functioned as the necessary psychological and rhetorical means for objectifying—and ultimately embracing—that which otherwise could not be acknowledged.
>
> (Castle 1993, 60)

However, I will invert Castle's theoretical paradigm by suggesting that Barnes, by contrast, presents a startling re-*embodiment* of the dead woman as a "repulsive" corpse. In *The Book of Repulsive Women* and in several poems from *A Book* (1923), Barnes's dead women pulse with life: their lustrous hair continues to grow, their corpses sprout flowers and weeds, they move and jerk about beneath the earth.[14] I argue that this grotesque embodiment of the dead woman represents Barnes's attempt to "re-flesh" the lesbian body and assert female homoerotic desire without the use of the spectralising metaphors that we find in Levy's work.

If we begin, then, with Levy, it is noteworthy that of the seventeen poems of which her "Love, Dreams, and Death" is composed, at least nine treat the theme of a dead/ghostly beloved. This focus on the apparitional muse com- mences with the fourth poem in the sequence, entitled "The Dream" (1889, 38). Carrying the epigraph "Believe me, this was true last night, / Tho' it is false to-day"—a quotation taken from A. M[ary]. F. Robinson's poem "Paradise Fancies" (1878) [15]—this poem begins with the speaker recounting a ghostly visitation experienced the night before:

> A fair dream to my chamber flew:
> Such a crowd of folk that stirred,
> Jested, fluttered; only you,
> You alone of all that band,

> Calm and silent, spake no word.
> Only once you neared my place,
> And your hand one moment's space
> Sought the fingers of my hand;
> Your eyes flashed to mine; I knew
> All was well between us two.
>
> (1889, 38)

Here, the ghost represents a familiar figure in the speaker's life, perhaps even a deceased companion. It is unclear, though, whether the phantasm represents a living or dead individual, and this is further complicated by another ambiguity: the gender of the speaking subject and the apparition, which remains unspecified throughout. This leaves the precise nature of the desire at the heart of the poem unresolved.

In the concluding section of the poem, the speaker awakes at dawn, still curiously affected by the dream, which lingers in their mind like a sweet scent: "The fair dream hovered round me, clung / To my thought like faint perfume" (1889, 38). Francis argues that this imagery of perfume flasks and "string[s]/ Of amber" (1889, 38) encodes the spirit as female: "The awakened speaker represents the residue the ghost leaves behind as a litter of cosmetics and decorations used in the production of femininity" (1999, 191). The next poem in the sequence, entitled "On the Threshold" (1889, 39), may be read as a continuation of the theme of the dead beloved. Again the (ambiguously-gendered) speaker narrates a dream in which the beloved appears dead: "garlanded / With blooms of waxen whiteness" (1889, 39), suggestive of bridal apparel. A later poem of the sequence, "In the Night," confirms the feminine identity of the beloved and continues the narrative of her death:

> What ails my love; what ails her? She is
>   paling;
> Faint grows her face, and slowly seems to
>   fade!
> I cannot clasp her—stretch out unavailing
>   My arms across the silence and the shade.
>
> (1889, 41)

It becomes clear, then, that the shadowy figure that visits the speaker nightly in dreams represents the ghost of a dead female beloved. Crucially, she appears at liminal times, such as twilight and dawn, when, according to folkloric beliefs, the boundary between the two worlds is thin.[16] This "in-between" state is described in "Borderland": "Am I waking, am I sleeping? / As the first faint dawn comes creeping / Thro' the pane" (1889, 42).

The persistent presence of the ghostly muse in these love lyrics has been analysed in light of Levy's apparently homoerotic inclinations. Levy's biographer Linda Hunt Beckman asserts that "Levy was a woman whose desire was homoerotic" (2000, 7), citing evidence of numerous homoerotic attachments throughout Levy's life, from letters that recount her youthful adoration for her school teacher, Miss Edith Creak, to her friendship with Vernon Lee, described in the poem "To Vernon Lee" (1889).[17] Whereas Melvyn New and Deborah Epstein Nord interpret her love lyrics as voiced by a male persona, numerous poems from Levy's *oeuvre*, including "Sinfonia Eroica," "In a Minor Key," and "To Lallie" can be analysed as evidence of Levy's homoerotic attachments.[18]

As I point out, Levy's decision to represent homoerotic desire using spectral metaphors can be explained using Castle's theory of the "apparitional lesbian." For Levy, the spectral metaphor enables her to write about communion with same-sex lovers, describing a desire that would perhaps not be permissible in more explicit terms. Semi-conscious states and dreams, for example, offer a space where possibilities can be realised, that would be condemned in waking life.[19] In this sense, Levy uses liminal states and spectres in a similar way to the "fantasias" constructed by late-Victorian female aesthetes. Talia Schaffer argues that such non-realist modes and "phantasmatic diction" permitted female aesthetes to write about "new sorts of gender politics. Writers situated a woman's desires in the unreal space of 'dream' and 'fantasy,' thereby preventing the reader from criticizing the character according to everyday nineteenth-century sexual norms" (Schaffer 2000, 51). Levy therefore makes use of the very strategy by which homoerotically-inclined women were "ghosted" in Victorian literary representations; that is to say, dematerialised in order to invoke an elusive yet persistently haunting female homoerotic desire. In this sense Levy anticipates some of the twentieth-century lesbian writers that Castle suggests harness the spectral metaphor. "Used imaginatively," Castle remarks, "the very trope that evaporates can also solidify" and it does so through the persistent haunting power of lesbian desire (1993, 46–7).

A "solidifying" of the spectral metaphor is also seen in Barnes's work. But here, the beloved is less a ghost, more a corpse. Rebecca Loncraine argues that Barnes's association of lesbian love with death functions as both: "a commentary on the 'unthinkableness,' in Victorian terms, of lesbian love" and a defiant resurrection of the lesbian: "the socially abjected, figured as the 'repulsive' corpse" (Loncraine 2003, 42). I, therefore, propose that Barnes's striking *embodiment* of the dead woman reflects a desire to "re-flesh" the lesbian body and articulate female homoerotic desire *without* spectral metaphors.

Barnes's series of poems about a dead beloved were published in her second collection, *A Book* (1923). Gillian Hanscombe and Virginia L. Smyers argue that eleven of these poems can be read as the story of Barnes's love for a woman named Mary Pyne: "[a]mong the collection's 20 poems, 11 can be sequentially read as the story of Djuna's love for Mary Pyne" (1987, 234). Pyne was a member of the Provincetown Players, a New York theatre group to which Barnes also belonged during the period 1915–1918. Hanscombe and Smyers suggest that *The Book of Repulsive Women* was written at around the same time that Barnes fell in love with Pyne, thus the poems may have been indirectly inspired by her (1987, 89).

Pyne certainly lived the kind of brief, tragic life described in *The Book of Repulsive Women*: she lived in poverty, supporting herself and her father by working as a cashier, dancehall instructor, waitress, and actress.

In 1915, Pyne married Harry Kemp, a fellow Provincetown player who styled himself as "the vagabond poet." In 1919, she contracted tuberculosis. Barnes nursed Pyne until her death, writing to her male lover Courtenay Lemon that: "Mary has been given up by 2 nurses, 2 doctors & a score of others at least 10 days back, but she still breaths [*sic*] – lies on her left side for the first time & is living on oxygen" (qtd. in Hanscombe and Smyers 1987, 90). Pyne died in November 1919, aged 25. Barnes's biographer Phillip Herring writes that Barnes tried to claim the body but was refused because she had no money (1995, 74)—an anecdote that quite literally underlines the connections between death, economics and female disenfranchisement. Barnes's grief over Mary Pyne continued to haunt her; Herring cites the painter Maurice Sterne who remembers Barnes "grieving over the death of this 'Titian-haired beauty' … 'sobbing painfully, her head buried in her arms, saying over and over that she would never get over the loss …'" (qtd. in Herring 1995, 74).

Of the several poems in *A Book* that can be related to this doomed love affair, a poem entitled "Six Songs of Khalidine" is perhaps the most striking. Published in 1923, but written in 1919, it is dedicated "To the Memory of Mary Pyne" and describes a bedside vigil beside a red-haired beloved:

> The flame of your red hair does crawl and creep
> Upon your body that denies the gloom
> And feeds upon your flesh as 'twould consume
> The cold precision of your austere sleep—
> And all night long I beat it back, and weep.
>
> (2005, 86)

Lillian Faderman singles out "Six Songs of Khalidine," with its grim scenario and gothic motifs, as a particularly objectionable example of Barnes's decadent influence: "the beloved's red hair flames and crawls and creeps, as in Verlaine's lesbian poems. Her fallen lids are stained with ebony … the setting comes directly out of nineteenth-century French novels of decadence" (Faderman 1985, 364). But Barnes's poem perhaps shares more similarities with the work of Charles Baudelaire and Algernon Charles Swinburne, in particular Swinburne's "The Leper" (2004, 113–17). "The Leper," published in Swinburne's controversial 1866 collection *Poems and Ballads*, takes the form of a dramatic monologue spoken by a "poor scribe" who suffers with obsessive love for a deceased woman. This woman scorned the speaker when she was alive but then grew to rely on him as she succumbed to disease. He hides her away with him and, once she has died, stays with her dead body, fixating on her decaying beauty, particularly her hair:

> Yet am I glad to have her dead
> Here in this wretched wattled house

Where I can kiss her eyes and head.
....
Six months, and I sit still and hold
    In two cold palms her cold two feet.
Her hair, half grey half ruined gold,
    Thrills me and burns me in kissing it.
                    ("The Leper" 2004, 113–16)

Hair is similarly fetishised in Barnes's poem, where the beloved's red hair takes on a life of its own and threatens to consume her weak body like a purging fire.[20]

Barnes's "Six Songs of Khalidine," and many other poems in *A Book*, focus on the uncanny vitality and eroticism of the dying and dead woman's body. In "Song in Autumn," for instance, the beloved feeds the "green / Long grasses" (2005, 88) and in "The Flowering Corpse," "Soft hairs blow" above her head and her "armpits bloom" (2005, 91). The uncanny vitality of the dead woman links to a popular myth surrounding the Pre-Raphaelite muse, Elizabeth Siddal. As the story goes, in 1869, Dante Gabriel Rossetti disinterred Siddal's body in order to retrieve the poems he had buried with her—only to find her coffin filled with a profusion of red-gold hair that had kept on growing after death.[21] Deborah Tyler-Bennett has pointed out that Barnes's portrayal of Mary Pyne engages with this by-then familiar public legend, placing Pyne in a pantheon of tubercular beloveds alongside Siddal and Edgar Allan Poe's gothic maidens. Tyler-Bennett argues that Barnes uses the Gothic mode to self-consciously question the ways in which women like Pyne and Siddal were, through their unearthly beauty and early deaths, fated to become static and unchanging products of the male imagination. She writes that Barnes "recognised how Pyne's 'Greenwich Village Beauty' status obliterated every other aspect of her personality" (Tyler-Bennett 2001, 99). Rather than endorsing the archetype of the tragic, red-haired beauty, Barnes uses it to indicate its limitations to the reader: her dead-woman muses constantly evade their living lovers; they are "hidden" beneath the earth, where their lovers cannot reach them.

In *H.D. and the Victorian Fin de Siècle* (1996), Cassandra Laity reveals that the modernist poet H.D. was particularly inspired by Elizabeth Siddal, who she felt had a grotesque beauty that could not be contained by the Pre-Raphaelite portraits in which she was represented. H.D. also idolised Greta Garbo for the same reason: "[b]oth women were considered to be sirens, of unconventional, larger-than-life beauty ... in possession of an intensity that radiated beyond the frame (celluloid or picture) of the male gaze" (Laity 1996, 144).[22] Therefore, if, as Loncraine argues, Barnes disinters the "repulsive" abject body of the lesbian in order to resurrect her, she perhaps also does so in order to suggest the impossibility of ever "capturing" this body in a fixed, stable representation. Barnes emphasises the perverse vitality of the flowering corpse, envisioning Pyne's body as feeding nature, while beneath the soil her armpits bloom with "passion flowers" ("The Flowering

Corpse" 2005, 91). This fertile, sprouting corpse disrupts and inverts the boundary between life and death, suggesting that however much one might seek to represent a woman, by killing her into art, she still exceeds such representation—she decomposes herself. Similarly, Daniela Caselli has noted that while Barnes's illustrations borrow Aubrey Beardsley's decadent black-and-white aesthetic, they do so only to disable it by blurring the neatness of the lines so that the colours "seep into one another and present the human form ... on the verge of dissolution" (2009, 76).

In representing the lesbian body as a perverse corpse that evades fixed representation, Barnes may be reacting to the increasing categorisation and pathologisation of the homosexual in the early twentieth century. During this period, definitions of sexual "deviation" and perversity proliferated via the works of sexologists and psychoanalysts such as Havelock Ellis, Richard Freiherr von Krafft-Ebing and Sigmund Freud.[23] These emerging sexological and psychoanalytical discourses presented problems as well as opportunities for homoerotically inclined individuals; they provided a language to express, but also to define and control genders and sexualities "outside of" heterosexuality (as Michel Foucault most famously argued in *The History of Sexuality*).[24] Therefore, while critics such as Faderman, Herring, and others have read Barnes's *The Book of Repulsive Women* as straightforwardly and audaciously presenting "lesbians" to the reader (for perhaps the first time), Caselli argues that Barnes "resists the spectacularization of 'the' lesbian ... and a revelation of the lesbian 'for who she is'" (2009, 77), arguing that while some poems in the volume: "undoubtedly lend themselves to being read as staging the birth of the lesbian; this ... is a difficult birth, which does not necessarily lead to lineage, but uses this 'repulsive' womanhood as the measure of a possible disruption of genealogy" (2009, 77).

We can detect a similar refusal to define or construct the lesbian in Levy's work. For example, Francis argues that in Levy's later poetry "subjectivities and forms of experience ... become increasingly less locatable, less intelligible within conventional accounts of sexual and social identification" (1999, 196). The poems of "Love, Dreams, and Death" sequence, with their ambiguous descriptions of dream-like states, liminal "borderlands," ungendered speakers, and disembodied encounters with feminine apparitions who may be alive or dead, invoke the spectre of the dead-woman muse as a way of expressing homoerotic desire, while radically questioning the fixed categories of both desire and gender. Francis finds such a disruption disturbing: "[t]hese poems are profoundly discomforting in the way they describe the breakdown of all possibilities of limitation or structuration, and the most significant casualty of this battle is sexual difference itself" (1999, 197).

Therefore, in both Levy's and Barnes's work, the dead-woman muse serves as the embodiment of a number of challenging contradictions regarding gender, desire and identity. In this sense, this muse is a figure that cuts across the major themes found in both their *oeuvres*. The dead woman signifies both the opportunities and dangers for women inhabiting the city space in the late nineteenth century; her new-found freedom to traverse the streets, and yet her dangerous circulation in a misogynistic system that still views women as consumable, replaceable objects. This dead woman also represents the apparitional lesbian: a figure for both the invisibility and persistence of female homoerotic desire. Finally, her body, resurrected as a "repulsive corpse" delineates the aspects of female subjectivity and sexuality that escape categorisation or containment. Read together, Levy's and Barnes's depictions of the dead woman, therefore, reveal the opportunities and dangers offered by the spectral metaphor; this trope that risks connecting lesbian desire pejoratively to death, destruction, and perversity also has the power to re-flesh a corpse.

Notes

1. Amy Levy (1861–1889) is perhaps most remembered for her novel *Reuben Sachs* (1889), which depicts Jewish life in London in the late nineteenth century. Her poetic volumes are *Xantippe and Other Verse* (1881), *A Minor Poet and Other Verse* (1884) and *A London Plane-Tree, and Other Verse* (1889). The corrected proofs for this final volume were discovered on Levy's desk when she committed suicide at the age of twenty-seven. Djuna Barnes (1892–1982) remains synonymous with her modernist masterpiece *Nightwood* (1936). Her distinctive prose style—also exhibited in *Ryder* and *Ladies Almanack* (both 1928)—frequently combines Gothic, Baroque, and Renaissance-inflected archaisms. Barnes also published journalism, drama, poetry, and illustrated her own works. *The Book of Repulsive Women* (1915) is, for example, accompanied by five drawings in a distinctive black-and-white style, reminiscent of Aubrey Beardsley's illustrations for *Salome* (1891).
2. As Renée L. Bergland observes, the ghostly trope has frequently been used to represent "political and economic power relations"—for example, the spectre of Communism haunting Europe at the beginning of *The Communist Manifesto* (2000, 7).
3. All subsequent references to Amy Levy's poetry are from *A London Plane-Tree, and Other Verse*. London: T. Fisher Unwin, 1889, unless otherwise indicated.
4. All subsequent references to Djuna Barnes's poetry are from Phillip Herring and Osías Stutman, ed. *Djuna Barnes: Collected Poems, with Notes towards the Memoirs*. Wisconsin: University of Wisconsin Press, 2005 unless otherwise indicated.
5. Joyce Zonana also addresses this question in relation to *Aurora Leigh*, arguing that Barrett Browning presents Aurora as a living "embodied muse" who incorporates the "masks" of womanhood into herself, uniting "spirit and flesh, heavenly and earthly" (1989, 251).
6. Faderman writes: "Djuna Barnes seems to have internalized the literary images of lesbianism ... although she did not let them lead to death" (1985, 364). Faderman argues that the lesbian poet Renée Vivien's internalisation of decadent influence literally contributed to her death (a result of anorexia, alcoholism, and drinking eau de cologne).
7. For example, Emma Francis draws a link between "In the Mile End Road" and Jack the Ripper's murders (see p. 91 of this chapter).

8. The legend of the Wandering Jew originates in the thirteenth-century manuscript *Flores Historiarum* by Roger of Wendover. After taunting Jesus during the crucifixion, the Jew is cursed to wander the earth until the Second Coming. For a history of developments of this legend, see Cohen (2007).

9. See Amy Levy's novel, *The Romance of a Shop* (1888), in which the heroine Gertrude, riding on the top of the omnibus, is met with "a look of speechless horror" from her well-to-do aunt (1993, 105).

10. This locale appears in another poem, "Ballad of a Special Edition," in which a newspaper seller spreads cries of "slaughter, theft, and suicide" in the East End: "He tramps the town from end to end. / How often we have heard it cried— / A double murder in Mile End" (1889, 23).

11. As Sander L. Gilman explains, the popular image of Jack the Ripper in the press was "a caricature of the Eastern Jew" (1991, 113), playing on anti-Semitic prejudices (aggravated by the wave of recent Jewish immigration to the East End) and suspicion surrounding ritual slaughter of animals and circumcision: "Jack the Ripper evoked in the minds of many the image of a foreign, syphilitic, mutilated butcher-Jew" (1991, 119).

12. For a related discussion of gendered economies in Jean Rhys's novels, see Cynthia Port, (2001) "'Money, for the night is coming': Jean Rhys and the Gendered Economies of Aging." *Women: A Cultural Review* 12 (2): 204–17.

13. In this way, we can observe parallels with Vernon Lee's "A Wedding Chest" which opens with an auction catalogue containing an entry for item "No. 428": the panel from an Italian wedding coffer which was used to store (and circulate) the corpse of an abducted girl (see Jane Ford's essay, "Greek Gift and 'Given Being,'" in this volume, 108–109).

14. In this sense, Barnes draws particularly on Baudelaire's experiments with the aesthetics of the corpse, such as in "Une Charogne" (A Carcass) which observes the perverse beauty of the rotting carcass and imagines the beloved "under blossoming grass, / As you moulder with bones of the dead" (1998, 63). The title of Barnes's "The Flowering Corpse" invokes Baudelaire's *Les Fleurs du Mal*, but she adapts his portrayal of the corpse from a "lecherous whore, / sweating out poisonous fumes" (59) to a more positive image of a body that nourishes the earth.

15. Robinson's poem appears in her debut volume *A Handful of Honeysuckle* (1878). Interestingly, before her marriage to James Darmesteter in 1888, Robinson was involved in a romantic friendship with the writer Vernon Lee. Levy met Lee in 1886 and became infatuated with her—perhaps a factor that influenced her choice of an epigram from Robinson.

16. Twilight also has lesbian connotations—seen, for example, in the title of a 1964 lesbian pulp novel *Twilight Lovers* (see Faderman 1991).

17. See Amy Levy's Letter 8, reprinted in Hunt Beckman (2000, 223–25). It is interesting to note that Levy uses a quotation from A. Mary F. Robinson—the former lover of Vernon Lee—to signal her own homoerotic desire.

18. See Deborah Epstein Nord (1990, 748) and Melvyn New (1993, 38). See also Linda Hunt Beckman's analysis of Levy's homoerotic poems (2000, 87–91).

19. For example, see Sheridan Le Fanu's "Carmilla" (1872) in which strange dreams, somnambulism, and vampirism provide metaphors for lesbian desire.

20. The poem also owes a debt to Robert Browning's "Gold Hair: A Story of Pornic" (1864) and "Porphyria's Lover" (1842).

21. See Jan Marsh, *The Legend of Elizabeth Siddal*. London: Quartet Books, 2010.

22. Castle's *Apparitional Lesbian* in fact begins with the ghost of Garbo: "One of the several ghosts haunting this book is that of Greta Garbo, who died in April 1990, just after I'd started working on the volume's signature piece, 'The Apparitional Lesbian'" (1993, 1).
23. See Krafft-Ebing's *Psychopathia Sexualis* (1886); Ellis, *Sexual Inversion* (1897) and Freud, *The Interpretation of Dreams* (1900) and *Three Essays on Sexuality* (1905).
24. Foucault describes the "*scientia sexualis*" (science of sexuality) of the nineteenth century as "a proliferation of discourses, carefully tailored to the requirements of power; the solidification of the sexual mosaic ... the mandatory production of confessions and the subsequent establishment of a system of legitimate knowledge and of an economy of manifold pleasures" (1990, 72).

Works Cited

Barnes, Djuna. 2005. "To a Cabaret Dancer." [1915] In *Djuna Barnes: Collected Poems With Notes toward the Memoirs*, edited by Phillip Herring and Osías Stutman, 53–4. Wisconsin: University of Wisconsin Press.

———. 2005. "The Flowering Corpse." [1923] In *Djuna Barnes: Collected Poems With Notes toward the Memoirs*, edited by Phillip Herring and Osías Stutman, 91. Wisconsin: University of Wisconsin Press.

———. 2005. "Seen from the 'L'" [1915] In *Djuna Barnes: Collected Poems With Notes toward the Memoirs*, edited by Phillip Herring and Osías Stutman, 49. Wisconsin: University of Wisconsin Press.

———. 2005. "Six Songs of Khalidine." In *Djuna Barnes: Collected Poems With Notes toward the Memoirs*, edited by Phillip Herring and Osías Stutman, 86–87. Wisconsin: University of Wisconsin Press.

———. 2005. "Song in Autumn." In *Djuna Barnes: Collected Poems With Notes toward the Memoirs*, edited by Phillip Herring and Osías Stutman, 88. Wisconsin: University of Wisconsin Press.

———. 2005. "Suicide." [1915] In *Djuna Barnes: Collected Poems With Notes toward the Memoirs*, edited by Phillip Herring and Osías Stutman, 55. Wisconsin: University of Wisconsin Press.

Baudelaire, Charles. 1998. "Une Charogne." [A Carcass, 1857] In *The Flowers of Evil*, translated by James McGowan, introduced by Jonathan Culler, 59–63. Oxford: Oxford University Press.

Bergland, Renée L. 2000. *The National Uncanny: Indian Ghosts and American Subjects*. Hanover, New Hampshire: University Press of New England.

Bronfen, Elisabeth. 1992. *Over Her Dead Body: Death, Femininity and the Aesthetic*. Manchester: Manchester University Press.

Caselli, Daniela. 2009. *Improper Modernism: Djuna Barnes' Bewildering Corpus*. Farnham, Surrey: Ashgate.

Castle, Terry. 1993. *The Apparitional Lesbian: Female Homosexuality and Modern Culture*. New York: Columbia University Press.

Cohen, Richard I. 2007. "The 'Wandering Jew' from Medieval Legend to Modern Metaphor." In *The Art of Being Jewish in Modern Times*, edited by Barbara Kirshenblatt-Gimblett and Jonathan Karp, 147–75. Philadelphia: University of Pennsylvania Press.

Endelman, Todd M. 2002. *The Jews of Britain: 1656 to 2000*. California: University of California Press.

Epstein Nord, Deborah. 1990. "'Neither Pairs Nor Odd': Female Community in Late Nineteenth-Century London." *Signs* 15 (4): 733–54.

Faderman, Lillian. 1985. *Surpassing the Love of Men: Romantic Friendship and Love between Women from the Renaissance to the Present*. London: The Women's Press.

———. 1991. *Odd Girls and Twilight Lovers: A History of Lesbian Life in Twentieth-Century. America* New York: Columbia University Press.

Foucault, Michel. 1990. *The History of Sexuality. Volume 1: An Introduction* [1976]. New York: Vintage.

Francis, Emma. 1999. "Amy Levy: Contradictions?—Feminism and Semitic Discourse." In *Women's Poetry, Late-Romantic to Late-Victorian: Gender and Genre, 1830–1900*, edited by Isobel Armstrong and Virginia Blain, 183–204. London: Palgrave.

Gilman, Sander L. 1991. *The Jew's Body*. New York: Routledge.

Goody, Alex. 2010. "Passing in the City: The Liminal Spaces of Amy Levy's Late Work." In *Amy Levy: Critical Essays*, edited by Nadia Valman and Naomi Hetherington, 157–79. Ohio: Ohio University Press.

Hanscombe, Gillian, and Virginia L. Smyers. 1987. *Writing For Their Lives: The Modernist Women, 1900–1940*. London: The Women's Press.

Hardie, Melissa Jane. 2005. "Repulsive Modernism: Djuna Barnes' *The Book of Repulsive Women*." *Journal of Modern Literature* 29 (1): 118–32.

Herring, Phillip. 1995. *Djuna: The Life and Work of Djuna Barnes*. London: Penguin.

———, and Osías Stutman, eds. 2005. *Djuna Barnes: Collected Poems With Notes toward the Memoirs*. Wisconsin: University of Wisconsin Press.

Hunt Beckman, Linda. 2000. *Amy Levy: Her Life and Letters*. Ohio: Ohio University Press.

Laity, Cassandra. 1996. *H.D. and the Victorian Fin de Siècle: Gender, Modernism, Decadence*. Cambridge: Cambridge University Press.

Levy, Amy. 1889. "Ballade of an Omnibus." *A London Plane-Tree, and Other Verse*, 21–2. London: T. Fisher Unwin.

———. 1889. "Borderland." *A London Plane-Tree, and Other Verse*, 42. London: T. Fisher Unwin.

———. 1889. "The Dream." *A London Plane-Tree, and Other Verse*, 38. London: T. Fisher Unwin.

———. 1889. "In the Mile End Road." *A London Plane-Tree, and Other Verse*, 50. London: T. Fisher Unwin.

———. 1889. "In the Night." *A London Plane-Tree, and Other Verse*, 41. London: T. Fisher Unwin.

———. 1889. "A London Plane-Tree." *A London Plane-Tree, and Other Verse*, 17. London: T. Fisher Unwin.

———. 1889. "On the Threshold." *A London Plane-Tree, and Other Verse*, 39. London: T. Fisher Unwin.

———. 1993. "Jewish Children." [1886] In *The Complete Novels and Selected Writings of Amy Levy*, edited by Melvyn New, 528–31. Florida: University Press of Florida.

———. 1993. *The Romance of a Shop* [1888]. In *The Complete Novels and Selected Writings of Amy Levy*. Ed. Melvyn New, 59–196. Florida: University Press of Florida.

Loncraine, Rebecca. 2003. "The Book of Repulsive Women: Djuna Barnes' Unknown Poetry." *PN Review* 29 (6): 40–5.

Marsh, Jan. 2010. *The Legend of Elizabeth Siddal*. London: Quartet Books.

Nead, Lynda. 2000. *Victorian Babylon: People, Streets, and Images in Nineteenth-Century London*. New Haven: Yale University Press.

New, Melvyn. 1993. Introduction. In *The Complete Novels and Selected Writings of Amy Levy*, edited by Melvyn New, 1–52. Florida: University Press of Florida.

Parsons, Deborah. 2000. *Streetwalking the Metropolis: Women, the City and Modernity*. Oxford: Oxford University Press.

Poe, Edgar Allen. 1846. "The Philosophy of Composition." *Graham's Magazine*, April: 163–67.

Port, Cynthia. 2001. "'Money, for the night is coming': Jean Rhys and the Gendered Economies of Aging." *Women: A Cultural Review* 12 (2): 204–17.

Rossetti, Christina. 2008. "In an Artist's Studio." [1856] In *Selected Poems*, edited by Dinah Roe, 49. London: Penguin.

Schaffer, Talia. 2000. *The Forgotten Female Aesthetes: Literary Culture in Late-Victorian England*. Charlottesville: University of Virginia Press.

Steptoe, Lydia [Djuna Barnes]. 1923. "What Is Good Form in Dying? In Which a Dozen Dainty Deaths Are Suggested for Daring Damsels." *Vanity Fair*, June: 73+.

Swinburne, Algernon Charles. 2004. *Major Poems and Selected Prose*, edited by Jerome McGann and Charles L. Sligh. New Haven: Yale University Press.

Tyler-Bennett, Deborah. 2001. "Thick Within Our Hair: Djuna Barnes' Gothic Lovers." In *Gothic Modernisms*, edited by Andrew Smith and Jeff Wallace, 95–110. London: Palgrave.

Vadillo, Ana Parejo. 2005. *Women Poets and Urban Aestheticism: Passengers of Modernity*. London: Palgrave.

Zonana, Joyce. 1989. "The Embodied Muse: Elizabeth Barrett Browning's *Aurora Leigh* and Feminist Poetics." *Tulsa Studies in Women's Literature* 8 (2): 240–62.

5 Greek Gift and "Given Being"

The Libidinal Economies of Vernon Lee's Supernatural Tales

Jane Ford

Nowhere in Vernon Lee's writing are objects more pernicious than when figured as gifts. Ostensibly benign acts of giving frequently emerge as baited offerings: offerings that have the potential to draw the recipient into a complex web of obligation, debt and depletion. In Lee's 1896 tale, "Prince Alberic and the Snake Lady," three figures at court offer up an extravagant medley of gifts in order to secure the young Prince's patronage; through their beneficence, they believed, "Alberic [would] be turned to profit" (Lee 2006d, 196). An earlier tale, "Lady Tal" (1892), describes how the eighteen year-old Lady Atalanta loses her aged husband within a year of their marriage; "Tal" is the beneficiary of her late husband's extensive wealth but is subject to a humiliating and punitive codicil (*á la* Edward Casaubon). Exposing a philosophy of giving that is honorific in nature and which tends towards the creation of obligatory attachments, the tales reveal Lee's mistrust of the practice of gift-giving; a mistrust which culminated in an attack on "making presents" in her 1904 work *Hortus Vitae*. Here, Lee's own "philosophy of presents" which laments the "specious air of … disinterestedness" attached to the gift anticipates Marcel Mauss in his belief in a "polite fiction" that conceals "obligation and economic self-interest": the driving force of gift-exchange (Lee 2008, 66; Mauss 2002, 4).

This chapter will argue that, in line with later theorists of the gift, Lee interpreted the circular or reciprocal structure of the gift-event as evidence of the activity's economic form. However, for Lee, the treachery of the gift exceeds the latent economy considered more recently in gift theory.[1] "Gift-giving" is a privileged form of symbolic activity in Lee's supernatural tales; an activity that, because of the discreet power-dynamics which underpin it, serves as a useful tool in her critique of patriarchy. Focusing on the supernatural tales, "A Wedding Chest" (1888) and "Dionea" (1890), I will examine two principal forms of gift-event: the devotional gift (including eucharistic and votive offerings) and the mythic "Greek Gift" (containing implicit allusions to the Trojan conflict).[2] I will argue that, for Lee, Christian and Greek epic narrative are kindred forms of patriarchal mythology that describe or support an economy of giving that involve the subjection and / or exclusion of women.

Lee's reference to the Judgement of Paris in "Dionea," for instance, advances a narrative key centred around the Trojan conflict: source of the original "Greek gift." The mytheme is an apt point of reference for Lee, since it dramatises those honorific and patriarchal dimensions of gift-exchange that are central to her own treatment of the theme. An epistolary tale composed of letters between a Dr Alessandro De Rosis and Lady Evelyn Savelli (Princess of Sabina), "Dionea" tells the story of a shipwrecked child found on the shore of Montemirto Ligure. In one episode "Dionea," now a beautiful and enigmatic woman, is discovered narrating a version of the Judgement of Paris to the village children. A favourite subject of Renaissance art, the Judgement of Paris is commonly cited as an example of Western visual power relations. Invariably depicting Paris in a seated or reclining position—and the naked goddesses assembled before him—popular representations of the myth reveal, to borrow a phrase from Daryl Ogden, the "supremacy of male eyes" (Ogden 2005, 1). Not only does the Judgement of Paris—and particularly its visual interpretations—portray Venus, Juno, and Minerva as surveyed, objectified entities, but Venus's gift of Helen presents woman as a mere commodity or given object within a culture of exchange defined by patriarchal values. Drawing on Laura Mulvey's seminal essay on cinematic scopophilia, Michael Squire bluntly remarks that "antiquity understood Helen as Mulvey's 'to-be-looked-at-ness.' She was the archetypal shaggable object – the passive pawn of patriarchal power passed from one owner to the next" (Squire 2011, 82).

The idea that female bodies might be conceived as things "given" and exchanged within a patriarchal system of exchange is one that is developed by Luce Irigaray in her essay, "Women on the Market." Using Marx's remarks on the form and nature of the commodity, Irigaray argues that women, far from being active participants within capitalist mechanisms of exchange, are structured as passive commodities (or "value-invested idealities") whose worth is determined by "masculine sexuality" (Irigaray 1985, 181). She points out that "[t]he economy—in both the narrow and the broad sense—that is in place in our societies thus requires that women lend themselves to alienation in consumption, and to exchanges in which they do not participate, and that men be exempt from being used and circulated like commodities" (172). The idea that woman is appropriated for her sexual and reproductive functions, is an important feature of Lee's own essay "The Economic Parasitism of Women," a piece originally written as a preface for the Italian edition of Charlotte Perkins Gilman's *Women and Economics* (1898).[3] Following Gilman, Lee considers the asymmetric relationship that has evolved between the sexes, arguing that the sequestration of woman from the activity of money-making, means that she has become "part and parcel of the home"—effectively "amalgamated with the man's property, a piece of property herself, body and soul" (Lee 1908, 270). This gender asymmetry, Lee remarks, might be figured as "a big man ... holding in his hand a little woman; a god (if we are poetical, and if we face the advantages of the case) protecting a human creature; or (if we are cynical, and look to the disadvantages) a human being playing with a doll" (Lee

1908, 270–71). For Lee, "animation" is merely a matter of perspective since, in relation to man, woman is both "human creature" and "doll" (indeed, in either condition, she is regarded as a commodity or "slave" to be "stolen or bought").

In similar ways, Lee's supernatural tales highlight this "thingness" of woman within a social (gift) economy that measures worth against those male-conceived markers of value: beauty and purity. Impressed with a representational value derived from mythic and art-historical indicators, the objects of Lee's aesthetic imagination explore a range of gendered subject positions. Her female *objets d'art*, imagined as corpses, sculptures and other motionless forms, emerge as surveyed entities—to use Lee's own words, "piece[s] of property" circulating within a misogynistic culture of exchange and valued for the erotic capital she affords her possessor (Lee 1908, 270).[4]

§

Like "Dionea," Lee's "A Wedding Chest" deploys mythic and art-historical images to launch its critique of male-dominated forms of exchange. The tale opens with the catalogue entry for an artefact housed at the Smith museum: the panel of a fifteenth century Umbrian wedding coffer, entitled, after Petrarch, "The Triumph of Love" (Lee 2006a, 229). Returning to its Renaissance setting and the narrative underlying the dismantled relic, the story reveals how Desiderio of Castiglione del Largo, craftsman of the coffer commissioned by a Messer Troilo Baglioni, is engaged to his employer's daughter, Monna Maddalena. Troilo, harbouring a libidinous desire for the affianced Maddalena and having the misfortune to see his advances rebuked, gives orders for her abduction on the eve of their wedding. A year following her disappearance, Maddalena is returned in the coffer, "naked as God had made [her], dead, with two stabs in the neck ... having on her breast the body of an infant recently born, dead like herself" (237). Attached to the coffer is a parchment bearing the inscription: "To Master Desiderio; a wedding gift from Troilo Baglioni of Fratta" (237). After a period of exile in Rome, the aggrieved Desiderio returns to exact revenge on Messer Troilo. Taking sacrament, Desiderio vows "never to touch food save the Body of Christ till he could taste the blood of Messer Troilo" (240). True to his word, on appertaining Troilo, who is "going to a woman of light fame," Desiderio delivers a fatal stab to his chest, declaring: "This is from Maddalena, in return for her wedding chest!" (241). Then, he "stooped over [Troilo's] chest and lapped up the blood as it flowed" (241).

Prior to Maddalena's abduction and in an attempt to win her favour, Troilo delivers a succession of curios, including the "knot of ribbons off the head of a ferocious bull, whom he had killed *singulari vi ac virtue*" (235).[5] Maddalena, not unaware of the contract embedded within the gift, "showed herself very coy and refused all presents which he sent her" yet, in so doing, poses a challenge to the natural economy of giving and one that would prove unwittingly fatal (235). As Mauss points out, "to refuse to accept is tantamount to declaring war; it is to reject the bonds of alliance and commonality" and certainly for Lee, the gift more frequently harbours an act of treachery than of beneficence (Mauss 2002, 17). It is unsurprising, then, that "A Wedding Chest" contains a sub rosa key to the pattern of self-interest and dissimulation that will characterise the tale's subsequent gift-events. The key resides in a panel depicting the region of happy love, one of "four phases of amorous passion" that ornament the wedding coffer (230–31). Here, Troilo is "depicted in the character of Troilus, son of Priam, emperor of Troy" (233). The story of Troilus, as we know, varies between sources, but one element these accounts share is the prophecy that Troy would survive should Troilus advance to the age of twenty. Cast in the figure of Troilus, Troilo's fate is thus aligned with the ancient city of Troy; both receive a gift that would signal their fall. The sequence of exchange—initiated with the return of Maddalena's body, "a gift of unspeakable wickedness for the father" and terminated with Desiderio's fatal blow, "from Maddalena, in return for her wedding chest"—is, more properly, a series of assaults in a larger context of conflict: a conflict that culminates, aptly enough, in a stratagem. Desiderio, on returning to Perugia, had "dyed his hair black and grown his beard, after the manner of the Easterns, saying he was a Greek coming from Ancona" (240). In this Trojan horse disguise, the craftsman makes a final, unequivocal return on Troilo's own bloody offering, advancing figuratively, and literally, a Greek gift.

The principle of reciprocity that is central to gift-exchange operates in tandem with the figures of blood and circulation in Lee's story. Actors in the triad formed of Troilo, Desiderio and Maddalena's father, Ser Piero Bontempi, for instance, pay and are restituted for their enterprise in blood; Troilo, makes a return on his seizure with the bloody remains of Maddalena, Desiderio "laps" up Troilo's blood in order to amortise (by proxy) the debt owed to Maddalena and Ser Piero, for his craven relinquishment of Maddalena, is struck "on the mouth till he bled" (236). In the mid to late-nineteenth century the blood-money analogy is often linked to economic distribution and circulation; notably, Herbert Spencer, in his essay "The Social Organism" (1860), aligns the "blood-discs" of the biological organism with coins or, money in the social one (Spencer 1883, 418). In recognition of the fact that in "the lower animals, the blood contains no corpuscles; and in societies of low civilization, there is no money," Spencer posits that "circulation" becomes apparent "only at a certain stage of [evolutionary] organisation" (Spencer 1883, 419).[6] "Circulation," then, insignia of biological and civilisational progress, operates in a sophisticated "body-politic" quite apart from the primordial economy of blood characteristic to Lee's gift-exchange. While Lee offers a consonant model of circulation, her tendency is not, as Spencer, to analogise but rather to *realise* the equivalence between blood and money in a de facto somatic currency.

Pointing to a haematic adaptation of the gift-exchange, the circulation of blood is linked to some striking moments of physical consumption and abnegation. Ser Piero, robbed of his daughter, "wept, and cursed wickedly, and refused to take food' (236) and likewise Desiderio vowed "never to touch food ... till he could taste the blood of Messer Troilo" (240). Fasting was certainly common in Renaissance Italy (in various seasons, including Lent) but while this physical abstention has a clearly Christological basis (to which I shall return), it is equally connected to economic circulation, specifically a violation of rules of economic exchange (Cohen & Cohen 2001, 103). As an unlawful seizure of capital, Troilo's abduction functions for Ser Piero and Desiderio as a direct inversion of the "consumption" principle while Maddalena's doll-like passivity renders her more properly commodity than human agent. In this way, physical abstention becomes the figurative expression of economic loss; the revelation that Ser Piero, being "the father of other children ... conquered his grief" (and with it, his appetite) moreover points to the fact that Piero's estate, possessed of surplus offspring, is capable of absorbing the cost of Troilo's extortion in a way that Desiderio, a mere craftsman, cannot (236).

Desiderio's own fast is conversely broken in a moment of vampiric mania when he "lapped up [Troilo's] blood as it flowed" from the wound in his chest (241). Patricia Pulham, in remarking the potentially homoerotic relations between Troilo and Desiderio, states that "Desiderio's vampire-like lapping of Troilo's blood arguably functions as an act of introjection which, given the 'two stabs' that mark Maddalena's neck, suggests a form of vampiric consummation of his relationship with Maddalena mediated via the androgynous body of Troilo's corpse" (Pulham 2008, 86). As an erotic act, Desiderio's assault is situated within a libidinal economy that conflates Christian and classical symbolism. Within the system of exchange that defines the relationship between father, son-in-law, and seducer, Desiderio's three fatal blows (delivered "in return" for Maddalena's chest) allude both to Trojan horse (with the connotations of sexual penetration this figure carries) and the holy trinity.

Evoking a range of quasi-Christian ritual, the literary vampire invariably assimilates the eucharist or Holy Sacrament into the broader economy of blood (capital). In "A Wedding Chest," it is the eucharist that emerges as the main tropological constituent, of which "the vampiric" is but one form of expression. Desiderio's final return on Troilo's "gift of unspeakable wickedness" is significantly prefaced by the communion he receives from Ser Piero's brother, the priest of Saint Severus (237; n.2):

> And he went to the priest, prior of Saint Severus, and brother of Ser Piero, and discovered himself to him, who although old, had great joy in seeing and hearing of his intent. And Desiderio confessed all his sins to the priest and obtained absolution, and received the body of Christ with great fervour and compunction; and the priest placed his sword on the altar, beside the gospel, as he said mass, and blessed it. And Desiderio knelt and made a vow never to touch food save the Body of Christ till he could taste the blood of Messer Troilo. (240)

For Desiderio, the eucharist operates as the symbolic settling of accounts. To receive the "gift" of sacrament is to enter a state of divine reciprocation. Indeed, according to the Christological economy of salvation, the self-sacrifice of Jesus Christ serves to discharge man's debt, in order that he stand free before God. Adalbert Hamman, writing on Saint Irenaeous, an early Christian thinker and Bishop of Lyons, points out that:

> For Irenaeus, the eucharist is the sacrament of the economy, or the unfolding divine plan, as revealed to us in the person and work of Christ. Faith and eucharist, eucharist and faith are inseparable and reciprocal: "our manner of thinking is conformed to the eucharist and the eucharist confirms our manner of thinking" (Adv, Haer.IV, 18,5). The eucharist is the center and the content of faith and contains the whole economy of the son of God.
>
> (Hamman 1978, 95)

Thought of in these terms, the eucharistic economy is necessarily a gift economy. The tautology "Faith and eucharist, eucharist and faith," as a statement of equivalence, affirms the principle of reciprocity built up around the divine beneficence of Christ. Like Marcel Mauss, who posits the absolute obligation to give and receive, Irenaeus acknowledges the tacit *quid pro quo* of the eucharistic ritual. Proclaiming that "the savior redeemed us with his blood and gave his soul for our soul, his flesh for our flesh," Irenaeus demands from the collective beneficiaries of this, the ultimate sacrifice, a faithful and commensurate return: flesh for flesh, soul for soul (Hamman 1978, 95).[7]

Desiderio, then, in what should properly be regarded as an act of debt-consolidation, receives sacrament and in so doing enters into a binary exchange that vanquishes all others. Thus pledging himself to God, Desiderio receives divine favour in the object of his sword, which is placed by the gospel and blessed. The fact that divine favour *is* conferred upon Desiderio is, as I point out, evident in the triadic structures that manifest around the sequence. The tripartite significance of Troilus's name, at once triad troil and Trojan, prefigures the trinity to be revisited upon him; for "three days and nights [Desiderio] watched and dogged [Troilus]" and on appertaining him, "ran his sword three times through his chest" (240, 241).

Lee's 1890 story "Dionea," reproduces some of the strategies of "A Wedding Chest," using mythic imagery to explore the economic relations between sexes. The eponymous foundling of Lee's tale is the subject onto which various male representational fantasies are transposed. The letters of Dr Alessandro De Rosis, which constitute the sole documentation of the epistolary tale, wistfully conflate the "squall" that casts Dionea onto the Ligurian shore with the "wicked sea" from which "Venus Verticordia" emerged in the classical age (Lee 2006, 77). As Catherine Maxwell and Patricia Pulham explain, Dionea's adopted village, Montemirto Ligure, translates to "myrtle mountain"; given that the myrtle is a shrub associated with Venus, the settlement may be counted among the many allusions that link Dionea to the goddess (Lee 2006b, 77n). Indeed, like her mythic counterpart, Dionea becomes muse—the erotic material which inspires the male artist's creative imagination.

As the tale records, the sculptor Waldemar and his wife, Lady Gertrude, make an extended visit to the Doctor and shortly after their arrival recognise Dionea as a suitable model for the artist. In fact, it is Lady Gertrude who procures Dionea for her husband. Cutting the figure of the vampire, Gertrude appears as a "pale, demure, diaphanous creature" who is "not the more earthly for approaching motherhood" (97). Morbidly anaemic, she scans the "girls of [the] village with the eyes of a slave-dealer" before alighting on the fleshly form of Dionea (97). Following a period of intensive activity, Waldemar's frustration surrounding the "superiority of the model over the statue" peaks; he becomes increasingly volatile and exhibits a peculiar interest in one of the Doctor's antiques: a Venus altar possessing "two little gutters ... for collecting the blood of the victim" (100–01). One evening, when Waldemar is working late—having "placed Dionea on the big marble block behind the altar [with] a great curtain of dull red brocade ... behind her"—Gertrude creeps downstairs to a desecrated chapel, Waldemar's temporary studio (103). A tragedy ensues, as the Doctor reports:

> We found her [Gertrude] lying across the altar, her pale hair among the ashes of the incense, her blood – she had but little to give, poor white ghost! – trickling among the carved garlands and rams' heads, blackening the heaped-up roses. The body of Waldemar was found at the foot of the castle cliff. He had hoped, by setting the place on fire, to bury himself among its ruins, or had he not rather wished to complete in this way the sacrifice, to make the whole temple an immense votive pyre? (104)

Economically dependent and relatively friendless, Dionea is theoretically vulnerable to the needs of the Doctor's wealthy and influential visitors, and certainly, Lady Gertrude's vampire-like pursuit, and ultimate purchase of Dionea's services (or, more accurately, her naked form), constitutes an act of subordination bordering on prostitution. However, in the visual power relations between artist and subject, Dionea emerges as victor, continually eluding Waldemar's attempts to fix her likeness in stone. As Catherine Maxwell remarks, "Dionea" deals with "uncontainable female energy," Vernon Lee's "strange, beautiful, demanding women [have] something about them that eludes fixed representation, and certainly possession" (Maxwell 1997, 265). The fire marks the apogee of the dialectic between sexes as Waldemar's "rapt[urous] contemplation" of the girl's beautiful form expends itself in what is, essentially, an act of sublime sumptuary destruction (98).

Dionea's victory, however, occurs only after Waldemar has disposed of his wife in sacrifice to the goddess and, in this way, fulfills his role as *pater familias*. As a corpse Gertrude is concretised in Waldemar's representational fantasy, and at the same time reduced to the status of (sacrificial) gift. Noting similarities between Dionea and Gertrude—both are likened to Madonnas—Pulham suggests that Lee "posits Dionea as a double ... of the artist's wife" (Pulham 2008, 141). It is interesting, therefore that Lady Gertrude's acquisition of Dionea is presaged in the Judgement of Paris, a tale which Dionea adapts for the village children. As we know, following Paris's judgement in Venus's favour, he abducts Helen of Sparta with the goddess's help: an act that supposedly ignites the Trojan conflict. Dionea's adaptation of the tale places Lady Gertrude in an analogous position both to Dionea and her prototype, Venus (who, like Gertrude, appropriates a fellow woman as gift for their male consort or lover). For Pulham, this "twinning" suggests a homoerotic attachment between women. Certainly, Gertrude's rapt contemplation of Dionea's beautiful body bears this reading out, but I would suggest that the doubling of these characters serves a further purpose. That is, in operating as double, Dionea realises her identity as Venus and embodies those qualities of sensuality and self-government that Lady Gertrude, in her position of wife, has sought to repress.

Pertinently, in her remarks on early representations of the Judgement of Paris mytheme, the classicist Jane Harrison—with whom, as Pulham points out, Lee was acquainted—notes a form of visual metonymy which makes it impossible to "distinguish the goddesses from the gifts they bring" (Pulham 2008, 109).[8] Harrison continues, "they are charities, Gift-bringers. They are their own gift" (Harrison 1980, 298). Harrison earlier remarks that the story "is sufficiently patriarchal to please the taste of Olympian Zeus himself" and, along similar lines, these comments draw attention to the ways in which the female body is reduced, in representational activity, to the status of object, gift or commodity (Harrison 1980, 292). Though Harrison's *Prolegomena to the Study of Greek Religion* was not published until 1903, there are interesting parallels between Lee's treatment of the idea of woman and gift in visual representation and Harrison's.

Lee would not be the first to deploy the figure of Venus to explore visual power relations. The eponymous Venus in furs of Leopold von Sacher-Masoch's 1870 novella has been read, for instance, as a "sublimated object of desire" within male "picture-making activity" (Stewart 1999, 76). As Suzanne Stewart remarks, Masoch's Venus is an archetype on which a "long catalog of literary and mythological references" are overlaid (77). The tale—which describes how the dilettante Severin becomes slave to his Venus-like lover Wanda—contains numerous pictorial reproductions which include a sculptural replica of a Florentine Venus and photographic copy of Titian's *Venus with the Mirror*. This art-historical Venus—having rather less to do with the desirability of the subject itself than with the "masochistic subjectivity" that demands her cold "self-sufficiency"—is "fixed," according to Stewart, in a synchronic moment of erotic picturing (73).[9] For Albrecht Koschorke too, the Hegelian dialectic suggested by Masoch's tale (the tale's unnamed narrator, it should be noted, falls asleep reading Hegel), reveals itself to be a rather less a fight-to-the-death of the sexes, than a "stagnant dialectic" (Koschorke 2001, 562–63). Like Stewart, Koschorke argues that male masochistic subjectivity creates a kind of immobility at the level of representation. Since the identity of the tyrannical Wanda is sustained by countless mythic references, "propagated through wall-paintings [and] mirror-images," Masoch's story does not, as one might assume, narrate the dialectical emergence of a conquering (gendered) consciousness but rather, a *mis an abyme* of "ecstatic stagnation" (553). Even within the masochistic framework of Masoch's tale, the projection of mythic and art-historical images onto the figure of Wanda mean that woman is stripped—in Hegelian terms—of being-for-self, which is expressed as pictorial stasis.

While, as I point out, Lee seeks to expose the paralysis of the female body within male representational frameworks, in "Dionea" it is not the logic of stasis that drives the dialectical tension between sexes, but a more dynamic one. While Dionea is the subject onto which various male representational fantasies are conferred, she is not (in the manner of Gertrude) immobilised by Waldemar's "picture making activity," offering instead a *fulfilment* of Masoch's suspended dialectic. Hegel's master-slave dialectic, which serves as a useful tool to describe the power-struggle between Dionea and her "proprietors," requires that the anthropogenetic desire or, "desire that generates self-consciousness," of a potential "master," assert itself over a "slavish" consciousness in order to achieve "recognition" as the ascendant conscious being.[10] Alexandre Kojève explains that "[t]he being that eats, for example, creates and preserves its own reality by overcoming a reality other than its own ... by the 'assimilation,' the 'internalization' of a 'foreign,' 'external reality'" (Kojève 1980, 4). So too does the ascendant party of Lee's tale, Waldemar, validate his own (artistic) consciousness by the consumption of an external reality: Dionea. In the following passage, which includes Kojève's own explanatory insertions, Hegel characterises the enslaved consciousness as:

> a consciousness that [being in fact a living corpse – the man who has been defeated and spared] does not exist purely for itself, but rather for another Consciousness [namely, that of the victor]: i.e. a Consciousness that exists as a *given-being*, or in other words, a Consciousness that exists in the concrete form of *thingness*.
>
> (Kojève 1980, 16)[11]

That the enslaved consciousness is not recognised as animate and exists, for the master, as mere "thing" or significantly "given" thing, has important implications for Lee's tale.[12] As the Doctor reports: "I could never have believed that an artist could regard a woman so utterly as a mere inanimate thing, a form to copy, like a tree or flower. Truly he carries out his theory that a sculpture knows only the body, and the body scarcely considered as human" (98). A "*given-being*," the product of Lady Waldemar's voracious "kindness," Dionea figures, for the artist, as no more than a "concrete form of *thingness,"* or "living corpse." The latter is significant, given the prevalence of the (eroticised) corpse in Lee's tales, because it highlights the striking lack of female agency. "A Wedding Chest," for instance, sexualises the naked corpse of Maddalena, and Lee's later tale, "Prince Alberic and the Snake Lady" (1896), similarly describes how the Prince's pet grass snake (his godmother, a woman that metamorphosises into reptilian form during daylight hours) reverts, in death, to the "body of a women, naked, and miserably disfigured with blows and sabre cuts" (Lee 2006c, 227).

The master-slave dialectic crucially requires that the enslaved party is not "recognized as an independent self-consciousness"; in fact, the slave is the only one of the two parties in possession of this kind of external recognition (Kojève 1980, 13). The upshot of this, according to Kojève, is that the master "is always enslaved by the world of which he is [ascendant] ... it is only his death that 'realizes' his freedom" (1980, 29). Waldemar's manifest failure to realise Dionea's form in clay, and the frustration culminating in his "obliteration" of the "exquisite" but nonetheless inferior duplicate, mirrors, in Hegel's dialectical relationship, the Master's inability to recognise the subordinate consciousness. Waldemar's fatal "recognition" of Dionea's true identity as Venus is reinforced by the contextual clues provided by her placement; posing the girl in the "old desecrated chapel ... that was once the temple of Venus," Waldemar illuminates her naked form "by an artificial light ... the way in which the ancients lit up statues in their temples" and before the altar of Venus procured from the Doctor (102, 103). As Dionea is revealed, in this way, as Venus, Waldemar faces "recognition" of another consciousness: a recognition that, as "Master," necessarily leads to his self-sacrifice. Thus Waldemar's "freedom" is, in Hegelian terms, a fatal and reciprocal recognition of the archetypal female psyche.

The master-slave dialectic does not, for the reason of competition, allow for the kind of reciprocal arrangement characteristic to the votive or eucharistic economies of "A Wedding Chest." As Kojève points out "the two [parties] do not give themselves reciprocally to one another, nor do they get themselves back in return from one another through consciousness" (1980, 14). Indeed, the "immense votive pyre" offered in worship, or acknowledgement of Dionea's ascendency is, as I point out, a uni-directional movement of capital: Waldemar's wife, the product of his labour and his props are all absorbed, exigently into an "immense" votive vortex (104). Significantly, Waldemar takes the life of his spouse in a sacrificial offering that, as gift of blood from wife to idol, has specifically vampiric overtones. Gertrude, found "lying across the altar," seeps blood—of which "she had but little to give"—onto "the carved garlands and rams' heads," a scene that strangely prefigures the anaemic bloodletting of Stoker's own Lucy Westenra (104). In this sense, Waldemar not only mediates the haematic exchange between Gertrude and Dionea, but reveals himself as proprietor of the "asset" thus disposed of. The offering, then, serves not to criticise the malign self-interest that debases gift and giving, but operates as an ideological inversion of the patriarchal economy of exchange that so often, in Lee's fiction, claims woman as its sacrificial gift. In Waldemar's moment of surrender, Dionea "dialectically overcomes" her oppressor and, in the Hegelian sense, "posits [*her*]*self* as a negative in the permanent order of things, and hereby becomes for [*her*]*self*" (Hegel 1977, 118). This is to say that Dionea, now capable of "negation," sets "at nought the existing shape confronting [her]"—the shape, that is, of patriarchy in the person of Waldemar—and in so doing becomes *herself*, the archetypal feminine icon: Venus. Dionea's liberation is symbolically affirmed in her escape on a Greek vessel that, set "full sail to sea," conveys the girl, braced against the mast with "a robe of purple and gold about her, and her myrtle-wreath on her head" (104). Gertrude, who is conversely victim of the patriarchy Waldemar administers, is curiously spectral; she is an unearthly "diaphanous creature" who, in death, resembles a "white ghost" with little blood to sacrifice to the goddess (97, 104). Gertrude's liminality, her wraithlike physicality bespeaks of her failure to break free from the bonds of servitude and acquire, like Dionea, phenomenal reality or, in Hegelian terms "being-for-self" (Hegel 1977, 118).

Transposing the gender of the sacrificial being, Lee imagines a theistic economy in which woman rules sovereign. According to Jane Harrison, writing shortly after Lee, "matriarchal theology," predates the "patriarchal mythology" of Hesiod and others (Harrison 1980, 283–84). Harrison points out, for instance, that where the goddess Pandora is conceived as "Earth-born" in primitive Greek culture, by the time of Hesiod's mythology, she is figured as "the handiwork of Olympian Zeus" (284). Harrison remarks: "Zeus the Father will have no great Earth-Goddess, Mother and Maid in one, in his man-fashioned Olympus, but her figure is from the beginning, so he re-makes it; ... she who made all things, gods and mortals alike, is become their plaything, their slave ..." (285). Lee's own particular reverence for the female gods of the Greek and Roman pantheon stems from a desire to re-instate the matriarch who, formerly ascendant, is displaced in the rise of patriarchal Christianity. Régis Debray articulates the demise of the female Gods, staking a position that appears to accord with Lee's own. He writes:

> If what was needed, whatever the cost, was a founding act of carnage, a union through murder, Freud, it would appear, confused genders: the cement of monotheism, the law of the Father, was made with the blood of the mother goddesses. The scapegoat strictly speaking should have been a she-goat. Sand and Sign restricted divinity to a regimen of dryness. Until the great turning point, however, divinity had been vitalistic and matrilinear: oral, visual, awash with rain, piss and milk, a source of nourishment ... the matricide occurred later.
>
> (Debray 2004, 158)

Rejecting Freud's proposition that the sacrifice of Jesus Christ represents an oedipal impulse that is revisited, symbolically, in the Christian eucharist,

Debray argues that the primordial deity was not a stale patriarch, but sundry fertile matriarchs, eliminated in the rise of the Christian religion. Like Debray who considers that Artemis is covertly re-imagined in the figure of the Virgin, Lee, in her preface to the 1927 version of "The Virgin of the Seven Daggers" similarly writes: "is she not the divine Mother of Gods as well as God, Demeter or Mary, in whom the sad and ugly things of our bodily origin and nourishment are transfigured … ?" (Lee 2006c, 245). Not only, then, does Debray share Lee's vision of a nourishing eternal mother concentred in the Holy Virgin, but also the conviction that within Christianity's theistic economy, the principal economic "players" are male. As is evident from my analysis of "A Wedding Chest," Lee shows herself particularly attuned to the patriarchy embedded not only within votive and eucharistic practices but in the broader Christological economy. The tale features the circulation of a female gift-object in a triad formed of Ser Piero, Desiderio and Troilus; the Holy Trinity revealed in these and in the tale's triadic structures, is associated with a male esoteric marketplace. Certainly, woman, who is powerless to participate in the exchange, becomes the erotic commodity circulated in an economy ostensibly presided over, or sanctioned by, God the father. While the Christological economy of salvation does, of course, evolve from an original act of *male* sacrifice, it operates in the context of a prototypical Maussian reciprocity (that is to say, the reciprocal obligation to give and receive). Freud notes that the Christian eucharist is a ritual whereby a "band of brothers … eats the flesh and blood of the son and no longer that of the father, the sons thereby identifying themselves with him and becoming holy themselves." He continues: "the reconciliation with the father is the more thorough because … there follows the complete renunciation of woman" (Freud 1919, 254). Thus the eucharist, through its primitive oedipal aspirations, actively excludes woman. But central to the idea of the Greek gift is the promise of a return—a sinister fulfilment of the economic logic of the praxis—and Lee capitalises on these mythic associations, staging a return of the repressed female subject. In "Dionea," Waldemar's self-sacrifice, intended to supply the votive flame, signals Lee's ideological reversal of this principle and works to reinstate the Eternal mother to her antecedent position. Moreover, the sacrifice betokens a grand act of overcoming. In the Hegelian sense I have described, woman throws off the yoke of patriarchy to become, effectively, idol of the marketplace; she is not the passive agent of "A Wedding Chest" but a locus point of economic activity, voraciously absorbing the gifts of man, life, and blood.

Notes

1. In *Given Time: Counterfeit Money*, Jacques Derrida considers the phenomenological impossibility of the gift outside of economic activity. He writes: "the gift, if there is any, would no doubt be related to economy" and certainly, if we are to believe the anthropologist and early theorist of the gift, Marcel Mauss, gift-giving is but another mode of economic circulation. For Derrida "economy

implies the idea of exchange, of circulation, of return" and thus the instant a gift-event commands reciprocal action—whether a symbolic or material return—it ceases to exist *as* gift; the latent egoism that drives the activity means that it belongs more properly to the realm of economic exchange (Derrida 1992, 6–7).

2. "A Wedding Chest" was first published in the journal *Art and Letters* 2 (1888): 5–16.

3. The Italian edition, *Le donne e l'economia sociale,* was published in 1902. Correspondence housed at Somerville College, Oxford reveals that Lee and Gilman were communicating about the volume in 1900. For an account of the nature of this correspondence see Patricia Pulham, 2003. "A Transatlantic Alliance: Charlotte Perkins Gilman and Vernon Lee." In *Feminist Forerunners (New) Womanism and Feminism in the Early Twentieth Century,* edited by Ann Heilmann, 34–43. London: Pandora Press.

4. Of course, the prevalence of human objects can, in part, be attributed to the materialist complexion of Lee's literary imagination. In her essay on Lee's ethics of consumption Kristin Mahoney, for instance, notes that Lee's "sensitivity to the separate life of objects" might be traced as far back as 1870 when her story, "Les aventures d'une pièce de monnaie" appeared in the Swiss journal, *La famille*—Lee was just 14 (Mahoney 2007, 40). For Mahoney, Lee's abiding preoccupation with economic themes (and the politics of consumption, in particular), culminates in a desire to shield aesthetic experience from the ahistorical consumerist impulse of the contemporary "desiring subject" (41). Mahoney argues that by insisting on the "re-auraticization of objects," Lee offers an "ethical corrective to the subjectivism of modern consumer practices" (39). But Lee's "sensitivity" to the object's "separate life" has implications beyond her ideas about ethical consumption. Lee dramatises *both* the sentience of the individual object and the object-ness of the individual life, creating a feedback relationship between subject and object—body and thing—which draws attention to a troubling uncertainty about what is, and what is not, the proper material of economic exchange.

5. In an "Account of the Spanish Bullfights" featured in an 1823 edition of *The Gentleman's Magazine,* an anonymous correspondent explains how "[t]he bulls each have a knot of ribbons of different colours fixed near to their shoulder, so that referring to a printed list, this badge declares their breed and province … The Piccadore will sometimes snatch the ribbons from his shoulder, which is considered as highly dexterous and greatly applauded" (1823, 301). Lee visited Spain between 1888–89 and refers to the bullfight in her preface to "The Virgin of the Seven Daggers" which she published in *For Maurice: Five Unlikely Tales* (1927). Here she articulates her "detestation" for the "Spanish cultus of death" which she suggests takes root in the "Spanish mud": a substance composed "half and half of *auto da fés* and bull fights" (Lee 2006c, 245). It is therefore probable that Lee, aware of the ritual, deploys the anatomical knot of ribbons to signal the malignancy of Troilo's gift, which is principally honorific in nature.

6. For a more detailed analysis of the blood-money homology—with special consideration to Georg Simmel, Arthur Crump, H. D. Macleod and George H. Pownall—see: Turley Houston, 2005, 118–19.

7. Interestingly, contemporary literary criticism tends to equate the literary vampire with late nineteenth-century economic activity, chiefly: market centralisation and corporate monopoly. Both Franco Moretti and Gail Turley Houston,

draw parallels between Stoker's *Dracula* (1897) and end-of-century economics. Moretti states that: "If the vampire is a metaphor for capital, [and for Moretti, it is] then Stoker's vampire, who is of 1897, must be the capital of 1897. The capital which, after lying 'buried' for twenty long years of recession, rises again to set out the irreversible road to concentration and monopoly" (Moretti 1983, 92). Similarly Turley Houston points out that "[t]he term 'Dracula' is ... an amalgamated corporation of vampires of which he is the brains; a process or procedure of (capitalist) infinite circulation (of the commodity of blood); and the extensive hybrid streams of consciousness (and blood) of a group of accountants (Van Helsing, etc.) who attempt to bankrupt the artificial personality of the incorporated Dracula" (Turley Houston 2005, 117). Certainly, following Marx's 1867 conceptualisation of capital as vampire (sucking the "living blood of labour"), the vampire figure is seen both to allegorise contemporary economic conditions, while also—in line with the rise of evolutionary economics in the latter part of the century—highlight a retrogressive or, devolutionary, movement in *fin-de-siècle* pecuniary arrangements (Marx 1973, 257).

8. Pulham points out that "Lee had met Harrison in London and was to write on Harrison's work, delivering a lecture entitled 'Sympathy verses Group Emotion, á propos of Miss Jane Harrison's Alpha and Omega' to the Cambridge 'Heretics' on 6 June 1915" (Pulham 2008, 109).

9. As Stewart points out, for Masoch, the "sublimatory process turns [the gaze of desire] into a substance, a Thing ..." (Stewart 1999, 63).

10. In the struggle that Hegel describes, the consciousness that exhibits a self-preservation instinct becomes, ultimately, the enslaved party in a symbiotic relationship. The desire to survive, notwithstanding potentially compromised conditions, leads the subordinate party to "recognise" the "supreme value" or, animal consciousness of the "master". This is pertinent for Lee's tale because the material conditions of Dionea's life depend entirely on her patrons.

11. This passage is translated as "a consciousness which is not purely for itself but for another, i.e. is a merely *immediate* consciousness, or consciousness in the form of *thinghood*" (Hegel 1977, 115).

12. Kojève translates the German "Seiendes" to "given-being" ("être-donné" in the original French) which has important implications for my own reading because it is precisely as a "gifted" consciousness or being that I read Dionea's involvement with the Waldemars. "Seiendes" which, more commonly denotes the state of being or existence can also refer to the act of coming into or, *giving* existence. It is evidently in this sense of "giving"—which accurately describes the subordination of the slavish consciousness—that Kojève has derived his meaning but we should be aware that, as James H. Nichols Jr., points out : "Kojève's translations of Hegelian terms are not the customary ones, but represent his interpretation of their meaning" (Nichols 1980, xiii). Thanks to Anna Pilz (University College Cork) for her help with the translated texts.

Works Cited

"Account of the Spanish Bullfights, in a Letter to a Friend." 1823. The *Gentleman's Magazine and, Historical Chronicle*, 93.

Cohen, Elizabeth S., and Thomas V. Cohen. 2001. *Daily Life in Renaissance Italy*. Westport: Greenwood.

Debray, Regis. 2004. *God: An Itinerary*. Translated by Jeffrey Mehlman. London: Verso.

Derrida, Jacques. 1992. *Given Time: I. Counterfeit Money*. Translated by Peggy Kamuf. Chicago: University of Chicago Press.

Freud, Sigmund. 1919. *Totem and Taboo: Resemblances between the psychic Lives of Savages and Neurotics*, Translated by A.A Brill. New York: Moffat, Yard & Co.

Gilman, Charlotte Perkins. 1994. *Women and Economics: A Study of the Economic Relation Between Women and Men*. New York: Prometheus.

Hamman, Adalbert. 1978. "Irenaeus of Lyons." In *The Eucharist of the Early Christians*, edited by Willy Rordorf, 86–98. New York: Pueblo Publishing.

Harrison, Jane. 1980. *Prolegomena to the Study of Greek Religion*. London: Merlin Press.

Hegel, G. W. F. 1977. *Phenomenology of Spirit*. Translated by A.V. Miller. Oxford: Oxford University Press.

Irigaray, Luce. 1985. "Women on the Market." In *This Sex Which Is Not One*, translated by Catherine Porter and Carolyn Burke, 170–91. New York: Cornell University Press.

Kojève, Alexandre. 1980. *Introduction to the Reading of Hegel: Lectures on the Phenomenology of Spirit*. Edited by Allan Bloom. Translated by James H. Nichols, Jr. Ithaca: Cornell University Press.

Koschorke, Albrecht. 2001. "Mastery and Slavery: A Masochist Falls Asleep Reading Hegel." Translated by Joel Golb. *MLN* 116 (3): 551–63.

Lee, Vernon. 2006a. "A Wedding Chest." In *Hauntings and Other Fantastic Tales*, edited by Catherine Maxwell and Patricia Pulham, 229–42. Toronto: Broadview.

———. 2006b. "Dionea." In *Hauntings and Other Fantastic Tales*, edited by Catherine Maxwell and Patricia Pulham, 77–104. Toronto: Broadview.

———. 2006c. "Preface to 'The Virgin of the Seven Daggers' (1927)." In *Hauntings and Other Fantastic Tales*, edited by Catherine Maxwell and Patricia Pulham, 243–48. Toronto: Broadview.

———. 2006d. "Prince Alberic and the Snake Lady." In *Hauntings and Other Fantastic Tales*, edited by Catherine Maxwell and Patricia Pulham, 182–228. Toronto: Broadview.

———. 1908. "The Economic Parasitism of Women." In *Gospels of Anarchy, and Other Contemporary Studies*, 263–97. London: Unwin.

———. 2008. *Hortus Vitae: Essays on the Gardening of Life*. Teddington: Echo Library.

Mauss, Marcel. 2002. *The Gift: Form and Reason for Exchange in Archaic Societies*. Translated by W.D. Halls. Oxford: Routledge.

Mahoney, Kristin. 2007. "Haunted Collections: Vernon Lee and Ethical Consumption." *Criticism* 48 (1): 39–67.

Maxwell, Catherine. 1997. "From Dionysus to 'Dionea': Vernon Lee's portraits." *Word & Image* no. 13, 253–69.

Marx, Karl. 1973. *Capital: A Critique of Political Economy*, Vol. I, part I. New York: Cosimo.

Moretti, Franco. 1983. *Signs Taken for Wonders: Essays in the Sociology of Literary Forms*. London: Verso.

Mulvey, Laura. 1985. "Visual Pleasure in Narrative Cinema." In *Film Theory and Criticism*, edited by Gerald Mast and Marshall Cohen, 803–16. New York: Oxford University Press.

Nichols, James H. Jr. 1980. Translator's Note in *Introduction to the Reading of Hegel: Lectures on the Phenomenology of Spirit* by Alexandre Kojève, xiii–xiv. Edited by Allan Bloom. Ithaca: Cornell University Press.

Ogden, Daryl. 2005. *The Language of the Eyes: Science, Sexuality and Female Vision in English Literature and Culture, 1690–1927*. New York: State University of New York Press.

Pulham, Patricia. 2003. "A Transatlantic Alliance: Charlotte Perkins Gilman and Vernon Lee." In *Feminist Forerunners (New) Womanism and Feminism in the Early Twentieth Century,* edited by Ann Heilmann, 34–43. London: Pandora Press.

———. 2008. *Art and the Transitional Object in Vernon Lee's Supernatural Tales.* Aldershot: Ashgate.

Spencer, Herbert. 1883. "The Social Organism." In *Essays: Scientific, Political and Speculative,* 388–432. V.I. London: William & Norgate.

Stewart, Suzanne R. 1999. *Sublime Surrender: Male Masochism at the Fin-de-Siècle.* Ithaca: Cornell University Press.

Squire, Michael. 2011. *The Art of the Body: Antiquity and its Legacy.* New York: I.B. Tauris.

Turley Houston, Gail. 2005. *From Dickens to Dracula: Gothic, Economics, and Victorian Fiction.* Cambridge: Cambridge University Press.

6 The Aesthete, the Banker, and the Saint

Economies of Gift and Desire in Lucas Malet's *The Far Horizon* (1906)

Catherine Delyfer

> In truth, one of his most characteristic and constant traits had ever been a certain longing for *escape*—for sudden, relieving interchange, even upon the spaces of life, along which he had lingered most pleasantly—for a lifting, from time to time, of the actual horizon. It was like the necessity the painter is under, to put an open window or doorway in the background of his picture, which, without that, would be heavy and inanimate; or like the sick man's longing for northern coolness, and whispering willow-trees, amid the breathless and motionless evergreen forests of the south.[1]
>
> (Walter Pater, *Marius the Epicurean*)

As one of the leading female novelists of the turn of the century, "Lucas Malet" (Mary St Leger Kingsley Harrison) authored an impressive body of work published between 1882 and 1931. Since the early 2000s, significant critical reassessments of her oeuvre have uncovered Malet's influence on novelists such as Thomas Hardy and Henry James and positioned her as a major bridging figure between literary aestheticism and modernism.[2] Lucas Malet's ninth published novel *The Far Horizon,* however, has received comparatively little attention. In its combined engagement with spiritual salvation and speculative banking, religious conversion and modern capitalism, art and the marketplace, this text constitutes a unique, if forgotten, late-aestheticist reflection on the status of self-interest and social good at the close of the Victorian era.[3] Building on a rich body of literature that is currently reassessing the role of women writers at the *fin de siècle*, and on the critical re-evaluation of the interplay between fiction and economic thought undertaken since the 1990s, this chapter considers how the circulation of self-interest, spiritual desire, libidinal energy, and monetary transactions intertwine, and how the logic of credit, gains, and losses eventually re-enthrones art and selfless love as the most treasured currencies of the modern age.[4]

Published four years after Malet's conversion to Catholicism, this novel is both aestheticist in its pictorial poetics and in its valorisation of art and mysticism, and modernist in its depiction of repressed, artistic subjects, urban solitude, nervous depression, and emotional aridity. With her characteristic blend of naturalism and aestheticism, partly inspired by Gustave Flaubert's notion (cited in the novel's epigraph) that beauty can be extracted even from the most prosaic aspects of existence,[5] Malet updates the figure of the *fin-de-siècle flâneur* for a proto-modernist readership. Not only does she select as her main aesthete a depressed, middle-aged bank clerk who has just been forced into early retirement, but she also de-genders the concept of *flânerie* to include the struggling female artist. Moreover, she takes a financial crisis (loosely modelled on the Panic of 1890) and the disastrous British defeats of December 1899 at the beginning of the second Boer war as key narrative turning points. In short, the author deliberately poises her tale at a critical intersection between individual self-doubt and a national crisis of confidence, in order to explore competing definitions of value and exchange: economic versus social, commercial versus cultural, monetary versus ethical.

As hedonistic consumerism, political uncertainties and economic downturn prompt her characters to pursue their erratic desires ruthlessly and without consideration for any higher collective goal, the social microcosm depicted in the novel appears to be on the verge of implosion. In this context, the visual trope of the novel's title, the "far horizon," thus captures the protagonist's search for a vantage-point that might enable him to rise above self-interest, materialism, and economism in order to encompass a broader, more rewarding vision of exchange in society. Implicit in this trope is the notion of an eschatological or messianic horizon beckoning to divine truth, i.e. a horizon of faith, towards which the main protagonist strives through aesthetic contemplation, conversion to Catholicism, and the adoption of a gift-oriented approach to the social economy. The latter has been described and theorised by economic anthropologists such as Chris Gregory and Marilyn Strathern. Strathern (1988, 143) explains that where commodity exchange "establishes a relationship between the objects exchanged," gift exchange "establishes a relation between the exchanging subjects." *The Far Horizon*, I argue, redirects our attention from a commodity-oriented economy, in which people "experience their interest in commodities as a desire to appropriate goods" to a gift oriented economy, in which "the desire is to expand social relations" (Strathern 1988, 143).

1. From *Homo Economicus* to *Homo Aestheticus*

The rise of commercialism and the development of a more permanent global market constituted the major economic transformations of the eighteenth century. In particular, the increasing commercial quality of society led to a redefinition of morality and virtue in ways that coincided with the new requirements of commerce. In a geographically large and diverse commercial world, the very notion of moral sentiment and the possibility for shared forms of moral sympathy or moral responsiveness became problematic. *Homo economicus*, Joan Tronto argues, thus emerged as "a calculating, measured fellow" (Tronto 1994, 35). Following John Locke's conception of individualism, Adam Smith theorised an economic world in which morality became more calculating and predicated on self-interest, though this was not necessarily seen as a negative shift.[6] In fact, building on Bernard Mandeville's political *Fable of the Bees* (1714), Smith's theory of the invisible hand in *The Wealth of Nations* (1776) proposed that "[b]y pursuing his own interest [the individual] frequently promotes that of society more effectually than when he really intends to promote it" (Smith 1838, 184). By the end of the eighteenth century and throughout the nineteenth century, however, moralists lamented that such a utilitarian approach heralded the end of true virtue and feared that competitive individualism would eventually extinguish sympathy and altruism altogether. In *Past and Present* (1843), Thomas Carlyle was alarmed by the thinning out of interconnections between individuals under the impact of Mammonism; with the disappearance of the feudal, hierarchical ties that once kept society together, people seemed to him linked by nothing except what he called the "cash nexus."[7] Later, Matthew Arnold and John Stuart Mill argued that such an evolution was tantamount to a loss of humanity, while John Ruskin and, at the close of the century, William Morris equally deplored the dehumanising tendency of modern industrial society to subsume all values under the values of the marketplace.

In the wake of the 1870s' so-called "marginal revolution," theorised by Victorian economists such as William Stanley Jevons, Carl Menger, and Léon Walras, economic man was seen not primarily as a producer, but as a consumer.[8] Indeed where the Classical school of economics described an economy based on production and economic surplus (considered the end of economic activity), for the Marginalists production was regarded as contingent on consumption.[9] Crucial to this turn in economic theory was the elimination of interpersonal comparisons. Rejecting the idea that any one person's desires or needs could be compared with another's, the Marginalists' theory focused on the isolated individual, giving rise to a hedonistic conception of man which led Thorstein Veblen to describe the modern subject (according to this rationale) as "a lightening calculator of pleasures and pains, who oscillates like a homogeneous globule of desire of happiness under the impulse of stimuli that shift him about ..." (Veblen 1898, 389).

The Far Horizon, set between 1899 and the death of Queen Victoria in 1901, is peopled with characters who are constantly engrossed in trying to maximise utility and material advantage. Their environment, which encompasses the entire topography of London and its suburban colonisation of the countryside (as described in the opening pages), bears testimony to the age of the "early Victorian speculative builder" (2). The language of economics permeates all of the social interactions portrayed; even the ties of affection are systematically assessed and accounted for as so many promising or failed pecuniary, emotional, spiritual, or political investments.[10] Many of the novel's characters are emphatically parentless and childless, solitary individuals evolving in a crowded and atomised urban setting as so many ruefully unattached monads. Some, like the retired bank clerk George

Lovegrove and the actress Poppy St John, vibrantly express their sadness at having no children, but most do not question the world-weary mood of the *fin de siècle* and tacitly endorse Herbert Spencer's notion that progress is always progress towards greater individualism, even though it might lead to anomie, isolation and rampant egoism.

The novel follows the experiences of the middle-aged bank clerk, Dominic Iglesias. Iglesias, who is forced into retirement, applies himself to the enjoyment of this unexpected leisure time. At the beginning of the novel, like Veblen's lightening calculator of pleasures and pains, Iglesias cannot help but feel satisfied at having secured for himself "the maximum of comfort and advantage which could be expected by a middle-aged gentleman, of moderate fortune" (2).[11] However, Iglesias's loss of his employment, subsequent discovery of a banking fraud and relationships with the socialist playwright De Courcy Smyth and his estranged wife, the actress Poppy St John all lead Iglesias to reassess his worldview. During the course of the novel, Iglesias's pursuit of "maximum comfort" is displaced by his selfless service to others and a renewal of the Catholicism of his youth.

Iglesias's relationship with the hapless De Courcy Smyth (a fellow tenant at his boarding house, Cedar Lodge) begins when he agrees to fund the playwright's latest venture. Notwithstanding his contempt for capitalist individualism, De Courcy Smyth cannot accept any gift (of food, sympathy, conversation, money, or patronage) from Dominic Iglesias without framing their relation as a business venture. Construing his own debt as an investment benefiting his creditor, De Courcy Smyth remarks "You would risk nothing, Mr. Iglesias. It would be an investment, simply an investment" (92); "you will see all your money back—see it doubled, certainly doubled, probably trebled" (129); "I do not even thank you" (132). In this exchange, however, Iglesias feels very much cheated. Although he helps the writer without expecting to make a financial profit, Dominic Iglesias nevertheless feels disappointed at being robbed of a symbolic gain, his own "personal reward" (133), that special "warmth" or "glow of satisfaction" (132) he had expected to derive from his charitable giving—a point I will return to later. In the absence of any gratitude from De Courcy Smyth, we are told, "the transaction left Dominic cold" (132).

Even the deep friendship that develops between Iglesias and Poppy St John (who is, unbeknownst to Iglesias, De Courcy Smyth's estranged wife) begins with Poppy's repeated promise to "play fair" with Dominic Iglesias. She agrees to be "useful to him in some ways" just as he "is useful to [her], awfully useful … I don't mean money, business, anything of the kind. I'm perfectly competent to manage my own affairs, thank you. But you're good for me, somehow. You rest me" (106). Whereas she is explicit about the fact that their exchange involves spiritual or emotional capital rather than money, her argument is nevertheless predicated on the logic of utility and accountancy; the vocabulary she uses to formalise their contract and clinch the deal of their friendship is strongly evocative of promissory notes and debt recognitions, as if no aspect of human psychology could escape the arid ethos of the market. In turn, this tirade prompts a response from Dominic Iglesias which also carries economic overtones. Like George Lovegrove, who sets "a wonderfully high value on Dominic's regard" (220), Dominic Iglesias agrees to a pact of friendship with Poppy implicitly in the name of the law of supply and demand, the rarity of the object determining its greater value: "I have very few friends. I should value a new one" (108). Again Dominic later remarks:

> you have been good enough to tell me that my poor friendship is of value to you. Does it not occur to you that yours is of far greater value to me? And that for many and obvious reasons—these among others, that while you are young, and have a wide circle of acquaintances, and a future to which, brilliant as you are, you may look forward with hope and assurance, I am absolutely alone in the world. (163)

In their dialogue, the economic metaphor is further extended as the delighted Poppy correlates her good fortune with the influence of the sun: clearly an allusion to William Stanley Jevons's controversial sunspot theory. Like Jevons who argued that certain types of sunspot activity generated meteorological changes that directly affected business cycle patterns, Poppy names the presence of an "anti-cyclone" (108) as the reason for Iglesias's changed attitude and her success.[12]

The logic of "economism," that is, in Regenia Gagnier's use of the term, "the tendency to interpret all phenomena in market terms," is captured in all its absurdity in the ridiculous yet touching character of Serena Lovegrove, a neurotic spinster (Gagnier 2000, 5). Hopelessly unproductive in commercial terms and un*reproductive* in the domestic sphere, she has nevertheless completely internalised the moral imperative of *homo economicus* as maximiser of self-interest. Serena is a character who perceives the world only insofar as it can be calculated as the interplay between individual decisions and personal interest. As a result, she spends her days unmasking self-interest all around her. She makes up for her own perceived redundancy by constantly engaging in mental (if not financial) speculation, compulsively decoding people's most insignificant actions, behaviours, or declarations as so many suspicious signs of egoistic motives. It is unfortunately a rather profitless occupation, for "her mind, like those of so many unoccupied, and consequently self-occupied, persons, was addicted to speculation of a minor and vacuous sort" (111). Furthermore, Serena's obtusely fanciful interpretation of people's interest in *herself* produces a kind of pathological logorrhea whose function is both to delay narrative progress and to create a fiction within the fiction. Being totally disconnected from the facts of the narrative, the private tale spun by Serena constitutes "a capital out of the non-existent" (296); that is, a sort of speculative bubble, which eventually bursts when she realises that Dominic never had any intention of marrying her.

Although tangential to the main plot, Serena Lovegrove's characterisation provides an interesting counterpoint to the type of conventional speculator represented by the banker Reginald Barking. But Malet's treatment of the unmarried, childless Serena also serves as a warning against the destructive effects of the invisibility imposed on a variety of "redundant" individuals, such as the retiree George Lovegrove, the unsuccessful writer De Courcy Smyth, or Dominic Iglesias's insane mother.

In fact, when the novel opens, Dominic Iglesias too feels the weight of his own superfluity, for in his position as head clerk of the bank Barking Brothers and Barking, he has been relegated to the margins of economic utility. [13] A victim of the generational gap, he has been discharged from work, his methods being now considered too outmoded to keep up with "the remarkable personal energy and strenuous transatlantic business methods" introduced by the young New-York-trained partner of the firm, Reginald Barking (16). Here, as in other speculation narratives of the period, such as Ouida's *The Massarenes* (1897), the United States is associated with boundless materialism, competitive individualism, and unscrupulous investment methods. Idle for the first time in three decades, Iglesias ponders "what in the world he should do with this gift of freedom, what he should do, indeed, with that which remained of his life" (15), before resigning himself to the feeling that "The routine has gone on too long" (29). He said to himself:

> "I have lost my pliability, lost my humanity. I am a machine now, not a man. To the machine, work is life. Work over, life is over; and the machine is just so much lumber—better broken up and sent to the rag-and-bottle shop, where it may fetch the worth of its weight as scrap-iron." ... "Unluckily there is no rag-and-bottle shop where superannuated bank clerks of five-and-fifty have even the very modest market value of scrap-iron!" he went on. "Of all kinds of uselessness, that of we godlike human beings is the most utterly obvious when our working day is past ..." (29)

Distinct echoes of Adam Smith, John Ruskin, and William Morris can be heard in Iglesias's lament. In *The Wealth of Nations*, Smith had observed that "the man whose whole life is spent in performing a few simple operations ... generally becomes as stupid and ignorant as it is possible for a human creature to become," whereas in the second volume of *The Stones of Venice* (1853), Ruskin had blamed laissez-faire economics for reducing the working man to the condition of a machine (Smith 1838, 327).[14] In his lecture, "How We Live and How We Might Live" (1884), Morris too had described the brutalising and divisive effects of the division of labour on which competitive capitalism relied, resulting in employees leading a "*mechanical* existence" and becoming "just a part of the machinery for the production of profit"(Morris 1896, 14). Yet Malet's clerk still has potential as a human being; such is the significance of Poppy St John's disbelief that, after thirty-five years of daily "drudgery" in a city bank, Dominic Iglesias should still look so "beautiful" and "distinguished," with "an air about [him] not usually generated by an office stool" (50). It is Poppy who predicts that he will rise, step into his "right place," and ascend his "throne," "by right divine" (159).

The lifestyle adopted by Iglesias after his dismissal might productively be read as an exemplar of the broader economic paradigm-shift from classic labour economics to consumption economics underway since the 1870s' marginal revolution. As the narrator remarks, "[t]hus had the chapter of labour ended, and that of leisure opened" (27). Despite some initial hesitation, not only does Iglesias finally choose to draw his retirement pension, but he decisively chooses to "spend" it too (32), in a vigorous attempt to transition from the productivist ethos of economic accumulation to an expenditure-based model of behaviour founded on hedonistic consumption. Unlike his childhood friend, George Lovegrove, who laments the passing of his working days, Iglesias desires to break free from his former existence and embrace an aesthetics of taste, pleasure, and consumption which he hopes will nourish his soul. Fending off his deepening "sense of isolation" (33), he resolves to dine at smart restaurants, sample theatres and music halls, and attend a polo match at Ranelagh, "that gallant and costly game beloved of Oriental princes" (38). He becomes keen on methodically subjecting himself to a strict regimen of "amusement,"

> that intangible yet very powerful factor in human affairs to which it is given to lift the too great weight of seriousness from mortal life, cheating perception of relentless actualities, helping to restore the balance, helping men to hope, to laugh, and to forget. Perceiving all which, conscious moreover of the near neighbourhood of Loneliness on the right hand and Old Age on the left, Iglesias began to bestow on these votaries of pleasure a more earnest attention, recognizing in them the possessors of a secret which it greatly behoved him to enter into possession of likewise. (26)

Not unlike Walter Pater's isolated individual who is startled out of his habits into a life of eager observation and quickened perception by the sudden acute sense of his own mortality, Iglesias here asks himself how he might make as much as possible of the Paterian "interval that remain[s]" (Pater 1904, 251–52). Soon realising that he has no interest in popular entertainment, he discovers the captivating pleasures of the myriad observations and kaleidoscopic visions afforded by *flânerie*.

In a utilitarian vision of London, natural and man-made beauty are typically presented as unjustifiable excess, senseless residue, surplus, for example in the opening pages of the novel when Dominic Iglesias, catching a glance at a panoramic view from his rented flat's window, sees the sky filled with the "smoky rose-red wastes" of the London sunset (1). The embittered writer,

De Courcy Smyth, subsequently sums up the tragic irrelevance of beauty, art and intellectual pursuits within *fin-de-siècle* British market society:

> [t]rade, commerce, finance, juggle with the names as you like, it all comes back to the same thing in the end, namely, the murder of intellect by money. Comes back to the worship of Mammon, chosen ruler of this contemptible *fin de siècle*, and safe to be even more tyrannously the ruler of the coming century. What hope, I ask you, is left for us poor devils of literary men? None, absolutely none. Just in proportion as we honour our calling and refuse to prostitute our talents we are at a discount. The powers that be have no earthly use for us. We have not got the ghost of a chance. (86)

Yet, whereas De Courcy Smyth basks in his artistic "martyrdom" (90), glories in his repudiation by his contemporaries, and generally embodies the Romantic attempt to affirm artistic value out of art's very irrelevance to the market, the bank clerk eventually turns out to be more sensitive than the *passéist* writer to the potentialities offered by modern urban aesthetics and its critical engagement with consumerism, hedonism, and ethics. This is made clear whenever Iglesias is described as indulging in what Ana Parejo Vadillo has termed "urban" aestheticism, that is, whenever he is caught in the act of perceiving "the city as both a cultural phenomenon and a work of art" (Vadillo 2005, 4). Indeed, thinking back to his younger days when he used to stroll through the city at all hours, from one job interview to another, he remembers being captivated by the impressionistic effects of electric lighting on the city (11–13). Now again, freed from the regular schedule of business hours for the first time in three decades, the retired clerk experiences London from atop an omnibus in the middle of the afternoon. As in Amy Levy's poem "Ballade of an Omnibus" or Oscar Wilde's "Symphony in Yellow," the painterly effects of the fleeting patches of colour and the quick glimpses of the city seen from the bus impress the viewer's sensitive mind with the modern aesthetics characterised by Vadillo as that of the turn-of-the-century "passenger." Iglesias's novel vision of the familiar streets encountered in his daily commute, from London to the middle-class suburb where he lives, awakens in him the perception of "a gayer, fiercer, simpler life, quick with violences of vivacious sound and vivid colour, the excitement of it heightened by clear, shining southern sunshine and blue-black shadow—a life undreamed of by conventional, slow-moving, rather vulgar middle-class London" (22).

Contemporary readers of *The Far Horizon* were very responsive to the subtle pictorial poetics deployed by Malet in this novel; one critic even observed that "no feature of this admirably woven tissue will be more apparent to artist-eyes than its London in all weathers—visual as Flaubert could render the lines, in a sense photographic but with mystery toning the crudeness" (Barry 1906, 143–44). Like the British *fin-de-siècle* poets Amy

Levy, Rosamund Marriott Watson, Alice Meynell, Mary F. Robinson, or Oscar Wilde—whose modernity was gauged, according to Arthur Symons, by their "capacity for dealing with London, with what one sees or might see there, indoors and out"—Malet shows her protagonist becoming fascinated with the "urbanscape" as a source of intellectual and aesthetic stimulation as well as a means of sharpening his own consciousness (Symons 1892, 184). Riding the omnibus, walking through the great city, or admiring the view from the actress Poppy St John's balcony, Dominic Iglesias becomes ever more attentive to London's various moods, the "pulsing" light of its dawn (37), its "raucous voice," its "heat and smoke" (40), its crimson and gold sunsets (56), its "breath," its palpitating "glare," its ceaseless traffic (135), and the various atmospheric and chromatic effects which bring out its mysteries and paradoxes. Moreover, in the narrator's description of the colours, lines, and angles of the metropolis as "the gigantic characters of some strange alphabet" (40), Iglesias's perception sometimes seems inflected by the Baudelairian hieroglyphic conception of the city as reservoir of symbols, while the excitement of his life-changing chance urban encounter with the "Lady of the Windswept Dust" is reminiscent of the French poet's "To a Passerby" (1861). The novelist thus suggests that Dominic Iglesias's new leisurely lifestyle has allowed him to mature into a modern version of Marius the Epicurean, that is, into an independent aesthete for whom, in Walter Pater's words,

> [l]ife in modern London even, in the heavy glow of summer, is stuff sufficient for the fresh imagination ... to build its "palace of art" of; and the very sense and enjoyment of an experience in which all is new, are but enhanced, like that glow of summer itself, by the thought of its brevity; which gives him something of the gambler's zest, in the apprehension, by dexterous act or diligently appreciative thought, of the highly coloured moments which are to pass away so quickly.
>
> (Pater 1885, 19)

But it is important to note that as an aesthete Iglesias cannot be reduced to an ivory-tower hedonist, an aloof spectator. His new-found independence gradually enables him to form more autonomous judgments and to engage with the world around him and its values with more critical acumen. As Jonathan Freedman has persuasively demonstrated, British aestheticism is in fact characterised by its vigorous "embrace of hateful contraries, the exploration of cultural contradictions," including the crucial question of the vexed relation between the categories of the aesthetic, the ascetic, and the economic (Freedman 1990, 8). It is, therefore, not surprising that the novel's aestheticist plot should become firmly imbricated within an economic tale, as the narrative gradually unpacks a densely woven comparative reflection on various forms of capital—financial, cultural, political, libidinal and moral.

2. Debt, Credit, Value

In the economic plot of *The Far Horizon*, Abel Barking, the senior partner of the bank which employed Dominic Iglesias for thirty-five years, represents financial capital, whereas the university-educated De Courcy Smyth articulates the snobbery of inherited cultural wealth. Both characters have in common the fact that they work progressively harder to deny the successive moral and financial debts they incur with Dominic Iglesias—and to some extent with his friend Poppy St John—strenuously misrepresenting them as favours bestowed by people of higher rank upon their social inferior. Politically, the same kind of paternalism and plain disregard for facts is illustrated in the novel by England's reaction to the South African Republics' declaration of war when it is announced in the papers, at the beginning of October 1899 (Chapter 14). The astute Iglesias—who is not English, but of Spanish and Irish extraction—regards this war as an inevitable result of Britain's recession: a recession he believes to be the result of both an inflated sense of nationhood and a market glut, or in Iglesias's terms, "wealth apoplexy" (142). Consequently, he is hardly surprised when Britain's imperial self-confidence is punctured in the immediate aftermath of the disastrous defeats of the "Black Week" of December 1899.[15]

More disturbing to the loyal bank clerk, is the fact that this is precisely the moment chosen by the young and ambitious Reginald Barking to announce in the newspapers the floatation of a new company in the process of acquiring control over extensive areas full of gold in Southeast Africa. While the prospects held out to investors are "of the most golden sort" (143), Iglesias recognises that in the current climate of political instability, such a scheme may well prove "one of those gigantic modern gambles of which the incidental risks are emphatically too heavy, since they more often than not make rich men poor, and poor men paupers, before they come through—if indeed they even come through at all" (144). Without disputing the existence of the precious metal, Iglesias is nevertheless acutely aware that its value and its convertibility for shareholders are entirely relative and conditional. As he points out, profit is dependent on "the results of such [mining] development when completed," "irrespective of the lapse of time required for such development; irrespective of possible and arresting accident; irrespective, too, of immediate and even protracted loss by the tying-up of huge sums of money which could yield but little or no return until the said process of development was an accomplished fact" (144). As it turns out, Dominic Iglesias's opposition to such reckless financial schemes is precisely what had caused him to be fired by Reginald Barking in the first place.

By stressing the gap that separates the monetary sign (the company share) from its referent (gold), the text thus calls attention to what Mary Poovey calls "the deferral or obfuscation of [the sign's] authenticating ground"— and, therefore, to the growing potential for a fiduciary crisis (Poovey 2008, 6). Indeed, not only does Iglesias deem such willful misrepresentation of the benefits to potential share buyers fraudulent, but he gradually comes to suspect that Reginald Barking has been operating unbeknownst to the supine elder partners. Iglesias speculates that Reginald must have "so deeply involved the capital and pledged the credit of the firm [Barking Brothers and Barking] that it became necessary to make a violent and doubtfully honest bid for popular support before the position of the said firm ... became desperate" (148). Employing the family bank's "unimpeachable respectability and solvency" as leverage towards the realisation of his own "dreams of power" (146), Reginald is in fact guilty of rogue trading. As the value of the shares continues to fall, the Barking Bank—once thought "as safe as the Bank of England" (153)—is now, together with all its clients, on the brink of ruin. A national financial collapse is in the offing. Reginald Barking's public disclaimers in the press about the solidity of the investment and the soundness of the House of Barking are transparent attempts to maintain the fiction of credit on which the establishment's fiscal trustworthiness is based. To make matters worse, the overstrained speculator soon succumbs to a nervous breakdown and is heard of no more. Disconnected as he is from the realities of modern banking, the bank's ageing senior partner is forced to appeal to his former head clerk for assistance. Moved by the old man's cry for help and by a sense of moral obligation to the shareholders, Dominic Iglesias agrees to be reinstated with enlarged responsibilities to manage the crisis. In doing so, however, he refuses any kind of monetary payment for his gift of time, labour, expertise, and, as it transpires, health.

Though Britain had been plagued by financial crashes since the South Sea Bubble of 1720 and throughout the nineteenth century, late-Victorian contemporaries of Malet had acquired a better grasp of how panics developed and spread. In his popular *Lombard Street* (1873), economist Walter Bagehot explained the workings of the monetary market in plain language and demystified the operations of the City for ordinary readers, while William Stanley Jevons's *Money and the Mechanism of Exchange* (1875) and *Primer on Political Economy* (1878) were also written in a fresh, popular style. Literary writers were quick to appropriate economic themes for fictional treatment, mining contemporary financial events for characters and plots. Margaret Oliphant's novel about the tangled history of a family bank, *Hester* (1883), for example, described how "once the first whisper of suspicion has been roused it flies fast, and the panic with which rural depositors rush upon a bank which has awakened the ghost of an apprehension, is even more cruel and unreflecting than other panics" (Oliphant 2009, 9). In 1897, George Gissing compared the money market to a "whirlpool" in a novel bearing that title. Following the rise and fall of the great financier Bennet Frothingham, Gissing's novel described how "Britannia Loan, Assurance, Investment, and Banking Company, Ltd" excited greed and speculative fever, "perturbing quiet industry with the passion of the gamester, inflating vulgar ambition, now at length scattering wreck and ruin" (Gissing 1897, 45). Malet herself must have been an attentive reader of economic commentary in the early 1900s, as she was then beginning to suffer under growing financial strain due to her brother Grenville's overambitious investments in Australia.[16] Reflecting on the frequent occurrence of economic crashes in the nineteenth century, Bagehot had described the characteristics of the panics of 1825, 1847, 1857, and 1866, linking them to outbursts of speculative mania due to unchecked greed, personal ambition, and a longing for action. The economist also outlined potential strategies to prevent episodes of economic crisis from spreading into full-blown irrational panics, for example by advising that the Bank of England should stave off such crises by serving as lender of last resort. It was precisely this doctrine which was implemented during the Baring crisis of 1890 and which, to a large extent, succeeded in containing its effects.

In the sense that they are fiercely ambitious protagonists who cannot discipline their urges or control their desire for success and recognition, both Reginald Barking and De Courcy Smyth are typical Bagehotian speculators. Disreputable and unscrupulous in the attainment of their goals, they crave instant gratification, whether in the form of money or fame, and see no reason to defer fulfilment. De Courcy's striking formulation is particularly clear on this point:

> I range myself alongside those heroes of literature and art, who, because they were ahead of the age in which they lived, were scorned and repudiated by their contemporaries; but they found their revenge in the worship of succeeding generations. My time will come just as theirs did. It must—I tell you it must. I know that. I am safe of eventual recognition; but I want it now, while I am alive, while I can glut myself with the joy of it. (90)

In *The Far Horizon*, however, the Bank of England does not intervene to stop the panic caused by Reginald Barking's wild speculative ventures; nor do any of the great financiers, such as Nathan Rothschild, who were involved in rescuing the Barings and restoring confidence in 1890. In Malet's novel, it is Dominic Iglesias, the son of a Catholic Irishwoman and a Spanish anarchist, who single-handedly restores the security of the bank. Thus, according to the terms of the novel, it is Iglesias who operates in the capacity of financial saviour. Yet unlike young Catherine Vernon in Oliphant's *Hester*, Iglesias has no monetary capital to speak of in order to back up the family bank and check a run on its reserves. So what precisely does his intervention signify?

One of the functions of literary writing, according to Mary Poovey, has always been to mediate value, whether it be understood as market value or some other *aneconomic* value. More specifically, Poovey analyses literature's capacity to "manage the troubling effects" of crises of value—such as the instability of paper credit in the nineteenth century—and the problematic of representation they made visible (Poovey 2008, 6). In that sense, literary writing has much in common with monetary instruments and economic commentary. While Poovey demonstrates that the generic continuum between these forms of writing was obscured in the course of the eighteenth and nineteenth centuries—as the opposition between fact and fiction gradually came to define the contours of financial versus imaginative writing—she also points out that episodes of fiscal crisis reveal the illusoriness of such boundaries. And when the fictions inherent in the modern credit economy are brought to light, society's economic and socio-political stability seems imperilled. Indeed

> [w]hen the problematic of representation becomes visible [in times of financial panics], this can have grave implications for a society's economic and political stability, for it can jeopardize the prevailing model of value, the conventions that facilitate trust, and the signs that convey creditworthiness—monetary, social, legal, and political.
>
> (Poovey 2008, 6)

Malet's panic-plot clearly disturbs the optimistic picture of British capitalism by showing the limits of its methods. Using Iglesias's intervention, the author not only interrogates the dominant system of value, but also, as I intend to argue, promotes an alternative model.

The novel's treatment of the character of Dominic Iglesias in fact literalises a transfer of value, or more exactly a displacement of creditworthiness. On a symbolic level, Iglesias is the outsider in whom the reader is asked to take the keenest interest and invest most of her assets. From a narrative point of view, his trajectory in the novel is conceived as a monetary curve charting the fluctuations of a currency whose ups and downs the reader is asked to follow. Iglesias is initially undervalued within the public economic sphere of British society, when as a young man his promising career opportunities are curtailed after he chooses to devote himself to supporting and caring for his insane mother, instead of going out into the world. Underemployed through the best years of his active life, Iglesias is finally discarded by Barking and Brothers just as Reginald becomes most influential. After Reginald Barking's disgrace, however, Iglesias, the "Hidalgo," slowly becomes a prized refuge value—as good as gold, the English bank's most solid asset and true bullion—serving as a rampart against bankruptcy and *dis*credit. Thus as the plot unfolds, "the values [a]re altered" (273). Importantly, by playing with the polysemy of the term "value," the author here binds together monetary, moral, and aesthetic stakes.[17] The narrative further emphasises the foreigner's new soaring desirability by having almost all the other characters' interests converge on his person: De Courcy Smyth becomes dependent on Iglesias's patronage to finance the first public performance of his play; Poppy St John relies on his support and encouragements to renounce her rich lover and work her way to artistic fame; George Lovegrove is saved from depression thanks to Iglesias's affectionate loyalty and intelligence, and Serena Lovegrove secretly hopes to marry him. Meanwhile, Dominic

Iglesias earns the respect of the City's leading financiers, who congratulate him on his successful management of the difficult crisis.

In the novel's depiction of the late-Victorian British credit economy, Iglesias stands out as the only character that is as good as his word. Scrupulously keeping his promises and commitments, honouring his debts (and those of others, including his father's), and postponing personal fulfilment for the sake of nobler aims, he comes to embody what the novel proposes should be the foundational values of a sound economy: not selfishness, greed, or hunger for quick rewards, but loyalty, sympathy, hard work, and self-denial. Crucially, this form of moral capital is intricately linked in the novel to what could be termed libidinal wealth. For while Malet takes care to construct her altruistic banker as a human saint, a desiring body, she also makes him fundamentally different from her other characters in that he remains, as Poppy St John observes, "innocent" (56), "an infant," and "a debutant" (105), i.e. a virgin. His capacity for self-discipline constitutes a claim to what John Kucich has termed "libidinal distinction."[18] Ultimately, it is by emulating Iglesias and achieving libidinal distinction herself that Poppy St John will find the energy to become a great artist at the novel's end.[19] By contrast, however, Reginald Barking's and De Courcy Smyth's frenzied impatience for success causes them to *spend, consume* (and thus waste) their libidinal energy all at once, instead of *saving* it, eventually leading the former to permanent nervous exhaustion and the latter to suicide. Malet's interpretation of the imbrications between the economic and sexual reflects the overlap between sexological and economic theories of spending which has been noted by Lawrence Birken. In particular, Birken reminds us that late-Victorian sexological thought was imbued with consumerist values:

> sexual science closely associated desire with "spending," assuming an innate tendency to spend or discharge energy. Defining energy itself as scarce, sexologists believed that the act of consumption involved a depletion of nervous energy and its transformation into activity. In contrast, the building up of energy was associated with the deferral of consumption.
>
> (Birken 1988, 42)

Implicit in this theory, however, was the idea that "the value of a deferred pleasure must be greater than that of an immediate pleasure" (Birken 1988, 44). So that at the end of the novel, when Malet has her protagonist die a sexually unspent man, and an un-repaid, un-thanked creditor to all those he has helped materially and morally, she is, in fact, confirming Iglesias's capacity for indefinite deferral of gratification, thus multiplying his value through eternity. This has important consequences. In the novel's economy, such a strategy of deferred returns is precisely what ensures that Iglesias's economic intervention is perceived as a *free* gift: a gift offered in the name of human friendship and based on what Iglesias calls "wise economies of proffered sympathy" (252). [20] In other words, such a strategy of deferral is essential in inscribing Iglesias's path of action as a disruption of the logic of capitalism.

Malet's choice to have this foreign, Romanist, celibate clerk assume liability for the novel's British merchant bank can thus be interpreted as an effective way of casting doubts upon the soundness and legitimacy of the nation's leading financial institutions. But it also suggests a rejection, or at least a revision, of a national identity based on competitive capitalism, Anglicanism, and domesticity. Ultimately and perhaps most importantly, it reveals the author's keen economic awareness of what constitutes the value of any currency. Indeed, quoting from a *Punch* article of 1857 Susan Walsh points out that money derives its power from "its two selves": "the moral plus the material." In a healthy economy, Walsh explains that banknotes, shares, or any other form of credit paper, therefore, signify "'the promise to pay *plus* the means of paying.' ('Promise to pay,' of course, [being] the ethical commitment stamped upon each Bank of England note …')." In *The Far Horizon*, this dual currency is embodied in Iglesias: his perfect combination of libidinal wealth, moral credit, and infinite ethical solicitude makes him, to borrow Susan Walsh's terms, the novel's true "man sterling," "the golden integer," "the bullion standing behind the paper," the "spirit inhabiting the body" (Walsh 2008, 2–3).

Furthermore, Malet complicates our understanding of her protagonist's economic achievement. Unlike the Bank of England or other banking institutions, Iglesias is not actuated by the desire to keep the nation's economy sound, and his success cannot be fully understood within the terms of capitalist economics: the banker's motivations are of a transnational, epistemological, aesthetic, and spiritual nature. Iglesias is in fact a semiotically-troubled protagonist who hankers after the lost unity of signifier and signified. Yearning for the "language of symbol" (79), "the language of the spirit," the "adjustment between the exterior and interior life" (89), he is particularly alert to the problematic of representation in general, that is to say, to the gap that separates the sign from its referent, from its ground of value or meaning. Just as he can see through political delusions, identify economic frauds, or decode the ironies of pictorial representation—when contemplating a portrait hanging in Abel Barking's office, for example— he is equally devoted to erasing these ironies in his own life, working to shape his public self to match his innermost beliefs and aspirations. On the one hand, such rigorous attempts at self-fashioning further underline the similarities between Iglesias and late-Victorian aesthetes who, following Walter Pater's ideal Hegelian vision of the Greeks in *The Renaissance* (1873), cultivated "the soil of their own individuality, creating themselves out of themselves, and moulding themselves to what they were, and willed to be" (Hegel qtd. in Pater 1904, 231). On the other hand, Iglesias's dream of an absolute and permanent convertibility of exterior/interior, signifier/ signified, paper/gold is what makes him "a poet" in his own right (140) as well as what leads him on the path to religious conversion. As a poet and as a Catholic convert, Iglesias operates according to an economic logic that radically disrupts or withdraws from capitalistic forms of circulation and exchange. Instead, he points towards a spiritual economy and the utopian possibility of the *aneconomic* Derridian gift.[21]

§

The Far Horizon explores the notion, already expressed in Malet's early fiction, that the saint and the great artist are made of the same mettle and serve as conduits for the revelation of higher truths, for they share similar faculties of perception and insight denied to ordinary mortals. In *The Wages of Sin* (1891), for instance, the narrator had forcefully declared that:

> [f]or [the great artist] the veils [are] withdrawn, the merciful veils which blunt perception and so help to keep us sane. To all those who are really alive, saint, sage, artist alike, each on their several lines, this condition is common at moments. It may be enchanting. It may be hideous. Perilous it must always be; for it oversteps the workable limits of human powers.
>
> (Malet 1902, 593)

In *The Far Horizon*, the main protagonist's "perilous" experiment is of an economic nature. It has to do with faith and the act of selfless giving, both of which lead him to reject exchange-based capitalist economics and to redefine value no longer as a relational or relative term, but as an absolute. Uniquely sensitive to his fellow humans' cries for help regardless of their merits or demerits—successively his mother, Poppy St John, George Lovegrove, De Courcy Smyth, and Abel Barking—and to the unrealised potential for beauty in human relationships, he gradually learns to give without any hope of immediate return or reward. Training himself to see, not human capital, but man for man's sake, Iglesias feels his relationship with each of the other characters alter, especially with Poppy, as he "ceased to consider her in relation to his and her broken friendship, or in relation to that which he so reluctantly divined of her private life. He contemplated her *in herself*" (206, emphasis added).

Soon after he loses his job, Iglesias derives his own sustenance from renewing and strengthening his ties with his mother's Catholic faith. Like Oscar Wilde's Christ-like perfect individual of the future in "The Soul of Man Under Socialism" (1891), Iglesias's value cannot be measured by material things, for in Wilde's words, although he has nothing, he "will have everything, and whatever one takes from [him], [he] will still have, so rich will [he] be" (Wilde 1915, 16). Sure enough, the more Iglesias gives, the more he has to give, observing of himself that: "It rejoiced him to find that now, as of old, the demand created a supply of silent but sustaining moral force, ready to pass into the sphere of active help should necessity arise" (157–58). Such a realisation eventually leads Iglesias to disengage himself from economic exchange after handling the Barking financial crisis. This transition is materialised in the novel when Iglesias takes the symbolic step of moving out of Mrs Porcher's boarding house and putting an end to his status as a "paying guest," to return to the memory-filled small flat he used to share with his beloved mother. Taking his family furniture and childhood toys out of storage, he surrounds himself with objects whose exchange value is insignificant, but whose emotional importance has become vital.

As an alternative to capitalist economics, Iglesias's economy of giving is hardly sustainable, for as Malet points out in the quotation above "it oversteps the workable limits of human powers." This gives Iglesias a pre-/ post-capitalist Morrisian aura, prompting both Poppy St John and George Lovegrove to compare their friend to a medieval knight in armour, a wonderful being, or a hero of an Arthurian romance. This justifies Poppy's feeling that Iglesias, in his utopian endeavour, is a "gentle lunatic" (208), belonging as he does "to another order of doctrine and practice to that current in contemporary society" (105). Yet to this utopian economy, based on the gift of beauty and selfless love, which Iglesias relates to his perfect relationship with his mother, Malet manages to give enduring appeal. For in stark contradistinction to Bernard Mandeville's and Adam Smith's virtuous beehive, the *fin-de-siècle* economic world of *The Far Horizon* is a destructive, exploitative system figured as a repulsive crowd of "gigantic black locusts, strong-jawed, pink-faced, and white-breasted, driven forth by a common hunger, rather cruelly active and intent" (204).[22] Who then would not be tempted to imagine with Malet the possibility of a generous economic actor? With the holy trinity of friends and disciples who sit in vigil over the dead Iglesias, who would not attempt to redraw the economic map of the world in the image of utopia? As Wilde famously remarks, "A map of the world that does not include Utopia is not worth even glancing at, for it leaves out the one country at which Humanity is always landing. And when Humanity lands there, it looks out, and, seeing a better country, sets sail. Progress is the realization of Utopias" (Wilde 1915, 28–9).

Notes

1. Pater 1885, 120.
2. On Malet's influence on James and Hardy, see: Schaffer 1996; Schaffer. 2000. On Malet as a bridging figure between aestheticism and modernism, see: Lundberg 2003; Delyfer 2011.
3. The novel's contemporary critics readily acknowledged its modernity and originality. For example, in March 1906, *The Bookman* called *The Far Horizon* "nothing if not up to date, touching on matters of modern finance, manners and morals, the modern church, and the modern theatre" (qtd. in Lundberg 2003, 297); the poet Madison Cawein wrote in *The New York Times Saturday Review*

of Books that "[t]o the prolific reader of the modern novel *The Far Horizon* must mark an epoch, both in point of distinction and of style ... It is a book for the future, and will grow in appreciation and popularity ... Mrs Harrison has achieved greatness" (Cawein 1907, 202).

4. On "Lucas Malet," see: Lundberg 2003. On the role of *fin-de-siècle* British women writers in general, see: Psomiades 1997; Schaffer and Psomiades 1999; Schaffer 2000; Vadillo 2005; Thain 2007a.

5. "Cherchons à voir les choses comme elles sont, et ne voulons pas avoir plus d'esprit que le bon Dieu! Autrefois on croyait que la canne à sucre seule donnait le sucre, on en tire à peu près tout maintenant. Il est de même de la poésie. Extrayons-là de n'importe quoi, car elle gît en tout et partout. Pas un atome de matière qui ne contienne pas la poésie. Et habituons-nous à considérer le monde comme un [sic] oeuvre d'art, dont il faut reproduire les procédés dans nos œuvres." [Let us try to see things as they are and not attempt to outwit God! People used to think that only sugarcane produced sugar, but now one can derive sugar from just about anything. The same is true of poetry. Let us extract it from everything, for there is poetry everywhere. There isn't an atom of matter that does not contain poetry. And let us learn to consider the world as an artwork whose processes we need to reproduce in our own works]. My translation. Gustave Flaubert, quoted as Malet's second epigraph in *The Far Horizon,* 1906.

6. See Birken 1988, 3–21.

7. Economic self-interest was also the object of much attention in nineteenth-century fiction, especially in the realist novel. See: Reed 1984; Brantlinger 1996; Walsh 2008; Wagner 2010.

8. On the marginal revolution see Birken 1988, 40–71; Gagnier 2000, 40–53.

9. Marginalism is a theory of economics which arose in the second half of the nineteenth century in response to classical economics, in order to explain why the value of goods or services did not necessarily depend on how much labour went into producing them, or on their intrinsic quality and usefulness, but simply on their levels of consumption, i.e. how desirable they were to consumers.

10. The use of economic language to describe exchanges of a social nature is a device that Malet has in common with her contemporary, Henry James. On James's use of the language of business see: Alberti 1991; Peiffer 2002.

11. All subsequent references to Malet's *The Far Horizon* (1906) are taken from the 1907 edition of the novel by Dodd, Mead and Company in New York.

12. In a series of papers published between 1875 and 1882, Jevons speculated that there was a connection between commercial crises and the cyclical variation of the number of sunspots. His reasoning was that sunspots affected the weather, which, in turn affected crops, which then could be expected to cause economic fluctuations. Although this theory was rapidly dismissed, Jevons was a highly respected economist and the first one to use statistical data to produce an account of the business cycle. For a thorough description of Jevons's sunspot theory, see: Morgan 1990, 18–26.

13. To early twentieth-century readers, the name of the novel's banking establishment, Barking Brothers and Barking, suggested obvious analogies with the then world-famous bank, Baring Brothers & Co. The oldest merchant bank in London, Barings had been responsible for the Panic of 1890. Incidentally, the name still carries equally relevant, albeit anachronistic, associations for early twenty-first-century readers, since the same bank was recently implicated in a

disastrous case of rogue trading which caused its collapse in 1995—an uncanny illustration of the Wildean aphorism about life imitating fiction.

14. Ruskin argued: "We have much studied and much perfected, of late, the great civilized invention of the division of labor; only we give it a false name. It is not, truly speaking, the labor that it divided; but the men; divided into mere segments of men, broken into small fragments and crumbs of life" (Ruskin 1899, 165).

15. The term "Black Week" was used to refer to the three devastating defeats the British Army suffered by the Boer Republics between 10–17 December 1899: the battles of Stormberg, Magersfontein, and Colenso, mentioned by Lucas Malet at the beginning of Chapter 18. These defeats served as an eye-opener for the British, who had thought that the war could be won very easily.

16. See Lundberg 2003, 134.

17. As a former painter trained at the Slade, Malet was fully aware that in drawing or painting the term "value" refers to a gradation of tone or colour luminosity and to the relation of these elements to the whole picture. The word is in fact often used in this explicit pictorial sense in *The Far Horizon*, as in the following examples: "Upon the grey pavements the bright-coloured dress of a woman—mauve, green, or pink—took on a peculiar *value* here and there, amid the generality of darkly clad pedestrians" (331, emphasis added); or "Huddled in a black velvet fur-lined sacque, reaching to her feet and abundantly trimmed with jet embroidery and black lace, she settled herself in her place. The soft fur was cosey against her bare neck. She felt chilly. Later she might peel, thereby exhibiting the *values* of the rest of her costume. But it was not worth while to do so yet" (191, emphasis added).

18. Kucich's concept has a distinctively Bourdieusian ring to it. Here, Iglesias differs from the ordinary man through his capacity for self-restraint, self-negation and repression. However his denial of vulgar, common or natural enjoyment (sex) implies an affirmation of the superiority of his more refined, disinterested, voluptuousness (Kucich 1897, 31). Indeed James Eli Adams suggests that such repression also functions as a sign of psychic depth and richly eroticised interiority (Adams 1995, 13).

19. She too thus becomes as good as gold. The producer Lionel Gordon exclaims: "She must be made to sign a three years' contract. If she can act like this there's nothing less than a cool half-million sterling in her" (385).

20. In his thoughtful reconsideration of the gift theories elaborated by Marcel Mauss and later by Claude Lévi-Strauss, Pierre Bourdieu has drawn attention to the role of time, delay and deferral in gift exchange: though a gift must be reciprocated, because of the social relations and obligations it defines, as Mauss and Lévi-Strauss have demonstrated, Bourdieu insists that for the gift to be identified as such this reciprocation must take place in due time and in a different form or location. In other words, the counter-gift must be both deferred and different, thus masking the underlying logic of interest at work in gift exchange (see Bourdieu 1977). In *The Far Horizon*, while Dominic Iglesias does receive much divine consolation in return for his charitable giving, he also performs exemplary disinterestedness in Bourdieu's sense because he is open to waiting for his true reward (which will only come after death, in God's Kingdom), thus making his gifts to the other characters appear gratuitous. As in Lucas Malet's earlier text *The Wages of Sin* (1891), the end of the novel marks the triumph of a spiritual economy.

21. See: Derrida 1995. An *aneconomic* gift is an absolute gift, that is, one which would not be followed by a counter-gift and, therefore, would break from the circle of exchange.

22. An interesting comparison could be made between this image of the crowds as cruel locusts in *The Far Horizon* and that of the crowds as retributive swarming bees in Malet's *The History of Sir Richard Calmady* (1901), especially in light of Marion Thain's study of apian aestheticism (Thain 2007b).

Works Cited

Adams, James Eli. 1995. *Dandies and Desert Saints: Styles of Victorian Manhood.* Ithaca: Cornell University Press.

Alberti, John. 1991. "The Economics of Love: The Production of Value in *The Golden Bowl.*" *The Henry James Review* 12 (1): 9–19.

Barry, William. 1906. "Lucas Malet's Saint and Sinner (*The Far Horizon*)." *Bookman* [London] 31, 183 (December 1906): 143–44.

Birken, Lawrence. 1988. *Consuming Desire: Sexual Science and the Emergence of a Culture of Abundance, 1871–1914.* Ithaca and London: Cornell University Press.

Bourdieu, Pierre. 1977. *Outline of a Theory of Practice* [1972], translated by Richard Nice. Cambridge: Cambridge University Press.

Brantlinger, Patrick. 1996. *Fictions of State: Culture and Credit in Britain, 1694–1994.* Ithaca and London: Cornell University Press.

Cawein, Madison. 1907. "Lucas Malet's Book for the Future: An American Poet Tells Why He Esteems "The Far Horizon" Above Other Recent Works of Fiction." *New York Times Saturday Review of Books*, April 6.

Delyfer, Catherine. 2011. *Art and Womanhood in Fin-de-Siècle Writing: the Fiction of Lucas Malet, 1880–1931.* London: Pickering and Chatto.

Derrida, Jacques. 1995. *The Gift of Death*, translated by David Wills. Chicago: University of Chicago Press.

Freedman, Jonathan. 1990. *Professions of Taste: Henry James, British Aestheticism and Commodity Culture.* Stanford: Stanford University Press.

Gagnier, Regenia. 2000. *The Insatiability of Human Wants: Economics and Aesthetics in Market Society.* Chicago: University of Chicago Press.

Gissing, George. 1897. *The Whirlpool.* London: Lawrence and Bullen.

Lundberg, Patricia Lorimer. 2003. *"An Inward Necessity": The Writer's Life of Lucas Malet.* New York: Peter Lang.

Malet, Lucas. 1902. *The Wages of Sin* [1891]. New York: Fenno and Company.

———. 1901. *The History of Sir Richard Calmady: a Romance.* New York: Dodd, Mead and Company.

———. 1907. *The Far Horizon* [1906]. New York: Dodd, Mead and Company.

Morgan, Mary S. 1990. *The History of Econometric Ideas.* Cambridge: Cambridge University Press.

Morris, William. 1896. *Signs of Change: Seven Lectures.* London: Longmans.

Oliphant, Margaret. 2009. *Hester*, edited by Philip Davis and Brian Nellist. Oxford: Oxford University Press.

Pater, Walter. 1885. *Marius the Epicurean: His Sensations and Ideas*, vol. 2. London: Macmillan and Company.

———. 1904. *The Renaissance: Studies in Art and Poetry* [1893]. New York: Macmillan Company.

Peiffer, Siobhan. 2002. "Commerce and Freedom in *The Ambassadors*." *The Henry James Review* 23 (2): 95–104.

Poovey, Mary. 2008. *Genres of the Credit Economy: Mediating Value in Eighteenth- and Nineteenth Century Britain*. Chicago: University of Chicago Press.

Psomiades, Kathy Alexis. 1997. *Beauty's Body: Femininity and Representation in British Aestheticism*. Palo Alto, CA: Stanford University Press.

Reed, John R. 1984. "A Friend to Mammon: Speculation in Victorian Literature." *Victorian Studies* 27 (2): 179–202.

Ruskin, John. 1899. *The Stones of Venice*, vol. 2 [1853]. Boston: Dana Estes Company.

Schaffer, Talia. 1996. "Some Chapter of Some Other Story: Henry James, Lucas Malet, and the Real Past of *The Sense of the Past*." *The Henry James Review* 17 (2): 109–28.

Schaffer, Talia and Kathy Alexis Psomiades, eds. 1999. *Women and British Aestheticism*. London and Charlottesville: University Press of Virginia.

Schaffer, Talia. 2000. *The Forgotten Female Aesthetes: Literary Culture in Late-Victorian England*. London and Charlottesville: University Press of Virginia.

Smith, Adam. 1838. *An Inquiry Into the Nature and Causes of the Wealth of Nations* [1776]. Edinburgh: Thomas Nelson.

Strathern, Marilyn. 1988. *The Gender of the Gift*. Berkeley and Los Angeles: University of California Press.

Symons, Arthur. 1892. "Mr Henley's Poetry." *The Fortnightly Review*, no. 58, 182–92.

Thain, Marion. 2007a. *"Michael Field": Poetry, Aestheticism and the Fin de Siècle*. Cambridge: Cambridge University Press.

———. 2007b. "Apian Aestheticism: Michael Field and the Economics of the Aesthetic." In *Michael Field and Their World*, edited by Margaret D. Stetz and Cheryl A. Wilson, 223–236. High Wycombe: Rivendale Press.

Tronto, Joan. 1994. *Moral Boundaries: a Political Argument for an Ethic of Care*. London: Routledge.

Vadillo, Ana Parejo. 2005. *Women Poets and Urban Aestheticism: Passengers of Modernity*. Basingstoke: Palgrave Macmillan.

Veblen, Thorstein. 1898. "Why is Economics Not an Evolutionary Science?" *Quarterly Journal of Economics* 12 (4): 373–97.

Walsh, Susan. 2008. "'Arithmetic of Bedlam!': Markets and Manhood in Charles Reade's *Hard Cash*." *Nineteenth-Century Literature* 63 (1): 1–40.

Wagner, Tamara S. 2010. *Financial Speculation in Victorian Fiction: Plotting Money and the Novel Genre, 1815–1901*. Columbus: Ohio State University Press.

Wilde, Oscar. 1915. *The Soul of Man Under Socialism*. New York: Max Maisel.

Part III
Queer Performativity

7   Living Parody

Eric, Count Stenbock, and Economies of Perversity

Matthew Bradley

Introducing the 1936 *Oxford Book of Modern Verse 1892–1935,* Yeats performed another variation on his "Tragic Generation" account of 1890s poetics:

> My father gave these young men their right name. When I had described a supper with Count Stenbock, scholar, connoisseur, drunkard, poet, pervert, most charming of men, he said, "they are the Hamlets of our age."
>
> (Yeats 1936, xi–x)

A casual mention by a canonical figure can be a great spur to critical curiosity. It was Yeats's remark that, in the 1960s, led the scholar John Adlard to become intrigued by the way that this almost totally *un*known figure was being taken as the symbol *par excellence* of a very *well*-known literary phenomenon of decadence. In 1969, Adlard wrote up what is still the only book-length study of Count Stenbock, in which he went on the hunt for the meagre facts of the Count's life and social circle. *Stenbock, Yeats and the Nineties,* is indicative of how much that one remark of Yeats's motivated the project. It is in fact the first quotation given in Adlard's volume, which begins proper like this:

> The man whose life I have tried to reconstruct was witty, imaginative, generous and very rich. He nevertheless achieved almost nothing. This was not altogether his own fault; he was a sick man, a pervert, and his life was short.
>
> (Adlard 1969, 1)

Yeats's word "pervert" rarely moves far from talk about Stenbock. In a 1992 reprint of one of Stenbock's volumes, Geoffrey Palmer introduced the Count as a man who had a mind "filled with werewolves and perverted desires," and for good measure calls Yeats's description of Stenbock "both truthful and kind" (Palmer 1992, v). In the introduction to his influential edited collection *The Fin-de-Siècle Poem* (2005), Joseph Bristow also points to the remark and uses it as emblematic of Yeats's myth-making about the period (Bristow 2005, 32). Bristow's volume actually set out to debunk the Yeatsian myth, or at least to variegate it, but Stenbock nevertheless finds himself again (and again thanks to Yeats), in the curious position of being aesthetically marginal, but symbolically central; only this time he is symbolic not of *fin de siècle* poetry, but of Yeats's narrow and partial narrative of it. Bristow does quote an example of Stenbock's work and offers a few summative comments, but he quickly moves on—understandably, given the collection's stated aim to move away from the myth that Stenbock is taken to symbolise. But ironically, this has the result that the Count once again remains almost pure sign, just as he does in Yeats's original—and also once again, he is taken as a representative figure in the introduction to a collection in which he is nowhere else represented.

It may be that we try to read the symbol—or indeed go beneath the surface—of Count Stenbock at our peril. Rupert Crofte-Cooke called him a "living parody of Ninetyism," "a mask, or perhaps a Pierrot" (Crofte-Cooke 1967, 250–1), a description which, like so much hostile early criticism of decadence, neatly captures that destabilisation of surface and depth—of truth and mask—which is such an enabling energy for the mode, and which has formed such a powerful dynamic in its critical rehabilitation. In particular, queer critics since the 1990s have found in decadent writing a subversive and powerfully anti-essentialist form of parodic performativity, what Jonathan Dollimore in 1991 famously called "sexual dissidence." Dominant/subordinate and normality/perversion hierarchies within the sexual economy are repeatedly unsettled by a "transgressive reinscription" of perversity as a paradoxically central dynamic within the cultural *status quo* (Dollimore 1991, 21–8). Ten years later, Dennis Denisoff in *Aestheticism and Sexual Parody 1840–1940* went further and argued that within nineteenth-century aestheticism this kind of destabilising parody could not be considered simply a one-way street, working as it did within a wider economy of (often apparently hostile) critics and parodists of the movement who, "[e]ven if they fully believed in essential configurations of human desire and attraction, ... were also catalysts for the denaturalization of gendered and sexual norms" (Denisoff 2001, 2). What I wish to examine in this chapter is the way in which these dynamics of parodic perversity form their own systems of value and their own processes of exclusion. Because for both his contemporaries and for modern critics, Count Stenbock seems somehow beyond the pale of that energising nexus of parody, perversity, and performativity emerging at the *fin de siècle*. He is the parody too far of a decadent movement that drew many of its significant energies from parody; the unacceptable face of unacceptability; the over-performed performance of identity; and, finally, a failure at what has been sometimes called the literature of failure.

Certainly, this was how Arthur Symons saw things in a short, unpublished article he wrote about the Count entitled "A Study in the Fantastic" (never published in Symons's lifetime, but included as an appendix to Adlard's book):

> Count Stanislaus Eric Stenbock was one of these extraordinary Slav creatures, who, coming to settle down in London after half a lifetime spent in travelling, live in a bizarre, fantastic, feverish, eccentric, extravagant, morbid and perverse fashion; after their own will, whim, caprice or fancy; self-centred, quite crazy enough to be aware of his singular madness which was always on him, always around him, like some cruel and poisonous exhalation that rises out of a mist-covered valley where assassins hide themselves in the act to slay him. Besides this he had weird propensities.
>
> (Adlard 1969, 89–90)

Perhaps surprisingly an actual Count, Eric Magnus Andreas Harry Stenbock was the son of an Estonian nobleman who had died (likely from alcoholism) before he was born, and a half-German, half-English mother. Growing up with his mother (and, from the age of four, an English stepfather), first in Cheltenham and then at Withdeane Hall in Brighton, he was sent to Wiesbaden in Germany for his schooling in 1875 and then later attended Balliol College, Oxford in 1879—where he was sent down after four terms for reasons unknown. His adulthood consisted of sporadic residence in London and the family home in Kolk, Estonia (Eric inherited the estates in 1885). However, between the lines of the bald biography, what Adlard managed to discover about the details of Stenbock's life only serves to make him more unreal, to seem even more Crofte-Cooke's "living parody." Like the hero of Huysmans's *A Rebours*, he was an eccentric remnant from the line of a mysterious aristocracy. Obsessed with the unhealthy and macabre (Stenbock left orders that after his death his heart should be sent to Estonia and displayed in a glass case), he out-Nervaled de Nerval by keeping not a lobster but a whole menagerie at his home (including a snake, tortoises, a monkey that cracked nuts in the dining room, and a dachshund named Trixie). Indeed, such was his devotion to the decadent cult of the artificial that he ran scent through his hair before meeting any hostess. By the time of his death, he was almost completely bald, and had by that time taken to dragging around a life-size doll with him in public and insisting that it was his son.[1] Other reports of his exploits by contemporary witnesses feel even more like attempts at bad parody. One priest who had railed against decadence in the periodicals, Father William Barry, apparently had a colleague who received Stenbock at his house one night only to be found dead the next morning (Barry 1926, 167). The Welsh poet Ernest Rhys (probably Stenbock's closest literary friend in *fin-de-siècle* London), told a similarly tall story in his memoirs that Wilde put out a cigarette on one of Stenbock's holy shrines, at which heresy Stenbock fainted dead away (Rhys 1931, 37).[2]

Moreover, if one were writing an over-determined parody of a late nineteenth-century decadent poet, it couldn't finish in a more fitting manner: after apparently attacking his father-in-law with a poker in a drunken rage, Stenbock collapsed and died on 26 April 1895, the first day of the Wilde trials (Adlard 1969, 84–5).

In a section in Dollimore's *Sexual Dissidence* (which Denisoff quotes), one well-known strategy of sexual dissidence—camp—is described as "undermining the depth model of identity from inside, being a kind of parody and mimicry which hollows out from within" (Dollimore 1991, 310). By the terms of this now-familiar argument, Stenbock should be the campest, most subversive, decadent of them all—because the hollowest. Yet for the most part, Stenbock seems to have encouraged not investigation or transgressive re-inscription, but rather a slightly embarrassed turning away. Like Enoch Soames, the failed decadent poet in Beerbohm's famous story, he doesn't make it into the index of Holbrook Jackson's *The Eighteen-Nineties* (Beerbohm 1919, 3). Indeed, what Jeremy Reed has called Stenbock's "hundred years of disappearance,"[3] the way in which he has evaded most historical accounts of the period, make him an all-too-tempting possible model for Soames. Moreover, in his article Symons is very clear that this neglect is, in his view, fully justified, and that Stenbock is a *curio* best only dimly remembered. He finishes with the declaration that "he was ... one of those conspicuous failures in life and in art which leave no traces behind them, save some faint drift in one's memory" (Adlard 1969, 94). And exactly that dynamic is observable within the scholarly recovery of decadence as a literary movement, which has been for the most part similarly content to let Stenbock moulder in what looks like well-deserved obscurity. Bristow's introduction to *The Fin-de-Siècle Poem* is a notable exception: Stenbock features in neither Dollimore nor Denisoff's books, but this marks them out only in being typical.

What is interesting, however, is precisely the difficulty that Stenbock seems to present for both decadence, and critical writing about decadence. Much has been said of the mode's destabilisation of depth-surface, of periphery-centre, of parody-seriousness, and of perversion-heteronormativity. Moreover, we are more sensitive than ever to the way in which decadence operates within an overall cultural economy. Most notably in recent times, Regenia Gagnier, in *Individualism, Decadence and Globalization* (2010), argues that decadence is both a response to, and an attempt to cope with, modernity's re-writing of the relationship of part to whole:

> Decadence was thus a pan-European and trans-Atlantic phenomenon that entailed a falling away from or a rejection that could also be a creative repudiation. In Baudelaire and Walter Pater it was overheard as a dying fall or cadence. In Nietzsche, it was a negation of the status quo, or a transvaluation of values. In Wilde, it was a dandiacal strategy of self-differentiation. What is essential is the non-absolute value of

this usage. Creative repudiation can mean creative destruction or war (Davidson) as easily as critique (Wilde, Nietzsche). Death can imply rebirth. As Baudelaire's figure suggested, the dominant organic metaphor of decay and degeneration could turn seamlessly into a cross-fertilized compost of amazing light and color. Decadence and Progress could be the same thing.

(Gagnier 2010, 90–1)

Yet what Stenbock shows is that decadence itself generates an economy of value: one in which perversity, enacted through strategies of parody and parodic subversion, is a currency whose value can apparently vary very widely. It is an economy with its own centres and its own peripheries. There are, it seems, acceptable and unacceptable forms of perversity and performativity within decadence—for both its writers and its latter-day critics. Stenbock alerts us to this by falling so firmly in the "unacceptable" category. Perhaps something of the distinction lies in the colloquial difference between being a writer who is said to embrace perversity, and a writer who is simply labelled a pervert. Decadence may embrace and perform "non-absolute value" usage, in Gagnier's terms, but that does not, of course, prevent it from creating value-systems of its own, just as the institutions of its study do.

Indeed, Stenbock provides a fascinating glimpse into how the development of an academic discourse around decadence has created its own fringes, its own variations of the dominant/subordinate and normative/perverse relationships. What looks like something of a vacuum of critical work on Stenbock from the point of view of mainstream *fin-de-siècle* studies actually masks a fascinating and colourful history in recent times. Websites and other forms of online tribute flourish,[4] and David Tibet, a musician, artist and committed Stenbock enthusiast, has reprinted a number of the works in short print runs (rarely more than 200), mainly through his record label and publishing house Durtro.[5] Interestingly, these well-presented new editions, mostly from the late 1990s and early 2000s, are themselves now becoming slightly mythical rarities. In an article on Stenbock by Rosalie Parker in *Book and Magazine Collector* in 2010, some of the Durtro editions are priced at over £100, as opposed to the £1–2,000 that some original Stenbock volumes can fetch (Parker 2010, 68). Tibet, with the band Current 93, has also recorded a volume of music inspired by a story of Stenbock's. Another member of Current 93, Michael Cashmore, released an EP in 2008 setting two of Stenbock's poems to music, in a collaboration with the singer Marc Almond.

My principal argument, however, is that Stenbock raises important questions about how value was—and is—assigned to the expression of perverse sexual and literary identities within decadence, and the tension he reveals between an apparently liberating discourse of subversive performativity and the way cultural capital accrues to the individual performances (or, more significantly here, doesn't accrue to them). In part, this is unwitting, in that we can read the near-comprehensive rejection of the man and his work by contemporaries and by posterity as revealing something of the limits of "acceptable" decadence within the movement's own parameters, but in part it is also detectable as a conscious strand in the work. Certainly Stenbock showed himself in sympathy with those whose "perversity" seemed unacceptable even for *fin-de-siècle* tastes: Simeon Solomon received both moral and financial support from him, as we know from a letter from Solomon to Robert Ross praising Stenbock's kindness after his conviction (Adlard 1969, 51).[6] Stenbock only published three short volumes of poetry and one volume of short stories in his lifetime, but throughout even this slender corpus, his difficult, nervous relation with performing a decadent identity makes itself clearly felt. Perhaps his most famous work remains the short story "The True Story of a Vampire," (1894) which anticipates Stoker's *Dracula* by three years in recounting the story of a vampire aristocrat delivered from Eastern Europe into the heart of the domestic sphere by thoroughly modern means of transport. Yet the story also sees Stenbock tentatively re-writing aesthetic and sexual perversity as a vampiric system of exchange, of gain and loss. Of course the figure of the vampire as a way of exploring the inequalities of systems of value at the *fin de siècle* has long been recognised,[7] but Stenbock raises the issue in unusually direct fashion:

> Our Vampire arrived by the commonplace means of the railway train, and in the afternoon. You must think I am joking, or perhaps that by the word 'Vampire' I mean a financial vampire. No, I am quite serious. The Vampire of whom I am speaking, who laid waste our hearth and home, was a *real* vampire.
>
> (Stenbock 1894, 121)

This is perhaps a rather surprising comment to the modern eye, both in its assumption that the economic metaphor would leap so readily to the reader's mind as the primary signification of the word "vampire" (a testament to how prevalent financial motifs were, however, in relation to vampirism in the late nineteenth century), and also because the story is not in fact about what we would understand as a "real" vampire at all. Although the titular vampire seems at least to possibly be one of the undead, blood is never mentioned, and there is no direct or indirect cue that actual blood-drinking is anywhere occurring. What Stenbock presents instead is a draining of vitality which operates through a relationship that expresses perverse (homo)sexuality through aesthetic performance. After disembarking from that "commonplace" railway train, Count Vardalek visits the household of Wronski, a Polish family living in a castle in Styria. On the first night of his stay, he plays a Hungarian csárdás (folk dance) on the piano. Gabriel, the shy and reclusive young Wronski son, is captivated by this "music which makes men mad," and, by way of response, proceeds to play an imitation of the same piece, but on "his fiddle and self-made xylophone" (137). Vardalek looks sad, and commiserates Gabriel: "Poor child! you have the soul of music within you" (138). What follows is a mysterious decline in Gabriel's health, the cause of which is only discovered when his sister (who narrates the story) passes Vardalek's room by chance one night to detect the visitor once more playing the piano, and drawing an entranced Gabriel to him. All Gabriel does is stand in the room while Vardalek plays, but it is a ritual that draws him on to growing weakness and eventual death. The homoerotic sub-text of the tragic "soul of music" shared by Gabriel and Vardalek through illicit meetings in the night is hard to miss (indeed it hardly qualifies as a subtext at all), but it is important that such eroticism is shown here explicitly as being mediated through aesthetic performance—and that Stenbock takes a tragic view of this connection. "My darling, I fain would spare thee," says Vardalek, while playing, "but thy life is my life, and I must live, I who would rather die" (143). This is a complex moment, economically speaking; "thy life is my life" seems on the edge of invoking a matrimonial model of property-in-common, and in terms of the way Vardalek sees vitality, it is Gabriel who is the rich man and Vardalek who is the pauper. Nevertheless, the overall frame of these encounters remains the combative, I-gain-you-lose frame of economic vampirism—so pointedly (over-pointedly?) discarded at the beginning of the story—and it persists as an awful reality within this mode of sexual transgression mediated by aesthetic means.

If we accept the proposition that Stenbock might be uncomfortable with the idea of a value-economy within a perverse aesthetic, then an important question arises. How far can skill in the performance of literary form be held as the standard by which performances of identity (perverse or otherwise) are to be judged? Or, to put it more bluntly, don't bad writers have a right to perform themselves and their sexuality, too? The fear of the connection between transgressive sexual identity and literary form is, I contend, both an animating and a (performatively) de-animating presence in Stenbock's work. The protagonists of a very large number of his stories and poems are innocents abroad like Gabriel, often pining lovers, or suicidal, sensitive souls far too good for this world of pain. Indeed, a number of them are also called Gabriel, with all that name's obvious associations with angelhood. For example, the Gabriel of "The Other Side" (1893), Stenbock's story for Alfred Douglas's periodical *The Spirit Lamp*, is typical in that for all his perverse desires (he dreams of crossing a brook from his village to a wilderness of wolf-men and women to pluck a beautiful "witch-flower"), he is easy prey for a rapacious world: "because he was less cruel and more gentle of nature than the rest," Stenbock tells us, "and even as a rare and beautiful bird escaped from a cage is hacked to death by the common sparrows, so was Gabriel among his fellows" (Stenbok [sic] 1894, 54). But the persistence of this martyr-figure across Stenbock's work, and the clear extent of his emotional investment in it, makes it tempting then to read Gabriel in "The True Story of a Vampire" as a self-questioning avatar of Stenbock himself, the performer of a second-hand, fiddle-and-home-made-xylophone version of decadent melodies originally played by someone else—and with the spectre of that someone else's presence at first registering as overwhelming, and then fatal.[8] In "The Other Side," a different, but equally bewitched, Gabriel, his vitality similarly diminishing, also feels "a will not his own perpetually over-shadow[ing] him" (Stenbok [sic] 1894, 62). If skill in literary form is one of the standards for "acceptable" perversity, and originality is a key constitutive criterion of that skill, then we might in fact be watching Stenbock asking him-self and us rather fearfully what happens to the performed identities of those whose performances are found *un*original, or indeed wanting in some other way. This is a particularly strongly felt dynamic in Stenbock's second volume of poems, *Myrtle, Rue and Cypress* (1883), which includes a poem called "The Vampyre," in which Stenbock ventriloquises a vampire's threat to his victim that he will "breathe with the breath of thy mouth" (Stenbock 1883, 55). The volume's overall emphasis is on the poet's sense of personal fear and pain, and the futility of his homosexual longings, either because he is forced into separation from his beloved ("I cannot sleep,/I cannot weep,/Bereft of his soft familiar face"),[9] or because homosexuality itself is so perverse it is akin to madness ("I know, I know that long ago/The moon with silver feet/Crept to thy bed, close to thine head,/And kissed thy forehead, sweet,/Giving thy lips strange wine to drink,/And alien flesh to eat.").[10] But Sten-bock also displays in *Myrtle, Rue and Cypress* not just anxiety of influence, but rather a hysterical outburst of it; poems entitled "The Aeolian Harp" and "The Nightingale" masochistically go out of their way to invite comparison with Coleridge's more accomplished originals ("What passion of music that moves to madness,/What secret thing doth thy song express,/What excess of joy, that is wellnigh sadness,/What agony bitter beyond redress?" he asks the Nightingale);[11] another poem, "Song XI" does Swinburne-by-keyword with talk of "a beauty that stings and burns me" and a heart "cast forth across the waves" (Stenbock 1883, 52). *Myrtle, Rue and Cypress* is not plagiarism in the breezy manner of Wilde's *Poems* (1881). Neither is it a parade of inauthenticity that could convincingly be read as subversive parody. When taken in combination with the collection's repetitive obsession with its own author's pain and sexual isolation, and Stenbock's obsession with the fig-ure of the martyr, it is certainly possible to read it as a histrionic display of the poet's own lack of originality, almost a plea for acceptance. Of course, homosexual martyrdom runs powerfully through much decadent discourse, arguably up to and including Wilde's famous decision to stay and face his inevitable prosecution for gross indecency. But in Stenbock, this sense of martyrdom seems to relate to his literary identity in a way that operates quite differently to Wilde. Even in great adversity, Wilde's sense of martyrdom fed his sense of personal artistic identity, as *De Profundis* attests. By contrast, before a reader even has a chance to judge Stenbock's poems as thinned-out and unoriginal, the author falls down before the punch is even thrown, the-atrically daring us to add to his pain and sense of exile by heaping on him, on top of everything else, our literary condemnation.

A sonnet in Stenbock's last collection *The Shadow of Death* (1893) is perhaps Stenbock's most explicit eruption of his sense of poetic ineptitude. "The Freezing of the Baltic Sea" is a poem that deals head-on with Stenbock's sense of what happens when the poetic expression of isolation and pain becomes impossible, when the poet literally has nothing to say. Taking the sea as our poetic repository for all the pains of life ("Who hath not lingered a little by the shore?/Seeking a symbol in the sighing of the sea" (Stenbock 1893, 53)), the poet is caught in what he declares to be a "[N]ovelty of horror" by the sight of the frozen Baltic, "silently stretching towards infinity," refusing him even this most conventional of poetic symbols. What you can do with your pain when you have no poetic outlet for it is the question being asked here, and again, almost in the manner of a plea for sympathy. Stenbock's answer may be a straightforwardly Christian one—in the midst of contemplating suicide he catches sight of one who "walked upon the waters, sombre, solemn, and slow" (Stenbock had by this time seemingly converted to Catholicism, and many of the poems in *The Shadow of Death* are religiously inflected)—but in asking the question and raising the possibility, we glimpse the poet's horrified sense that he cannot contribute.

The concept of shame has been of great significance to queer readings of decadent literature, and has been convincingly shown as one of the principal mechanisms by which sexual dissidence is performed within the decadent mode. Eve Kosofsky Sedgwick has characterised shame as a performance which makes identity; we look out at a disapproving face, we feel the affective weight of our isolation and our separation from others, we flush, we feel hot, we glance down. But we also, in that moment, make our identity precisely *because* we've separated it from something or someone else, and moreover a something or someone which by definition refuses us legitimacy (because they/it must be condemning us for us to be feeling shame at all)—it is a sensation, she says, "whose very suffusiveness seems to delineate my precise, individual outlines in the most isolating way imaginable" (Sedgwick 2003, 37). Ellis Hanson saw the essentially theatrical impulse to performing one's own shamefulness (and the process of *being shamed*), as key to the decadent sensibility. For Wilde in particular (although he is emblematic of the wider decadent tendency towards what Hanson calls the "dialectic between shame and grace"), shame is "less an affect than a performative possibility, less a force of nature than an effect of language, less a moral predicament than an artistic opportunity for self-fashioning" (Hanson 1997, 86).[12] Stenbock's marginality may perhaps be because he represents a peculiar anxiety within decadence of a performance of vice and of shame which remains stubbornly thin, stubbornly de-energised; in which identity remains unmade, and the liberating, transformational process that shame is meant to kick-start appears to stall.

Stenbock's poems certainly never seem to let the poet's overwhelming sense of shame help individuate himself. Indeed, perhaps their most notable feature—repetitiveness—militates precisely against such development, as the motif simply recirculates again and again. But they do add an unusual and striking element into decadent poetry's shameful mix: they are, at many points, preoccupied with the prospect of *laughter*. In the very first volume *Love, Sleep and Dreams* (1881), the opening series of poems labelled "A Decade of Sighs on a Lost Love," Stenbock's voice is in the tenor of what was to become his usual pain-wracked innocent, who muses on his toxic love and the lover who has abandoned him:

> The bitter cup you gave to me,
>   Unto the dregs I quaff,
>   And you stand by and laugh:
> And all men laugh too, seeing me;
>   You laugh, all laugh, I laugh,
> Whilst from my heart a secret flood
> Flows on for ever, of tears, of blood.
>   (Stenbock 1992, 8)

That a response to his performative shame may be a kind of derisive laughter ("all men laugh too, seeing me;") is something that Stenbock returns to frequently. In a poem clearly drawing from Swinburne's "Anactoria," "The Unwept Tear," the poet dreams of hell, but a hell with no tears, only laughter: both the endless mocking laughter of the demons, and the hollow and insane laughter of the sinners ("Almost too horrible to hear,/Too terrible to tell,/The song about the unwept tear,/And the laughter heard in Hell" (Stenbock 1992, 16). *Derisive* laughter, of course, is an awkward kind of condemnation, in that it threatens to rob shame even of the dignity of tragedy, constantly foregrounding the sense of its ludicrousness.

   This, perhaps more even than the issue of originality, taps into Stenbock's anxiety about the connection between literary form and a performative sexual perversity. As is well-known, the word "decadence" derives from the Latin "decadēre," a "falling down" or "falling away," a point emphasised by Alex Murray and Jason David Hall in the introduction to their recent collection *Decadent Poetics: Literature and Form at the British Fin de Siècle* (Murray and Hall 2013, 1). But there are different ways of "falling down" or "falling away," some of them more attractive than others (Murray and Hall's way is for decadent literature to be engaged in intensely questioning the very frameworks by which simplistic ideas of decay and "falling away" circulate). Perhaps a factor at play in the perversity-economy of decadence— and which I think we find in Stenbock, and certainly in responses to him— is the most unredeemed literary form of "falling away" of all: *bathos*, the movement from high to low, the fall from sublime to the ridiculous. Parody is energising: critically speaking, it now might almost be said to be a rather safe form of subversion. Perhaps more difficult for decadence is the spectre of a kind of bathetic performativity which limits and *de*-energises, a performativity where we're reminded forcibly that most performances suggest an audience, who might well deliver an unfavourable or hostile verdict; a perversity which threatens to re-write the "tragic generation" as farce. In his introduction to *Love, Sleep and Dreams,* Geoffrey Palmer judged that Stenbock "tried to be deliciously wicked but his antics were comic rather than Wildean" and that "he only succeeded in becoming a *pathetic* copy of more talented natures [emphasis added]" (Palmer 1992, v). It may be, however, that to consider Stenbock as a *bathetic* figure within decadence may prove more fruitful.

As far back as Pope, bathos has been associated with a type of decadent artificiality. The genius in the art of bathos, Pope says ironically in his *Peri Bathous* (1728) fully grasps the modern boredom with nature:

> Nothing seemed more plain to our great authors, than that the world had long been weary of natural things. How much the contrary is formed to please, is evident from the universal applause daily given to the admirable entertainments of harlequins and magicians on our stage. When an audience behold a coach turned into a wheelbarrow, a conjurer into an old woman, or a man's head where his heels should be; how are they struck with transport and delight? Which can only be imputed to this cause, that each object is changed into that which hath been suggested to them by their own low ideas before.
>
> He ought therefore to render himself master of this happy and anti-natural way of thinking to such a degree, as to be able, on the appearance of any object, to furnish his imagination with ideas infinitely below it. And his eyes should be like unto the wrong end of a perspective glass, by which all the objects of nature are lessened.
>
> (Pope 1993, 201)

Artificiality is not a transgressive cultural strategy or a signifier of aesthetic purpose, it is a route to commercial success. While it appears to transvaluate the world, to make it strange, in reality it only reassures its audience by re-explaining the unfamiliar in already-familiar terms. So when a "true genius" of bathos looks at the sky, says Pope, he immediately thinks of something he already knows, say a piece of blue fabric or a child's mantle, drawing his experiences, however sublime, constantly to the level of the mundane or everyday. For nineteenth-century decadence, so invested in artificiality as a transgressive cultural strategy, bathos might be said to be something of a lethal a *doppelgänger*. It is rarely, if, ever mentioned in critical connection with the mode, although it is one of the many faults identified in the *Athenaeum*'s hostile review of Wilde's *Poems* (reprinted in Beckson 1970, 25). Yet like decadence, bathos as a literary-critical practice exists on an uneasy cusp between the description of a style and the condemnation of a fault. Also like decadence, it regularly slips between its linguistic, stylistic, and cultural applications. Perhaps most of all, however, bathos seems corrosive to the performed perversity of decadent sexuality. Sexuality of any kind, of course, is always vulnerable to certain kinds of ironic comedy, and particularly the idea of bathos as a move from orgasmic high to comic low (something the continued popularity of the literary "bad sex prize" confirms). The enactment of desire, the having of sex, very easily seems ridiculous when it's not you enjoying it, or indeed writing about it—and bathos is particularly damaging for a perverse sexuality that operates through the mechanism of performative shame because it so decisively shifts the emphasis away from the paradoxically enabling dynamic between "shamed" subject and disapproving observer. It stresses instead the ironic distance and condemnation of that observer—whose viewpoint, by means of a focus on literary style, becomes unquestionable and authoritative. The energising relationship between shamed subject and shaming observer is fatally weakened, and the perverse dynamic (at least on an individual level) is all but dissolved. Bathos offers perhaps the most literal type of deflationary pressure in a literary economy where perversity and performativity are the units of value.

One of Stenbock's stories gives us a notable example of performative shame turning into seemingly unintentional farce. Lady Margaret, a character in Stenbock's story "The Child of the Soul," is so jealous of the seemingly homoerotic bond between her husband and a young male composer that she arranges to be caught having sex with him:

> My object was that Henry should discover the treachery of his friend. Then perhaps he would kill him. He might then kill me too for all I cared. I desired to be caught *in flagranto delicto*, and that desire at least was accomplished.
>
> (Stenbock 1999, 30)

Self-evidently it's a performance of sexual transgression and sexual shame, but one which is inauthentic, a setup, overly-staged and ludicrous in effect. It doesn't even work, as Lady Margaret's husband, Lord Kilcoran, seems fonder of his friend than ever. Things drift even further to the comic when we learn almost straight away from Lady Margaret that, thanks to a heart complaint, the young composer died anyway—from having sex with her:

> Here I was surprised to see an actual blush on her face, invariably of an ivory pallor. "You are the wife of a doctor," [Lady Margaret is addressing Lady Randall, the story's main narrator], she continued hesitatingly, "so you must know that certain exertions may have fatal consequences ..." (31)

The comedy of this performance is only increased by the tragic seriousness with which it is apparently presented.

As Sara Crangle and Peter Nicholls remind us in the introduction to their collection of essays on bathos, both implicit and explicit theorists of the term from Longinus onwards draw into question the assumption that "to miss a high aim is to fail without shame" (Crangle and Nicholls 2010, 2).

Or, perhaps, as in this case, to fail with the *wrong sort* of shame. Bathos confronts us with the possibility that not all falls are Icarian ones when looked at through an appropriately distanced lens, and that a seriousness that fails isn't always the path to camp glory. It's a possibility that Susan Sontag recognised in "Notes on Camp" in 1964:

> In naïve, or pure, Camp, the essential element is seriousness, a seriousness that fails. Of course, not all seriousness that fails can be redeemed as Camp. Only that which has the proper mixture of the exaggerated, the fantastic, the passionate, and the naïve.
>
> (Sontag 2013, 266)

The way that Stenbock introduces the toxic idea of the *wrong* mixture, an "unredeemed" performance of perverse identity, a failed seriousness which misses even the aim of converting itself into camp subversion, is perhaps one of the reasons why Yeats, Symons, and the others seem to hold him at such a distance.

It is all too easy to identify examples of bathos as a stylistic feature in Stenbock's poetry. Again over-performing his literary debts—this time to Baudelaire's famous exhortation to drunkenness "Enivrez-Vous" in *Le Spleen de Paris* (1869)—we might take the final lines of "Paidika," Stenbock's hymn to the beauty of a young boy (its title is taken from a Greek term for the younger partner in a homosexual relationship between man and boy):

> Oh, give me to drink, for nothing
> My thirst can satiate;
> I drink, I have drunk, and am drunken,
> I am wholly inebriate.
>
> (Stenbock 1992, 21)

The literary faults here need hardly pointing out. There is obviously the awkward syntax ("give me to drink"?), but also the strange way the attempt to delineate a decadent intoxication with the *paidika*'s beauty degenerates into something sounding suspiciously like a grammar exercise ("I drink," "I have drunk," and I "am drunken") before culminating on the entirely flat line, "I am wholly inebriate." The poem certainly feels parodic, but it never really crosses into dissidence, or camp: it induces a smile almost unequivocally at Stenbock's expense. The shame here, we feel, is in having written this at all. The feeling subject retreats from our attention, he feels less real to us; in a way we want to read on, but we also want to turn away, almost embarrassed for the author. Examples of these kinds of stylistic "fall" in Stenbock's poetry, where high sublimity of emotion seems to collapse under the weight of banality of expression, are extremely common within a corpus, which Palmer calls with some justice "thin, sentimental, formless and repetitive" (Palmer 1992, v).

Yet simply listing examples of what we might take to be bathetic writing in Stenbock is surely to acquiesce in the assumption that literary style is the formal criterion by which we mark acceptable or unacceptable modes of sexual dissidence, the very assumption that Stenbock himself raises as a problem. Stenbock is certainly alert, if not over-sensitive, to the dynamics of different kinds of sinking or falling; the "Finale" to the "Sighs on a Decade" sequence piles fall upon fall ("The fallen petals of the rose,/The fallen feathers of the dove,/And the time of swiftly-falling snows,/Are strewn on the tomb of Love" (Stenbock 1992, 12)). In both the *Myrtle, Rue and Cypress* and *Shadow of Death* collections, falling is everywhere; feet, flowers, snow, ashes, the sun, tears, the poet, everything seems to be constantly sinking (the word "fall" and its derivatives appear 28 times in one volume, 38 in the other). One of Stenbock's recurring poetic images is the "dead sea fruit," or the apples of Sodom, an image from the Song of Moses in Deuteronomy 32: 32,[13] where the "strange fair apples" of homosexual love reveal themselves to be nothing but ashes when eaten, a form of forbidden fruit which brings no pleasure but only disappointment, even death.[14] And just as Stenbock seems to want to display his sense of inauthenticity and his lack of talent as a kind of martyrdom, so many of his poems seem to similarly invite us to condemn them for a "fall" from repetitive overwrought emotion to a kind of blank, baffling tepidity. In one of the poems in *Myrtle, Rue and Cypress*, the poet asks of his beloved:

> What – shall we laugh or weep, dear,
> Remembering all our pain?
> (Stenbock 1883, 6)

In a way, Stenbock raises the age-old problem in literary study as to what we should do with "bad" literature. To claim Stenbock as an unjustly neglected author is a near-impossible task (although as I hope I have suggested, his work is perhaps a little more self-aware than it is usually given credit for). What most critics of Stenbock have opted for, then, is what one might call the "campfire" approach, where the flame of awareness about a writer is kept alive by the continual re-telling of the sad, sometimes silly tales of his life and times. That is not, of course, an unworthy historical aim (I have employed it at the beginning of this chapter), but Palmer's introduction to the 1992 reprint of *Love, Sleep and Dreams* (Stenbock as "a pathetic copy of more talented natures") alerts us to the potential contradictions within it as a mode of literary criticism. Having mined Stenbock's eccentric life for all the anecdotal humour he can, Palmer goes on to utterly repudiate the very work that he is helping to reprint and re-circulate (poetry that is "thin, sentimental, formless and repetitive," in his own words). But perhaps there is an exploratory space between an over-optimistic claim of unjust neglect and the half-mocking ritual of the campfire. A writer like Stenbock can help us re-think not just decadence's relationship with wider cultural economies, but how the literary movement and its criticism have created their own such economies. Stenbock perhaps gives us a clue to the mechanisms by which "value" within the perverse decadent aesthetic has been established; how sexual dissidence holds—or doesn't hold—its legitimacy in a critical economy of sexual subversion conducted through literary means. In other words, how one might fall from an enabling perversity to being dismissed as a pervert. For some, Count Stenbock was the hollowed-out symbol of decadence. Yet it may be that his critical "disappearance," and the atmosphere of low comedy that continues to surround him and his work is, paradoxically, one of the decadent movement's darker shadows—a farcical haunting by a performance of self that doesn't reveal a shameful but liberating unworthiness, but which is simply declared unworthy; a performance that can't even raise the energy required for a boo from those who watch, but simply an ironic, maybe even an embarrassed, smirk—and a turning away. This, from a typically self-castigating sonnet in Stenbock's last volume:

> So shalt thou suffer without sympathy,
> And should'st thou stand within the street and say:
> "Look on me, ye that wander by the way,
> If there be any sorrow like to mine."
> They shall not bind thy wounds with oil and wine,
> But with strange eyes downcast, shall turn from thee. (Stenbock 1893, 55)

It is a cry largely unheeded by modern critics. Even those who might have been most expected to play the Good Samaritan have been largely content to leave Stenbock lying there, while—perhaps a little nervously—they walk by on the other side.

Notes

1. These biographical details are from Adlard 1969, 85, 36–7, 78.
2. Also cited in Adlard 1969, 63–4.
3. This is the title of the short biographical piece on Stenbock in Reed's book *Angels, Divas and Blacklisted Heroes* (Reed 1999, 109–115).
4. See for example, http://www.mmhistory.org.uk/cce/Jo/index.htm.
5. For details of Tibet's work, and his interest in Stenbock, see www.davidtibet. com. Tibet is currently editing the collected works of Stenbock, although this much-delayed project too has attained an almost mythical status.
6. Mary Costelloe described Stenbock's rooms in his castle at Estonia as combining a menagerie of lizards, snakes and toads with "worse still – a collection of Simeon Solomon's morbid and pessimistic pictures" (Costelloe 1980, 19).
7. See for example Moretti 1983, 83–108, Houston 2005, and Ford 2013, although none of these works discuss Stenbock's story.
8. This is to read against the grain of what looks like a strong case for Stenbock as self-identifying with the vampire, and not just because Vardalek is also a Count. Timothy D'Arch Smith, for example, argues for Vardalek-as-author because of the "something serpentine" that is said to be Vardalek's chief characteristic, given that Stenbock's self-adopted emblem was a snake (Smith 1970, 38).

9. "Song IX" (Stenbock 1883, 41).
10. "The Lunatic Lover" (Stenbock 1883, 42).
11. "The Nightingale" (Stenbock 1883, 18).
12. Hanson never mentions Stenbock in his nonetheless wide-ranging study.
13. "For their vine is the vine of Sodom, and of the fields of Gomorrah: their grapes *are* grapes of gall, their clusters are bitter ...".
14. "The Ballad of the Dead Sea Fruit" (Stenbock 1992, 13). Interestingly, another poem to deploy this motif, "The Lunatic Lover," ends in even more uncertainty and confusion, from the reader's point of view. In the original printing, after the final lines, "Fruit from the tree by the Dead Sea/Whose fruit is death to eat," there is a note appended which reads simply "We have deemed it more judicious to represent the rest of this poem by * * * * *." It is unclear to me quite what this indicates, and whether the "we" is an affectation by Stenbock or a genuine publishers' addition.

Works Cited

Adlard, John. 1969. *Stenbock, Yeats and the Nineties*. London: Cecil and Amelia Woolf.

Barry, William. 1926. *Memories and Opinions*. London and New York: G. P. Putnam.

Beckson, Karl, ed. 1970. *Oscar Wilde: The Critical Heritage*. London: Routledge and Kegan Paul.

Beerbohm, Max. 1919. *Seven Men*. London: William Heinemann.

Bristow, Joseph, ed. 2005. *The Fin-de-Siècle Poem: English Literary Culture and the 1890s*. Ohio: Athens University Press.

Costelloe, Mary. 1980. *Christmas with Count Stenbock*. Edited by John Adlard. London: Enitharmon Press.

Crangle, Sara, and Peter Nicholls, eds. 2010. *On Bathos: Literature, Art, Music*. London: Continuum.

Crofte-Cooke, Rupert. 1967. *Feasting with Panthers: A New Consideration of Some Late Victorian Writers*. London: W. H. Allen.

Denisoff, Dennis. 2001. *Aestheticism and Sexual Parody 1840–1940*. Cambridge: Cambridge University Press.

Dollimore, Jonathan. 1991. *Sexual Dissidence: Augustine to Wilde, Freud to Foucault*. Oxford: Clarendon Press.

Ford, Jane. 2013. *Vampiric Enterprise: Metaphors of Economic Exploitation in the Literature and Culture of the Fin de Siècle*. University of Portsmouth: unpublished doctoral thesis.

Gagnier, Regenia. 2010. *Individualism, Decadence and Globalization: On the Relationship of the Part to the Whole 1859–1920*. Basingstoke: Palgrave Macmillan.

Hanson, Ellis. 1997. *Decadence and Catholicism*. Cambridge, Massachusetts: Harvard University Press.

Houston, Gail Turley. 2005. *From Dickens to Dracula: Gothic, Economics and Victorian Fiction*. Cambridge: Cambridge University Press.

Moretti, Franco. 1983. *Signs Taken for Wonders: On the Sociology of Literary Forms*. London: Verso.

Murray, Alex, and Jason David Hall. 2013. *Decadent Poetics: Literature and Form at the British Fin de Siècle*. Basingstoke: Palgrave Macmillan.

Palmer, Geoffrey. 1992. Introduction to *Love, Sleep and Dreams*, by Stanislaus Eric Stenbock. Norfolk: Hermitage Books.

Parker, Rosalie. 2010. "Count Eric Stenbock." *Book and Magazine Collector,* no. 317, 62–9.

Pope, Alexander. 1993. "Peri Bathous; or Martinus Scriblerus, His Treatise of the Art of Sinking in Poetry." In *The Oxford Authors: Alexander Pope,* edited by Pat Rogers, 195–239. Oxford: Oxford University Press.

Reed, Jeremy. 1999. *Angels, Divas and Blacklisted Heroes.* London: Peter Owen.

Rhys, Ernest. 1931. *Everyman Remembers.* London and Toronto: J. M. Dent.

Sedgwick, Eve Kosofsky. 2003. *Touching Feeling: Affect, Pedagogy, Performativity.* Durham and London: Duke University Press.

Smith, Timothy D'Arch. 1970. *Love in Earnest: Some Notes on the Lives of Uranian Poets from 1889 to 1930.* London: Routledge and Kegan Paul.

Sontag, Susan. 2013. "Notes on Camp." In *Susan Sontag, Essays of the 1960s & 70s,* edited by David Rieff, 259–74. New York: The Library of America.

Stenbock, Eric, Count. 1894. *Studies of Death: Romantic Tales.* London: David Nutt in the Strand.

Stenbock, Count Stanislaus Eric. 1893. *The Shadow of Death: A Collection of Poems, Songs, and Sonnets.* London: The Leadenhall Press.

Stenbock, Stanislaus Eric. 1883. *Myrtle, Rue and Cypress: A Book of Poems, Songs and Sonnets.* London: Hatchards.

Stenbock, Stanislaus Eric. 1992. *Love, Sleep and Dreams.* Edited by Geoffrey Palmer. Norfolk: Hermitage Books.

Stenbock, Stanislaus Eric, Count. 1999. *The Child of the Soul And Other Stories.* London: Durtro.

Stenbok [sic], Eric. 1893. "The Other Side: A Breton Legend." *The Spirit Lamp* 4 (2): 52–68.

Yeats, W. B., ed. 1936. *The Oxford Book of Modern Verse 1892–1935.* Oxford: Clarendon Press.

8 Camp Aesthetics and Inequality
Baron Corvo's Toto Stories

Kristin Mahoney

In 1895 and 1896, in the immediate wake of the Wilde trials, the *Yellow Book* published six short stories by Baron Corvo (Frederick Rolfe, 1860–1913). These stories detail the erotically charged interactions between an English gentleman and a group of Italian adolescents as they roam the Italian countryside. The young Italian peasants wait upon Don Friderico, carrying his books and photographic equipment as he wanders the Alban hills. His particular favourite, Toto, recounts stories to the older man that intertwine myth, saints' lives, and Italian folklore, while dressed in the white clothes his patron has demanded he wear: "a silk shirt with all the buttons undone and the sleeves rolled up, showing his broad brown chest and supple arms" (Corvo 1896, 95). Though these stories were published at a volatile time, they were nevertheless warmly received. John Lane chose to publish a collected edition of *Stories Toto Told Me* in 1898 as well as an enlarged and revised collection of Toto stories, *In His Own Image*, in 1901. In the later stories, the power imbalance between the boys and their master is further foregrounded and eroticised. Toto's body, the reader is told, "undulate[s] deliciously" as he is forced to model for his master, and, when Don Friderico is displeased with his actions, he makes Toto kneel at his feet, takes his throat between his hands and throttles him (Corvo 1901, 71).

It is difficult to imagine what might have made these stories seem acceptable to Lane, who dismissed Aubrey Beardsley from his position as art editor of the *Yellow Book* due to his associations with Wilde. In this chapter, I explore the possibility that the stories' reliance on an erotics of inequality allowed them to read as comfortably conservative despite their transgressive representation of desire between men. The issue of class miscegenation had been central to the Wilde trials, as his attackers expressed dismay concerning his voluntary contact with social inferiors. Wilde's avowed disregard for class difference was part of a larger discussion concerning eroticised and democratic comradeship taking place at the turn of the century, which operated as an implicit critique of traditional class hierarchy. Corvo's stories, on the other hand, revel in hierarchy. He takes pleasure in power imbalance, extolling those relationships between older men and adolescent boys that rely upon an ethics of obedience, humility, and reverence for rank. These young men are not to be "raised up," educated, and mentored to occupy a position of equality because Corvo does not conceive of friendship between men in terms of its progressive or democratic possibilities; rather, he celebrates a form of same-sex desire that reinscribes hierarchy.

However, the political implications of Corvo's representations of eroticised hierarchy can potentially be read in another light. While Corvo hailed from a middle-class background, he spent the majority of his adult life impoverished and often homeless. Nevertheless, he insisted that he held socialism in disdain and explicitly denounced democratic principles in works such as "Towards Aristocracy," an unpublished poem conceived as a "counter-blast" to Carpenter's *Towards Democracy* (1883–1902).[1] Given that Corvo suffered, starved, and ended up in the workhouse, his investment in highly conservative and oppressive class ideologies seems surprising. I argue that Corvo's Toto stories "camp" and critique inequality by enacting exaggerated, near ridiculous scenes of hierarchy and injustice. The stories emerge within this reading as the poignant fantasies of a fundamentally disempowered subject, rather than cold and cruel articulations of elitism. The camp scenarios in the Toto stories, which allow the impoverished Corvo to imagine himself into a dominant position, highlight what Susan Sontag refers to as "Being-as-Playing-a-Role," demonstrating the performative nature of class identity, allowing Corvo to engage in what amounts to class drag (Sontag 1982, 109). In addition, the power imbalances in the stories are so exaggerated, they seem to parody the very concept of inequality, exposing the absurdity of hierarchy by forcing it to its extremes. While at first glance these works might appear less pleasing and progressive than those works that integrated socialism and same-sex desire by Corvo's *fin-de-siècle* peers, attending to Corvo's formulation of camped and eroticised inequality allows for insight into the existence of the diverse range of politicised discourse surrounding same-sex desire and class hierarchy at the turn of the century.

In Regenia Gagnier's *The Insatiability of Human Wants*, Baron Corvo is cast as the worst sort of Decadent, one who desires above all "control, stability, and distance from others" a foil to all those "genuinely democratic and progressive writers" of the *fin de siècle*, such as Edward Carpenter (Gagnier 2000, 150). According to Gagnier, Corvo "bears all the marks of the most conservative Englishness: love of hierarchy and of ritual for its own sake, obsession with private property (including the Beloved), general inflexibility, and a deluded self-sufficiency" (151). He possesses a "rigid need to control the Other" and is guided by a "fantasy of exact exchange in social relations," a psychological structure Gagnier associates with his dealings with male prostitutes and his tendency to engage in relations "pathologically mediated by monetary exchange" (151, 146, 154). She describes his vision of desire as "love-as-domination" and argues that his pleasure arises only from hierarchical scenarios in which he is entirely in control of and utterly distant from his inferiors (151).

The Toto stories do, in many ways, seem to bear out Gagnier's allegations. Don Friderico governs the Italian teenagers in his service quite firmly, and a rigid system of hierarchy underwrites the operations of the homosocial community he has created. Even the early stories published in the *Yellow Book*, which focus primarily on Toto's tales of the saints and spend less time detailing the interactions between Toto and his master, reveal that Don Friderico has propagated a dynamic of order and control. The introductory passages of "About Beata Beatrice and the Mamma of San Pietro" (1896), for example, indicate much about the arrangement that exists between the narrator and Toto. It is in this story that the reader is first told that Don Friderico has ordered Toto to wear white, revealing clothes and that Toto prostrates himself before the narrator in agony when he is frightened that he might have displeased him. As the story opens, Toto confesses to "la sua excellenza" that he wishes to bring his beloved, Beatrice, into their circle, and the confession is accompanied by the following scene: "He flung himself down on the ground. He kissed my hands, and kissed my feet, and wept" (Corvo 1896, 94). While he is abject before his master, the story also reveals that Toto in turn has "half-a-dozen creatures of his own rank under his command, all chosen for some singular quality; and it was their business to … wait upon [Don Friderico] while [he] loafed the summers away in the Alban hills" (95–6). In this way "About Beata Beatrice" establishes that Toto and his peers operate according to an ethos of duty and obedience while the narrator remains at once haughtily detached from, yet titillated by, the interactions between his servants.

The stories published in the subsequent 1901 collection provide further insight into this dynamic of excessive hierarchy, abjection, and discipline, opening with an account of extreme penance and physical abuse. The first story in *In His Own Image*, "About the Fantastical Fra Guilhelmo of the Cappuccini," tells of the "sound and solemn" flagellation Toto received at the narrator's hands as a punishment for his involvement with another "hussy" named Fiammina. This beating was so severe "as to impress Frat' Agostino, who was present on the occasion in an official capacity, with the notion that we English regarded the function as possessing something of a sacramental nature—indeed he spoke afterwards of the twig as the outward vehicle of inward invisible grace." Toto responds with masochistic glee to his role in this sadistic/voyeuristic scenario of flagellation witnessed by an enthusiastic priest: "[He] took the thrashing in his habitual sweet-tempered way, and bore me no malice for shedding his blood. He said that he knew himself to have been wrong; anyone could see that with half an eye: and if he escaped punishment, he would become a sinner of vast dimensions as time went on" (Corvo 1901, 4).[2] The beating is in fact understood by Toto as a kindness: "Naturally, he preferred to be flayed by me, because I was his patron who wished him well into the bargain" (5). Toto accepts and revels in the punishment he receives from his master.

While the community Don Friderico has fostered is a small one, it is one in which rank and hierarchy are rigidly enforced, and inferiors are continually educated by superiors concerning their rights and duties. Toto mimics and reproduces his master's sadistic taste for discipline and lords over the boys beneath him with a short temper. His ardent humility regarding Don Friderico is matched in enthusiasm only by the level of fury he feels when he believes the boys beneath him have offended his master. In "Why the Rose is Red," for example, Toto erupts in anger when Guido and Ercole set Don Friderico's table with red roses, a flower "stained with blood—the blood of Holy Innocents," which must, therefore, be understood as a "badge of infamy" (Corvo 1901, 72). When he first spots the flowers, he immediately becomes "livid, stiff and stark, convulsed with silent rage" (66). He forces the boys upon their knees to beg for pardon from "la sua excellenza," and he visits the butcher to obtain a sinew of bullock with which he plans to "flay the hides off Guido, [his] brother, and off Ercole of Rome, in order to appease la sua excellenza" (72). Inequality seems to beget inequality, as Toto's reverence for Don Friderico inspires an excessive need to dominate and control his charges.

Punishment similarly seems to generate punishment within the stories, for Toto's enthusiastic impulse towards discipline generates the potential for additional discipline. He himself must be brought under control; in asserting his right to flay the boys, he has exceeded the boundaries of his position. The narrator interrogates Toto concerning Guido and Ercole's offense, referring to Toto as "Beast" and demanding to know what the boys could have possibly done to necessitate such a scene. When he refuses to confess, Don Friderico forces Toto to model for him, imbuing Don Friderico with the power to objectify the young man. The sadistic scene is further eroticised as Toto disrobes, "undulate[s] deliciously, and stiffen[s] into the pose" (Corvo 1901, 69). Watching him model so obediently, the narrator insists he now has his "lion in a leash" (69). However, as he sketches, he notes that Toto continues to tremble with anger and realises he "must chain this lion more securely" (71). He forces the boy to kneel at his feet and takes his throat between his hands, questioning him further while throttling him when he sees anger in his glance. Finally, "two emotions [course] processionally through [Toto's] eyes. First, penitent appeal. Second, veneration" (71). Order is restored. The passionate attentiveness to hierarchy and rank within the stories yields boundless opportunities for offense, reprimand, penance, and submission.

The pleasures associated with power and rigid hierarchy are a prominent preoccupation in Corvo's work, and his photographs often seem to echo the eroticised modeling scenario represented in "Why the Rose is Red." Corvo was a practitioner of "Arcadian" photography, in which young male models were photographed outdoors in the nude or in vaguely classical costume, often in Mediterranean settings.[3] He produced a large body of Arcadian photography, an accomplishment for which he was recognised in the art journals of the 1890s. "The Nude in Photography," an 1893 essay in *Studio*, for example, referred to him as "an amateur photographer, who brings artistic instinct into play, and knows the right moment to choose for representation" (108). Many of his most well-known photographs were taken after his expulsion from Scots College in Rome, where he had been a candidate for the priesthood. Following his departure from the college, he was taken up by the Duchess Carolina Sforza-Cesarini, who invited him to stay at her villa at Genzano and, according to Corvo, bestowed upon him the title "Baron."[4] It was during this time that Corvo encountered the Italian adolescents, Toto Ephoros and his six friends, upon which the Toto stories focus, and he painted and photographed the boys during this period as well. An album at Oxford contains the largest collection of Corvo's prints, and there is an additional collection of photographs in the Martyr Worthy Collection at Columbia University. The captions for these photographs indicate that at least one of the photographs pictures Toto himself, reclining, naked, with a sprig of leaves covering his genitals, and others feature his brother as well at Tito Biondi, another member of their circle.[5] The pictures highlight the power dynamic that so often underwrote the production of Arcadian photography, foregrounding the disempowerment of the boys by binding them or placing their hands behind them. The young models, subjected to the gaze of the older photographer and the presumably older audience for the photographs, are often in "presenting" poses, their arms behind their heads (Figure 8.1), or tied to a tree, evoking St. Sebastian (Figure 8.2).[6]

Figure 8.1 Frederick Rolfe, *Boy with Straw Hat*, 1890. Reproduced by permission of the Bodleian Libraries, University of Oxford. MS. Walpole c. 12, fol. 2.

Figure 8.2 Frederick Rolfe, *St. Sebastian*, 1890. Reproduced by permission of the Bodleian Libraries, University of Oxford. MS. Walpole c. 12, fol. 17.

In an 1891 letter to the Uranian poet Charles Kains-Jackson, Corvo asserted that he never made friends with the boys. He rather made them his "bondslaves": "Then I worship their beauty. When my knees get stiff or I am bored I kick them to Gehenna or Sheol. Then I go on sweet remembrance till I find another idol. But I am not a scrap sentimental about them *to* them (though I often said to Toto 'ah how lovely you are' and he replied 'Eccelenza, si.')" (Rolfe 1891). While the pictures often reference the Grecian spirit, they do not employ a pedagogic eros. The boys are not to be mentored. They are bondslaves and erotic objects to be enjoyed and discarded until the photographer can "find another idol."

The photographs might be more patently erotic in their investigation of the operations of power, but, as I have tried to emphasise, the Toto stories themselves dwell on bodies and pleasure in an only slightly more subtle way. There is a bit more "undulating deliciously" in the later stories, but even those published in the *Yellow Book*, in the months immediately following the Wilde trials, dare to discuss Toto's "broad brown chest and supple arms" and his "lithe young figure, tense and strung up" (Corvo 1896, 95, 93). In "About the Lilies of San Luigi," which was published in the October 1895 issue of the *Yellow Book*, Toto describes Saint Sebastian (who had at this time already become a key figure in gay iconography and whose name Wilde would take during his expatriated years following his release from prison) in the following terms: "He was so beautiful and muscular, and straight and strong, and his flesh so white and fine, and his hair like shining gold, that no one had ever thought of him as being naked" (Corvo 1895, 216).[7] Much is made in this story of Sebastian's shamelessness and the embarrassment his nakedness causes to the pious Saint Luigi, who implores Sebastian to don a surplice. Sebastian and his beloved friend Saint Pancras tease Luigi, tossing the surplice between them and gazing at Luigi with "merry laughing eyes" (217). These are, as Frederick Roden has described them, tales of "naked boy-saints frolicking in paradise" (Roden 2002, 248). They invite readers to consider male bodies and masculine beauty in unmistakable terms during a period when such statements might be regarded with great suspicion and, even more strikingly, in the pages of a periodical in the process of retreating from the front lines of the war on sexual and gender ideologies.

It has become a critical commonplace to note the shift in tone and editorial practices at the *Yellow Book* in 1895. As Linda K. Hughes argues the periodical has often been "approached in terms of a historical divide: B.T. and A.T., before and after the trials of Oscar Wilde" (Hughes 2004, 849).[8] Following the announcement of Wilde's arrest, in what Sally Ledger has described as a "moral rearguard action," John Lane fired Aubrey Beardsley, who had illustrated Wilde's *Salome* (Ledger 2007, 6).[9] According to E. F. Benson, after Beardsley's dismissal, the *Yellow Book* "turned grey overnight" (qtd. in Fraser 1974, 13). A contemporary reviewer said that the April 1895 issue that followed Beardsley's dismissal was "so proper that it might, without seeming impropriety, be taken up the river in a boat and read, yellow and unashamed, beneath some overhanging willow, or on some riverside lawn" (qtd. in Ledger 2007, 21). Margaret Stetz and Mark Samuels Lasner have recently worked to complicate the notion that the periodical became entirely "colorless" after Beardsley's dismissal. New opportunities for women artists and illustrators opened up at the *Yellow Book* once Beardsley was no longer the art editor, and New Woman writers continued to publish in the magazine following the Wilde controversy. In addition, Stetz and Lasner assert that the periodical did not "[succumb] wholly to censorship and caution after Wilde's arrest."[10] Nevertheless, though accounts of a complete and utter overnight transformation of the *Yellow Book* might have been exaggerated, the public humiliation of Wilde did have an impact on the periodical. As Linda K. Hughes has argued, the representation of masculinity in the issues published after the trials seemed somewhat anxious and reactionary: "In response to the link between sodomy and yellow books, decadence and degeneration, which press coverage of Wilde's arrest had established, male contributors to volume 5 erupted in a frenzy of hyper-masculine verse" (Hughes 2004, 856). Sexual controversy might not have disappeared entirely from the pages of the *Yellow Book* after the trials, but a new sense of danger did accompany the representation of desire between men during this period.

Despite the odds, Corvo's Toto stories remained exempt from the "moral rearguard action" that occurred in the months and years following the trials. The stories appeared in pairs in the October 1895, April 1896, and October 1896 issues, and the public greeted them with warmth. *The Literary World* referred to those published in April 1896 as the "most arresting pages" in the volume ("The Quarterlies" 1896, 487). Henry Harland, the *Yellow Book's* literary editor, in an editorial written under the pseudonym "The Yellow Dwarf," encouraged the magazine to "cultivate that admirable Baron Corvo whose contributions to your seventh volume no pressman noticed and no reader skipped" (Harland 1896, 21–2). The collection that appeared in 1898 also attracted favourable press attention that represented the stories as pleasing, sweet, and quite tame. In an 1899 review, the *Literary World* stated that "the stories suggest admirably the Italian temperament and atmosphere, and are told so artistically that Toto's familiar use of sacred persons amuses without shocking" ("Current Fiction" 1899, 187). An earlier review in the same periodical noted, "The stories differ in length, but not in merit. They are simple, direct, and utterly satisfying" ("Stories Toto Told Me" 1898, 177). The review in the *Freethinker* does the most to acknowledge the spirit of the stories, referring to them as "sly," "quaint burlesque," and "daintily blasphemous": "as satirical as Heine, as profane as Voltaire, and as modern as Catulle Mendes." However, while the impish quality of the tales is highlighted, they are not deemed truly troublesome or offensive: "There is a laugh on every page, and a smile in every line" ("Book Chat" 1898, 652).

The critical response to the 1901 collection is even more striking, for, while published six years after the trials, the stories in the later book go much further in terms of courting controversy. This content was by no means invisible to Corvo's contemporaries. Henry Harland, who had so enjoyed the earlier stories, declined to be the dedicatee of the new collection because the stories had a "flavor" he did not like.[11] A letter from Corvo states that "H. Harland proclaimed my book in M.S. to be [pederastic]" (Benkovitz 1976, 12).[12] Kenneth Grahame wrote to Lane in a letter concerning the manuscript, carefully marked "confidential," that there was "a good deal of *boy* in it—passion of boy. Lithe limbs of boy, subtle curves of boy, tawny skin of boy + so on." Grahame nevertheless advised Lane to publish the work as his "line has always been to discover + deal with the individual note" (qtd. in Guager and Jacques 2009, 176). This "passion of boy," however, went largely unnoted in published reviews of the collection. The reviewer for the *Academy* saw in the stories a reflection of the fact that the Italian peasant "is the most delightful folklorist in the world":

> Nothing could be more charming than the folklore that emerges after so many centuries of Christianity, not stifled but transmuted, in which, as on the canvases of the primitive Tuscans, the buoyant figures of smart angels, gay little virgins, pugnacious boy martyrs ... sport and make merry among the fadeless flowers under the benign gaze of the Padre Eterno and the Signor Cristo. ("In His Own Image" 1901, 533)

The reviewer does note that the storyteller has retained "all that was graceful and picturesque and pure in the paganism from which he is the most genuine of converts," which can be understood as an encoded allusion to the pleasure that is taken in male bodies within the stories ("In His Own Image" 1901, 533). Similarly, the *Star* notes that the collection "has flashes of tender poetry, and there is in it a rollicking hilarious wistfulness which is curiously new and strange," highlighting the presence of something eccentric in the book ("Advertisement for John Lane" 1901, 274). However, the Toto stories were spared the critical outrage that greeted, for example, the first issue of the *Yellow Book* or the courtroom analysis undergone by *The Picture of Dorian Gray*.

Perhaps it was the prominent display of what Gagnier refers to as "the marks of the most conservative Englishness" that spared the Toto stories from the persecution visited on Wilde's works (Gagnier 2000, 151). As Ruth Livesey's study of socialism has demonstrated, forms of sexual and economic/political dissidence were frequently intertwined at the *fin de siècle* (Livesey 2007). Utopian thinkers such as Edward Carpenter linked the socialist reimagining of economic life with a rethinking of private and sexual relationships. The Wilde trials revealed an escalating anxiety about this twinned contestation of class and gender ideologies at the turn of the century. While same-sex desire was certainly the issue on trial at the Bailey, the question of class difference also played a prominent role in the proceedings. As Randolph Trumbach notes, though the young men Wilde visited were significantly younger than him, during the trials, "the differences in age were not treated as any more startling than those in class" (Trumbach 1999, 105). Edward Carson, the defence counsel for the Marquess of Queensberry, consistently highlighted the class position of the young men. In discussing Alfred Wood, for example, Carson demanded to know whether it occurred to Wilde "as being a strange thing to take a man of his position and give him supper and then give him money?" (Holland 2004, 119). When inquiring about Edward Shelley, who was employed by Elkin Mathews and John Lane, Carson referred to Shelley as "a youth of his class" and an "office boy" (136–37). Carson responded to the news that Wilde had given Alfonso Conway a walking stick by exclaiming, "For a newspaper boy. Just look at that!" (148). Wilde fanned the flames of Carson's outrage by insisting that class categories meant nothing to him. He contested Carson's insistent derision of Shelley's clerk position at the offices of Lane and Mathews, asserting that "to be connected in any capacity with a bookseller's shop is a high privilege" (127). Carson demanded to know if the conversation of Conway was "literary," and Wilde replied that it was "quite simple and easy to be understood." When Carson pressed, "He was an uneducated lad, wasn't he?" Wilde replied that he was not cultivated. When laughter erupted, Wilde reprimanded, "Don't sneer at that. He was a pleasant, nice creature" (145). Finally, during one of the most well-known moments in the trial, while questioning Wilde about his relationship with Charles Parker, Carson demanded to know, "What was there in common between you and this young man of this class?" to which Wilde replied, "I recognise no social distinctions at all of any kind and to me youth—the mere fact of youth—is so wonderful that I would sooner talk to a young man half-an-hour than even be, well, cross-examined in court" (175).

Helena Michie and Morris B. Kaplan have suggested that the horror expressed concerning the class difference between Wilde and the young men reflected concerns about the exploitation of working-class men by decadent gentlemen. Michie notes that "newspaper reports of the trial often relied on an idiom of protection, through which Wilde was presented as failing in his duties as member of the upper class" (Michie 1999, 418). However, while the public might have been concerned about the innocence of these young men, the fact that Wilde found these young men interesting at all, the fact that he insisted that he "recognised no social distinctions of any kind," must have been all the more troubling. At a moment when socialist discourse and discourses concerning same-sex desire were intersecting in ever more radical ways, Wilde's insistence that love between men could make class hierarchy irrelevant would have sounded increasingly familiar and disturbing. As Colin Cruise notes, at the *fin de siècle*, "male-male relationships in all their variety—social, sexual, moral, theological—were to take on a millenarian, revolutionary note: they would *change* things" (Cruise 2004, 144). In his famous speech concerning the "love that dare not speak its name," Wilde stressed the pedagogic eros that can exist between an older and a younger man, the extent to which love between men of different ages might follow a democratic and educational model and foster mentoring and growth. In these assertions Wilde drew on a larger late-Victorian discourse concerning democratic friendship and its potential to initiate radical changes within the larger culture. John Addington Symonds, for example, wrote approvingly of Walt Whitman's ideal of amatory friendship, a mode of "Democracy" that might "extend 'that fervid comradeship,' and by its means to counterbalance and to spiritualise what is vulgar and materialistic in the modern world."[13] Edward Carpenter, who also derived much inspiration from Whitman, promoted an idea of comradeship that could overcome social barriers by cultivating connections between middle-class men and working-class youths. As Timothy D'Arch Smith notes, Carpenter's *Towards Democracy* is inspired by his "passion for the youthful worker and his admiration for the unsophisticated mind and handsome body of the underprivileged but 'natural' young man, untrammelled with the social conventions and artificial behaviourism imposed by education" (Smith 1970, 22). He celebrates connections with, and desire for, the worker, praising "the love of men for each other—so tender, heroic, constant" that it "overleap[s] barriers of age, of rank, of distance" and operates as the "flag of the camp of freedom" (23).

Corvo, on the other hand, expressed explicit distaste for Carpenter's ideals. After reading *Towards Democracy*, he wrote to Richard Dawkins that, although he found "some perfectly sumptuous verses" in the poem, its doctrine was "damnissimable" (qtd. in Benkovitz 1977, 228). In his semi-autobiographical *The Desire and Pursuit of the Whole* (1934), Corvo describes his "counterblast" to the poem:

> Crabbe had written, on the tablets of his mind, as something to be done on a fitting occasion, a big book of verses as a counterblast, magnificent hexameters, bright iambics, melodious hendecasyllabics—a whole new duty of man, from the gardener's boy and the scullery-maid, and the chauffeur and the typist, and the shopman and the factory-girl, and the man and the woman up to the King and the Pope, in their progress *Towards Aristocracy* on the road which leads to The Best.
>
> (Rolfe 1934, 238)

He often railed against the escalating democratic spirit of the day, espousing a harshly conservative vision that celebrated the rigid preservation of class hierarchy. In a 1907 letter to a collaborator, Harry Pirie-Gordon, Corvo wrote:

> It's a matter of principle with ME not to yield a single inch to dirty Demos, not to have any sort of truck with the beast excepting when I have him on a chain. And I affirm that concession is wicked and shameful, and all attempts to improve him by equality fatuous and futile. Drive your beast, lash him well, and make him go your way if you can: but don't attempt to run in harness with him, unless you want him to swallow you down his miry throat.
>
> (qtd. in Benkovitz 1977, 228)

His contempt for the pedagogic eros, for the idea that one might improve and educate an inferior, runs counter to every element of Carpenter's thinking. He performs in his letters and his novels a rigidly unsympathetic and conservative persona. He insists he feels nothing for the suffering of the poor and rejects entirely the concept of equality.

Corvo, however, spent the majority of his life in dire economic circumstances. Much of his most frequently discussed privations occurred during the final years of his life in Venice (1908–13), when he slept aboard a boat and was attacked by rats and crabs as he struggled to continue writing. However, he was also often troubled, deprived, and in need of charity during the 1890s, the period when the Toto stories, which espouse such rigidly conservative ideas about class and hierarchy, were composed and published. Following his expulsion from Scots College, Corvo was homeless and penniless until the Duchess of Sforza-Cesarini arrived in Rome to offer him refuge. When he returned to England in 1890, his finances again took a turn for the worse. He was often without lodgings and forced to borrow money from numerous acquaintances. In an 1893 letter to Wilfred Meynell, he described himself as "a shabby, badly dressed person with a wan face haggard with the worry of 7 years torment and insufficient food" (qtd. in Benkovitz 1977, 65). During the winter of 1894–5, he wore unchanged light summer clothes, he often had no place to sleep, and he was forced to eat food from the gutter (Benkovitz 1976, 73). Ella D'Arcy, who encountered Corvo at receptions for the *Yellow Book* hosted at Henry Harland's home, insisted that he must have slept in doss houses or on the embankment and stated that he left "singularly lively traces of his presence in Harland's armchairs" (Benkovitz 1976, 108; 113). After leaving London, he lived in "humble poverty" in Holywell, and he wrote from Holywell to John Lane in London that all he desired was "to be picked out of this hole where I am buried, and to be given a chance to use myself" (Benkovitz 1976, 91). In 1898, he was forced to stay in the workhouse in Holywell, Wales.

Corvo's poverty is central to the mythology that has surrounded the author and his work since his death. Early biographical treatments of Corvo by Shane Leslie and A. J. A. Symons emphasise that he frequently starved, that he was often miserable and always frustrated. In his *Quest for Corvo* (1934), the first major biography of the author, Symons cites an 1898 article from the *Aberdeen Free Press* that describes Corvo's humiliating eviction from his lodgings in his pyjamas. He stresses how frequently Corvo was forced to draw on the charity of others, how often he was "penniless" and "friendless" (Symons 1934, 106). However, these early biographical treatments rarely note the dissonance between Corvo's avowed elitism and his actual circumstances. In a review of *The Quest for Corvo*, Shane Leslie refers to Corvo as "the most aristocratic of English writers," reproducing Corvo's cantankerous claims about his own exceptional status (Leslie 1934, 94). Again and again, early "Corvines" highlight Corvo's avowals of nobility without investigating the incongruity between his harsh and reactionary ideas about inequality and the direness of his financial situation. Regenia Gagnier's treatment of Corvo contributes to this critical tradition. She notes that Corvo was "for long periods homeless" and wrote "the suffering of those who sleep on the streets; who watch helplessly the disintegration of their clothes" (Gagnier 2000, 154). These facts do not, however, lead to a reassessment of Corvo's strange "love of hierarchy" (151). It is simply noted that he often relied on the money of others to "maintain rank": "His *aristos* was heavily subsidized" (154). The strangeness of his persisting enthusiasm for hierarchy at a moment when his privations were growing more severe is disregarded.

Corvo's espousals of fanatically conservative ideals are often so excessive that they seem to border on the ridiculous, and I would like to consider the possibility that there is something more at play here than rigid conservatism. It might be useful to read the fetishisation of obedience and rank in the Toto stories as a manifestation of camp aesthetics. I would not be the first to suggest that Corvo's work may be categorised as camp. Philip Core, for example, describes him as "nineteenth-century camp at its churchiest and most hysterical." This reading of Corvo does not, however, do much to decipher the political implications of Corvo's camp aesthetics. His "bogus title" is listed as one of the central elements of his particularly *fin-de-siècle* brand of camp, which at least begins to gesture toward the role of performative superiority in Corvo's strange parody of hierarchy and subordination (Core 1984, 162).

Nevertheless, the possibility that the shrill enactment of oppressive scenarios in his fiction might be at once humorous and politicised is not entertained. I would like to suggest that the complex class politics of the Toto stories can only come to light when read through a camp framework. Read in any other way, the stories can only confirm Gagnier's categorisation of Corvo as representative of the most conservative Englishness and the worst sort of elitist decadence. Read as camp, the stories emerge as thoughtful and playful responses to the experience of hardship, oppression, and invisibility.

The Toto stories implement camp in a peculiarly funny and poignant interrogation of the operations of power in a culture marked by injustice and inequality. As many critics have suggested, camp aesthetics are particularly useful in theorising pain and power. Jack Babuscio suggests in his discussion of "Camp and the Gay Sensibility" that themes such as "the interdependence of sex and power, love and suffering, pleasure and pain; ... the value of the pose as an escape and protective shield; [and] the inevitability of inequities within relationships so long as love, ego, or insights are distributed in unequal proportions ... carry a special resonance for the gay sensibility" (Babuscio 1993, 30). The Toto stories dwell on this very set of thematic concerns. While the narrator represents himself as sadistic and in possession of complete authority, the stories' intense preoccupation with control and domination signal anxiety about humiliation and abjection as opposed to authentic authority. Rather than capitulating to the pain of acknowledging his humble position, Corvo chooses in these stories to occupy a pose, to perform complete control and superiority, in order to insulate himself from the trauma of his troubled circumstances. This camp posturing of exaggerated superiority is so extreme that it reads like a parody of the concept of rank. Camp enactments of social roles highlight the arbitrariness and constructedness of those social roles. As Susan Sontag asserts in "Notes on Camp" (1964), "Camp sees everything in quotation marks. It's not a lamp, but a 'lamp'; not a woman, but a 'woman.' To perceive Camp in objects and persons is to understand Being-as-Playing-a-Role. It is the farthest extension, in sensibility, of the metaphor of life as theater" (Sontag 1982, 109). Corvo's fantasies of power and control, of being waited on hand and foot by entirely obedient boys, highlight Being-as-Playing-a-Role and speak to the arbitrariness of social hierarchies. These are impersonations, class drag: the enactment of a fantasy inversion of existing structures.

Victorian works of flagellation literature are, as Steven Marcus asserts, frequently preoccupied with fantasies that involve acting, role playing, or impersonation. However, as Marcus notes, the majority of flagellation literature in the nineteenth century addresses itself to upper-class men who attended

public school, and "for this literature perversity and social privilege are inseparable markers of distinction" (Marcus 1964, 253). These works often invite
the reader to identify with the boy being flogged, allowing an empowered
readership to engage in a fantasy of disempowerment. Corvo seems to have
inverted this characteristic of the genre, crafting works that facilitate fantasies
concerning power, authority, and control designed to appeal to a readership
for whom such fantasies would provide a welcome escape.

The Toto stories may also be understood as an exaggerated performance
of existing inequalities that highlight the folly of those injustices. As Scott
Long argues, certain varieties of camp imitate "the oppressive mechanism
only to expose it by forcing it to its extremes: the tragedy grows so grotesquely great that only madness can persist in the attempt to domesticate
it." The scenes of exaggerated inequality in the Toto stories force the reader
to consider questions of rank and hierarchy, to question the validity of any
situation in which one individual is empowered while another is entirely
abject. Long asserts that the reverence for and devotion to absurd scenarios
in camp operates as acts of "mockery and defiance against the configurations of power that control the labels and signs of absurdity" (Long 1993,
79). If the celebration of rank and punishment in the Toto stories appears
excessive or absurd, the representation of the characters' acceptance of such
a system raises questions concerning the logic of the hierarchies that underwrite any class system.

The fact that Corvo's early biographers along with recent critics such as
Gagnier have read his work as elitist or marked by an aristocratic aesthetics,
however, would imply that the stories are not advertising themselves clearly
as camp. According to Long's definition, the camp moment exists within the
spectator. Camp is, in his eyes, a dialectical process. The opposition between
the absurd and the serious must first be established:

> Then [the camp process] gestures toward a point—a moment of con-
> sciousness, a shock, a synthesis—from which that opposition can be
> seen as absurd in turn, based on a higher and more encompassing
> sense of absurdity, since it includes far more in its sway: it separates
> the beholder in a vertiginous moment from a whole encrusted body of
> cultural dictates and values.
>
> (Long 1993, 79)

In Long's vision, the response this shock or synthesis elicits from the audience is the moment when camp comes into existence. If turn-of-the-century
readers and twentieth-century critics all refused to undergo the transformation of consciousness the stories might have initiated, then, according to
this formulation, the camp of the Toto stories is incomplete. The concept of
inequality survived Corvo's camp critique intact, which allowed the stories
to be read as inoffensive and conservative by late nineteenth and early twentieth-century readers and offensively conservative by recent critics.

I am reluctant, however, to cast the stories as failed camp. With the proper critical apparatus in play, with sufficient knowledge of Corvo's larger body of work and the circumstances under which the stories were composed, the camp process described by Long can be completed. However, the critical conversation surrounding Corvo has worked to inhibit this process. His works were initially enshrined and celebrated by a group of men, such as A. J. A. Symons and Shane Leslie, who chose to highlight Corvo's elitism, to take it seriously, and to disregard the manner in which his circumstances might have inflected his approach to questions of inequality and oppression. These early critical moves have had a lasting effect on the understanding of Corvo's work in the twentieth and twenty-first centuries, which has in turn limited the opportunities for reassessments of his work. Corvo is often dismissed and disregarded because of his political reputation. He does not seem to present the pleasing opportunities for recovery that many of his more radical or progressive *fin-de-siècle* peers offer. In addition, the complexity of his political positioning can only emerge when individual works are understood as part of a larger argument that occurs across his oeuvre, that includes his correspondence and the critical responses of his peers. I would like to suggest, however, that reading Corvo's works in camp terms alongside the works of what Gagnier describes as the "genuinely democratic and progressive writers" of his era allows for a richer picture of the *fin de siècle* to emerge, one which acknowledges the complex web of conversations occurring around the topics of class and economics during this period (Gagnier 2000, 150). The most attractive or pleasing parts of that conversation might occur in works such as *Towards Democracy* or "The Soul of Man Under Socialism." Texts like the Toto stories, on the other hand, reveal the poignant operations of a defiant subjectivity endeavoring to establish his own value as an individual within a culture that has argued in material terms that he has none. Corvo does not turn, as Carpenter or Morris did, in the direction of cooperation and comradeship. He turns instead to camp and the opportunities the camp aesthetic provides for performing and questioning power and hierarchy.

Notes

1. This work has never been found, but it is referred to in Rolfe's semi-autobiographical work, *The Desire and Pursuit of the Whole, a Romance of Modern Venice* (1934, 238). *The Desire and Pursuit of the Whole* was published posthumously.
2. Corvo's eroticised representation of flagellation should, of course, be understood in relationship to the genre of flagellation pornography that circulated in the nineteenth century. As Steven Marcus notes, there was a "vast literature of flagellation produced during the Victorian period." Much of this literature seemed to address itself to the higher gentry and nobility and assume "that its audience had the common experience of public school." Marcus also argues that this body of literature, in which boys are often beaten by "women on to whom masculine characteristics have been grafted or imposed" or in which "a little

boy is being beaten—that is loved—by another man," seems to at once express and disavow same-sex desire and "represents a kind of last-ditch compromise with and defense against homosexuality" (Marcus 1964, 252; 253; 260). Corvo seems to be simultaneously playing with the genre's association with class privilege and rendering its homoerotic subtext more explicit.

3. The most well-known turn-of-the-century Arcadian photographers were Guglielmo Plüschow and Wilhelm von Gloeden.
4. For further discussion of the Duchess Carolina Sforza-Cesarini, see Scoble 2009.
5. It should be noted, however, that the captions are not in Corvo's hand.
6. As David Rosenthal notes, "presenting" poses were more common in the female nudes of the period (Rosenthal 2008, 51).
7. For a discussion of Saint Sebastian as a *fin-de-siècle* homoerotic icon, see Kaye 1999.
8. Though Wilde had never published in the *Yellow Book*, when he was arrested, he was holding a copy of *Aphrodite* by Pierre Louÿs bound in a yellow cover. The headlines had simply announced "OSCAR WILDE ARRESTED: YELLOW BOOK UNDER HIS ARM," and the fictitious connection between the periodical and Wilde quickly became solidified in the public imagination (Sturgis 1998, 238). This had an immediate effect on the publication. The publisher John Lane claimed, "It killed *The Yellow Book*, and it nearly killed me" (qtd. in Ledger 2007, 5).
9. Lane had succumbed to pressure from Alice Meynell as well as William Watson, who telegraphed Lane that all Beardsley's designs must be excluded from the *Yellow Book* or he would sever his connections with the publisher.
10. As Stetz and Lasner note, contributions such as "P'tit Bleu" by Henry Harland, which appeared in the January 1896 issue, dealt with potentially controversial material, such as the eroticism of music-hall performances, while at the same time bowing partially to conventional morality by representing the reformation of a Latin Quarter dancer. As they argue, "'P'tit Bleu' embodied the sort of literary compromise that appeared to be necessary in the first year after Wilde's arrest, but a compromise that was by no means a surrender" (Stetz & Lasner 1994, 34; 36).
11. See Rolfe's discussion of these events in the semi-autobiographical *Nicholas Crabbe; or, the One and the Many, a Romance* (1958, 119).
12. In the original letter, which was written to Arthur Stedman, Rolfe used the Greek term for "pederastic.".
13. For further discussion, see Dellamora 2004, 24. Symonds himself celebrated the democratic potential of erotic connections with working men in works such as "In Venice" (1880) and "In the Key of Blue" (1893). Howard J. Booth argues that, in his Venice writings, Symonds "explored how the reciprocated look—usually driven by desire for other men—could help effect connections between … different classes" (Booth 2013, 171).

Works Cited

"Advertisement for John Lane, Publisher, London and New York." 1901. *The Academy*, no. 60, 274.

Babuscio, Jack. 1993. "Camp and the Gay Sensibility." In *Camp Grounds: Style and Homosexuality*, edited by David Bergman, 19–38. Amherst, MA: University of Massachusetts Press.

Benkovitz, Miriam J. 1976. "Arthur Stedman and Frederick Rolfe, Baron Corvo," *Columbia Library Columns* 25 (2): 3–17.

Benkovitz, Miriam J. 1977. *Frederick Rolfe, Baron Corvo: A Biography*. London: Hamilton.

"Book Chat." 1898. *Freethinker*, no. 18, 652–53.

Booth, Howard J. 2013. "John Addington Symonds, Venice and the Gaze." *English Studies* 94 (2): 171–87.

Core, Philip. 1984. *Camp: The Lie That Tells the Truth*. New York: Delilah.

Baron Corvo [Frederick Rolfe]. 1896. "About Beata Beatrice and the Mamma of San Pietro." *The Yellow Book*, no. 9, 93–101.

Baron Corvo [Frederick Rolfe]. 1895. "About the Lilies of San Luigi." *The Yellow Book* 7: 214–224.

Baron Corvo [Frederick Rolfe]. 1901. *In His Own Image*. London: John Lane, The Bodley Head.

Cruise, Colin. 2004. "Baron Corvo and the Key to the Underworld." In *The Victorian Supernatural*, edited by Carolyn Burdett, Nicola Bown, and Pamela Thurschwell, 128–48. New York: Cambridge UP.

"Current Fiction: Stories Toto Told Me." 1899. *The Literary World* 30: 187.

Dellamora, Richard. 2004. *Friendship's Bonds: Democracy and the Novel in Victorian England*. Philadelphia: University of Pennsylvania Press.

Fraser, Harrison, ed. 1974. *The Yellow Book: An Illustrated Quarterly: An Anthology*. New York: St. Martin's Press.

Gagnier, Regenia. 2000. *The Insatiability of Human Wants: Economics and Aesthetics in Market Society*. Chicago: University of Chicago Press.

Guager, Annie and Brian Jacques, eds. 2009. *The Annotated Wind in the Willows*. New York: Norton.

Harland, Henry [The Yellow Dwarf]. 1896. "A Birthday Letter." *The Yellow Book*, no. 9, 11–22.

Holland, Merlin. ed. 2004. *The Real Trial of Oscar Wilde*. New York: Harper Perennial.

Hughes, Linda K. 2004. "Women Poets and Contested Spaces in 'The Yellow Book'." *Studies in English Literature 1500–1900* 44 (4): 849–72.

"In His Own Image By Frederick Baron Corvo." 1901. *The Academy* 60: 533–534.

Kaye, Richard. 1999. "'A Splendid Readiness for Death': T. S. Eliot, the Homosexual Cult of St. Sebastian, and World War I." *Modernism/Modernity* 6 (2): 107–34.

Ledger, Sally. 2007. "Wilde Women and *The Yellow Book*: The Sexual Politics of Aestheticism and Decadence." *English Literature in Transition, 1880–1920* 50 (1): 5–26.

Leslie, Shane. 1934. "Tracking Down a Literary Mystery." *Saturday Review of Literature* 11 (8): 89, 94.

Livesey, Ruth. 2007. *Socialism, Sex, and the Culture of Aestheticism in Britain, 1880–1914*. Oxford: OUP.

Long, Scott. 1993. "The Loneliness of Camp." In *Camp Grounds: Style and Homosexuality*, edited by David Bergman, 78–91. Amherst, MA: University of Massachusetts Press.

Michie, Helena. 1999. "Under Victorian Skins: The Bodies Beneath." In *A Companion to Victorian Literature & Culture*, edited by Herbert Tucker, 407–24. Malden, MA: Blackwell.

Newton, Esther. 1993. "Role Models." In *Camp Grounds: Style and Homosexuality*, edited by David Bergman, 39–53. Amherst, MA: University of Massachusetts Press.

Roden, Frederick. 2002. *Same-Sex Desire in Victorian Religious Culture*. New York: Palgrave Macmillan.

Rolfe, Frederick. 1958. *Nicholas Crabbe; or, the One and the Many, a Romance*. London: Chatto & Windus.

Rolfe, Frederick. 1891. Rolfe to Charles Kains Jackson, 8 December 1891. Quoted in Benkovitz, 1977, 48.

Rolfe, Frederick. 1934. *The Desire and Pursuit of the Whole, a Romance of Modern Venice*. London: Cassell and Company.

Rosenthal, Donald. 2008. *The Photographs of Frederick Rolfe*. Hanover, NH: Elysium Press.

Scoble, Robert. 2009. *A Duchess and Her Past*. Portsmouth: Callum James Books.

Smith, Timothy D'Arch. 1970. *Love in Earnest: Some Notes on the Lives and Writings of English Uranian Poets From 1889 to 1930*. London: Routledge & K. Paul.

Sontag, Susan. 1982. "Notes on Camp." In *A Sontag Reader*, 105–119. New York: Farrar, Straus, Giroux.

Stetz, Margaret, and Mark Samuels Lasner. 1994. *The Yellow Book: A Centenary Exhibition*. Cambridge: Houghton Library.

"Stories Toto Told Me." 1898. *Literary World*: 377.

Sturgis, Matthew. 1998. *Aubrey Beardsley: A Biography*. Woodstock: Overlook Press.

Symons, A. J. A. 1934. *The Quest for Corvo: An Experiment in Biography*. New York: Macmillan.

"The Nude in Photography: With Some Studies Taken in the Open Air." 1893. *The Studio*, no. 1, 104–08.

"The Quarterlies: The Yellow Book." 1896. *The Literary World*, no. 27, 487.

Trumbach, Randolph. 1999. "London." In *Queer Sites: Gay Urban Histories Since 1600*, edited by David Higgs, 89–111. New York: Routledge.

Weeks, Donald, ed. 1978. *Two Friends: Frederick Rolfe and Henry Harland*. Edinburgh: Tragara Press.

9 "Our brains struck fire each from each"

Disidentification, Difference, and Desire in the Collaborative Aesthetics of Michael Field

Jill R. Ehnenn

This chapter explores the Michael Field collaboration as a partnership that appropriates and queers heteronormative conventions in order to negotiate late-Victorian paradigms of gender and sexuality, authorship and subjectivity, and aestheticism and decadence. In Katharine Bradley and Edith Cooper's private and published texts, we see two lovers and aesthetes who celebrate womanhood in their verse yet often prefer the company of men and who express concerns about their daily life, their future as poets, and the future of poetry, itself. We hear them articulate forceful opinions about the aesthetic and decadent movements with which they were associated—such as deploring the *Yellow Book* while admiring Baudelaire and Verlaine. And we observe their interactions with aesthetes like Oscar Wilde, Bernard Berenson and notably, the artist-couple Charles Ricketts and Charles Shannon, who helped them design their books, jewels and home so that all aspects of their life would follow Pater's dicta "to burn always with that hard gemlike flame" as they pursued "poetic passion, the desire for beauty, the love of art for its own sake" (Pater 1986, 219–20). What interests me most regarding these texts are Michael Field's representations of desire, especially within the framework of difference.

As the earliest literary historians and critics who "recovered" Michael Field's work have noted, the coauthors' published and private writings employ a rhetoric of sameness, merging and marriage. More recent studies, however, draw upon their original diaries and letters in addition to the bowdlerised extracts used by the earlier critics.[1] Thus the growing body of scholarship on "the Michaels" has moved beyond initial portraits of their relationship as one of shared subjectivity and "perfect absolute equality" (Faderman 1981, 213).[2] In what follows, I build upon this recent work, examining some of Michael Field's lesser-studied verse alongside their extensive collaborative journals. As I read both literary and autobiographical texts as textual performances with queer implications for theorising nineteenth-century representations of joint authorship and same-sex love, I will complicate previous observations about the "woman-identified" qualities of sameness and romantic friendship so frequently associated with Michael Field. Then, I will elucidate the important role of more sexually dissident concepts such as bisexual, non-monogamous desire within a long-term same-sex relationship, intergenerational erotics, role play, and cross-gender identification. As I will demonstrate, it is precisely in and through the complexities of their relationship to each other, to authorship, and to art, that Michael Field's partnership and writing manifest many of the contradictions now associated with aestheticism.

My arguments follow the work of David Halperin, who describes queer as a site of becoming, as well as the theories of Alexander Doty, for whom queer is a verb, an anti-heteronormative way of seeing and being in the world.[3] As I will show, recognising how Bradley and Cooper's textual performances anticipate what today we call queerness permits a richer understanding of how this late-Victorian couple found ways to navigate—within their cultural and historical context—the relationship between subjectivity and sexuality, as well as the effects of subjectivity and sexuality upon partnership and authorship. Additionally, such an analysis attempts to circumvent some of the problems inherent in terms like "romantic friendship," which has been critiqued by Chris White and Martha Vicinus, among others, as disavowing the sexual aspects of same-sex relationships. My frame avoids ahistorical usage of the term "lesbian," and the related connotation of an identity politics which their journals suggest would be inaccurate. Thus, when I refer to the Michael Field texts (including their name-as-text) as queer, I invoke a strategic and shifting way of seeing and being in the world that breaks up identity categories and the foundational assumptions of the sex/gender system that keeps those categories in place.

To that end, I employ Jose Esteban Muñoz's concept of queer disidentification as a useful lens that helps us understand how sameness and difference function for Michael Field, creating a space for an ongoing self-fashioning of subjectivity and sexuality that helps the coauthors navigate and nurture their long-term personal and professional partnership. As we will see, the relationship between Bradley and Cooper, especially the expression of that relationship on the page, becomes a contradictory field upon which aestheticism's use of femininity becomes, as Kathy Alexis Psomiades puts it, the driving force "to manage the contradiction between artistic autonomy on the one hand and art's necessary commodification on the other" (1997, 33). Notably, the differences and tensions expressed in Field's writing are also the embodiment of culturally dissident desires, rather than of "woman-identified" qualities of romantic friendship admired by Victorians and cultural feminists alike. The coauthors thereby subvert what Gayle Rubin, in "Thinking Sex," identifies as a "hierarchical system of sexual value," which privileges monogamous, reproductive heterosexuality and demonises all other forms of desire (1993, 11). In this observation, my study is consonant with Yopie Prins's important analysis of *Long Ago* (1889), in which she examines Field's figures of doubling and interweaving and contends: "[t]hrough the Greek fragments of Sappho, Bradley and Cooper enter a space for the interplay between sexuality and textuality, allowing various sexualities to emerge and finding new ways to engender the lyric as a genre"

(1999b, 94). Here I seek to consider textual practice and strategy at various stages in Michael Field's career and their work in multiple genres, including, but also subsequent to, their foundational work in verse with Sappho.

As we study literature of the past, and perhaps redraw the map of the literary canon, we are accompanied by the critical apparatus and concerns of our own time, with all their biases. Early feminist critics observed fruitful parallels between Michael Field's rhetoric and cultural feminism. Now, however, it becomes impossible to ignore Michael Field's evocations of conflict and difference, usefully read through more recent theoretical insights. If we continue to privilege representations of "essential oneness" in Michael Field texts, or even if we conclude, "[a]s open as they were about their mutual love, they were as markedly discrete about possible inequalities or irritating difference dividing them" (Laird 1995, 120), we acknowledge only a portion of the interesting complexities within Michael Field's life and work. What follows, then, will address Bradley and Cooper's innovative collaborative aesthetics—how they refashioned themselves on and off the page through the performance of dissident desires and productive differences. I also suggest that once we complicate statements like "we are Michael Field," we must rethink the theoretical possibilities they portend, vis-à-vis studies of women's literary collaboration, queer theory, and *fin-de-siècle* aestheticism.[4]

1. Strategic Sameness

At first glance, *Works and Days*, Michael Field's remarkable shared diaries (1888–1914), *do* suggest much in the way of personal and professional merging. There, Bradley and Cooper (Michael and Henry) share information most partners might not. A poem or reflection in the hand of one of "the Michaels" does not guarantee that the scribe was the original author or thinker, and sometimes the handwriting is not easily attributable to one or the other. Manuscript sources also reveal Bradley's early fascination with Spinoza, who "with his fine grasp of unity says, 'If two individuals of exactly the same nature are joined together, they make up a single individual, doubly stronger than each alone,' i.e., Edith and I make a *veritable Michael*" (original emphasis. Field 1933, 16). Similarly, Cooper laments when Bradley visits a friend, "I am away from my own identity."[5] Such statements contribute to Michael Field's "tropes of likeness," which Ruth Vanita has shown follows Shakespearean models of love that feature a homoerotic economy of likeness in opposition to heterosexuality (102).

As in the following poem, which Bradley shared with Robert Browning in an 1886 letter, the poets often claim their bond and similarities reinforce one another and eventually their work becomes indistinguishable:

> By time set a space apart
> We are bound by such close ties
> None can tell of either breast

The native sigh
Who by
To learn with whom the Muse is guest
How sovereignly I'm blest
To see and smell the rose of my own youth
In thee, how pleasant lies
My life, at rest
From Dream, its Hope exprest
before mine eyes![6]

Here, this poem asserts that similarities counter age difference, as boundaries between work and rest, reality and dream, past and present are blurred in one sensation-filled moment of suspended youth. Bradley's musing on New Year's Eve, 1891: "[we] are knit up into one living soul,"[7] and the closing lines of *Underneath the Bough*'s (1893) famous poem "A Girl," have also encouraged literal interpretations of Michael Field's rhetoric of merging and likeness:

Such: and our souls so knit
I leave a page half writ-
The work begun
Will be to heaven's conception done
If she come to it.
                    (88, ll. 10–14)

These images should not, however, be interpreted too simplistically. Careful readers of *Works and Days* will recognise, as Virginia Blain argues:

They lived together, worked together, wrote together, holidayed together, slept together, were converted together, and almost died together, in what seems a perfect orgy of togetherness; yet they were never simply one person. In fact, they were two quite different people, with quite different poetic talents and impulses. (1996, 242)

In light of Cooper and Bradley's differences, which the next section will unpack in greater detail, Michael Field's "tropes of likeness" can be understood beyond the literal in two ways: the first, as conscious strategy against difficulties they faced as female, and collaborative, authors. Their concerns are clear in this 1890 letter to Vernon Lee:

It cannot be too frequently repeated that belief in the unity of M.F. is absolutely necessary. Alike for the advancement of his glory. And attaining of his favour. He is in literature one. Where the secret of this chance dualism is not known, the wise and kind preserve it. And every public reference to him should be masculine. But I need scarcely warn Vernon Lee on this point?

As I have previously argued, Bradley and Cooper here remind Lee, a fellow author, that she should understand the importance of keeping safe their singular, masculine *nom-de-plume* because the public presumes that literary authorship is the realm of male solitary genius (Ehnenn 2008, 33–4). They emphasise their point by employing Biblical rhetoric and intoning Trinitarian economies. Indeed, their urgent plea to Lee is justifiably prescient, considering Michael Field's loss of popularity after their female, dual identities were discovered. An 1896 diary entry bemoans:

> We ask why have we so many enemies? We make out that the nom-de-plume was a cause of enmity, the way it was kept, the way it became known, the way it was unacknowledged and acknowledged, "One lady in literature is unmanageable enough-but two!!"[8]

In *Women Coauthors*, which focuses on psychosocial interaction in order to "read coauthored texts as a study of relationships" and reconsiders theories of the "relation between power and desire in writing," Holly Laird analyses Michael Field's insistence on their unified, male persona and concludes "the Fields surrendered themselves to the very conventions that they seemed to defy" (1995, 5; 13; 117). Instead, I would like to suggest that, far from surrender, Michael Field performs strategies resembling queer disidentification, which José Esteban Muñoz defines as "the way that identity is enacted by minority subjects who must work with/resist the conditions of (im)possibility that dominant culture generates" (1999, 6). Muñoz's work also provides an alternative to arguments about essentialist vs. constructivist formations of identity, since disidentificatory strategies produce identity "at the point of contact between essential understandings of self ... and socially constructed narratives of self" (6). This is particularly useful for theorising Bradley and Cooper's self-representations, because their writing tends to embrace certain kinds of identity politics in ways that prefigure cultural feminism (such as their frequent elision of women and Nature and elevating "femininity" above "masculinity"); yet their texts simultaneously assert that other aspects of gendered and poetic identity are linked to arbitrary social norms. So, to apply Muñoz's ideas to the Vernon Lee letter quoted above, Michael Field's assertions about their authorial identity replicate that which excludes them but with a disidentificatory twist; they denaturalise the authorial model even as they inhabit it. The *belief* in their unity as Michael Field is necessary: "He," is "in literature," if not in reality, "one."

The second way we can understand Bradley and Cooper's metaphors of merging is to understand them as legitimising their same-sex relationship in a heteronormative world. As previous critics have noted, Michael Field, like many romantic female friends in the eighteenth and nineteenth centuries, often represent their relationship as a sacred union or marriage. For the coauthors, this is a useful way to celebrate their precious moments of privacy and passion and to envision their relationship as independent from the other members of their household. Bradley makes a characteristic diary entry in June 1893 while the rest of the household travels: "Father and Amy started for Scotland yesterday. Henry and I are living in the deepest conjugal bliss;" the following year Cooper similarly reflects upon a recent "weekend in Nature" near Stonehenge: "Life! but how we have lived—we such a grateful and renewed pair of lovers."[9]

These marriage metaphors, some with and some without a rhetorical insistence on unity, also endorse their same-sex partnership as collaborative authors. For example, Bradley, in an early letter, writes to Cooper about negative feedback:

> Sweet wife. The hardships of early married life are beginning. Let us bear them together bravely and growing the dearer to each other for the derision of the world. Then has nothing happened to us but what is common to all poets: let us rejoice to share of their bitter herbs of adversity."[10]

The rest of the letter makes suggestions about improving their writing. Thus, the model of marital problem-solving provides reassurance for both authorial and relational challenges. Bradley's often-quoted 1886 journal entry juxtaposing their partnership with the Brownings' functions similarly: "Oh! love. I give thanks for my Persian: these two poets, man and wife, wrote alone; each wrote, but did not bless or quicken one another with their work; *we are closer married*" (original emphasis. Field, 1933, 16).[11] This marital comparison elevates the love between Bradley and Cooper to almost mythic proportion, while also sanctifying, eroticising, and rendering it productive with the phrase "bless or quicken."[12] By adopting the label that sanctions compulsory reproductive heterosexuality, the "Poets and Lovers"-as-"Michael Field" legitimise their personal and professional relationship, its value, and its productivity. They accomplish this latter point especially, by appropriating society's belief in woman's innate desire to reproduce and nurture: "To be happy women must be serving by creation—slow, quiet, development of germs to organisms, They are more of the Earth than men are—They must be mothers in body or brain. Corn & grape! – The child or The Poem!"[13]

At first, Bradley and Cooper's appropriation of the marriage trope seems to reinforce many of the values and social benefits of heterosexual marriage, to function as a sweet and genuine expression of love, and thus to resemble other (accepted) romantic female friendships of their day. However, as their infamous 1892 response to Havelock Ellis's wedding indicates, they envision their "marriage" quite differently from the traditional institution, with which they find much fault: "This is a true account of the modern Sacrament of matrimony. It is revolting. 'Free love, free field' is sacreder."[14] It is instructive, in this context, to contemplate the logo Michael Field commissioned from Selwyn Image in the early 1890s: the thyrsus, interlaced with rings (Figure 9.1):

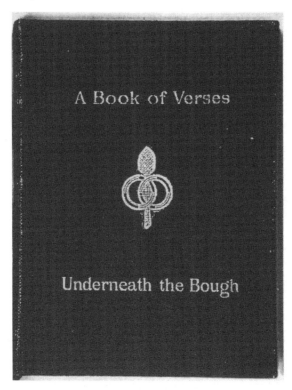

Figure 9.1 Thyrsus symbol from the cover of *Underneath the Bough*.

Functioning as shorthand for their personal and professional union, the symbol graced the cover of *Underneath the Bough* and interior pages of other Michael Field texts. It appeared on stationary, was used in initial correspondence with new acquaintances, and was stamped on their luggage. The logo combines eternally united wedding rings with the staff of Dionysus, symbolic of ecstatic abandon, sacred rites and fertility; it also is reminiscent of the ankh, the cross and the *chi rho*, with all their attendant evocations of resurrection. A telling reference to the image appears in 1896, when after a wonderful day outdoors with Cooper, Bradley finds the sign of the cross insufficient to express their worshipful, creative joy in each other and in Nature. She rhapsodises, "what better than our own sign – the inwoven rings and the thyrsus – in token of our worship and praise and bliss."[15] Thus, as the coauthors do elsewhere in words, Michael Field's visual proxy combines both Pagan and Christian tradition in a skillful disidentificatory appropriation that enables Bradley and Cooper to represent themselves precisely at the site where two powerful and potentially limiting narratives of femininity converge. Personified as Bacchic Maenads and bound in a sacred union, they are dangerous women creating through "the brain" if not through "the body," yet celebrating both.[16] Instead of allowing traditional narratives to compromise them, Bradley and Cooper's ringed thyrsus is a visual text that makes concrete what they most desire: eternal union as "Poets and lovers," in and through the name of Michael Field and the immortality of "his" poetry.

Michael Field's thyrsus, chosen with such deliberation, casts a judgmental shadow as Cooper reacts to Ellis's wedding:

> [The bride] stands like a willing victim, but a victim to the first Great Illusion. I feel as though I am assisting at some rite of an old world. The Illusion is strong as the Earth, but the worship paired to it must have new forms or new freedom if it is to be living as the power it celebrates. Then comes all the deformation of love by cake, champagne, stupid hopes, emphasis of the new condition. Ugh! But the cake is excellent.[17]

The next day, perhaps inspired by all that conventional marriage does *not* represent to them, they pledge themselves to one another in their own way. Cooper writes, "My love and I go to the Station that I may see her off to Dover. We swear with the bright world round us that we will remain Poets and Lovers whatever may happen to hinder or deflect our lives."[18] On the train Bradley penned their now most anthologised poem, "It was deep April," which was first published in the thyrsus-decorated *Underneath the Bough* (1893):

> It was deep April, and the morn
> Shakespere was born;
> The world was on us, pressing sore;
> My Love and I took hands and swore
>   Against the world to be
> Poets and lovers evermore,
> To laugh and dream on Lethe's shore
> To sing to Charon in his boat,
> Heartening the timid souls afloat;
> Of judgment never to take heed,
> But to those fast-locked souls to speed,
> Who never from Apollo fled
> Who spent no hour among the dead;
>   Continually
>   With them to dwell,
> Indifferent to heaven and hell.

In this context, this poem does not merely pledge female marriage, brave and impassioned and beautiful though that pledge may be. It is an innovative manifesto for survival that discloses a deep-seated and inseparable desire for both authorship and interpersonal communion yet an uncanny anticipation that they must be/become a Foucauldian author-*function*, "Michael Field," in order to fulfill their dreams: to live in worship of each other and of beauty in the "new forms and new freedoms" that are as "living as the power [marriage] celebrates."[19] And so "It was deep April" appeals to multiple sources for legitimacy: the national bard, Greek mythology, the institution of marriage.

"My Love and I" are placed in a creative space at mid-spring, but also a liminal one—between life and death, heaven and hell—aware that their resolve in their project and their alliance is as unyielding as the judgment they will undoubtedly face. Read as disidentification, what becomes most remarkable about this lyric is its re-signification of contradiction. It engages the speakers' mixed emotions and the world's ambivalent responses, thereby functioning like the thyrsus in the above example where Bradley chooses "our own sign" over the cross. In its mix of wistful nostalgia, passionate commitment ceremony, and artistic self-promotion, Michael Field sings of the desire to have what they want and be what they feel they are, despite the world's hostility, and yet be joyful. The voice is playful, yet determined—fully aware they are courting the dangers of earthly reprobation—yet more worried about the damnation of literary oblivion. Under the sign of the rings and the thyrsus, the vital authority rests within. It is no wedding license but rather documents a new rite: a joint performance of self-(re)creation.

2. Dissident Desires and Productive Differences

Michael Field's diary excerpts about Havelock Ellis's wedding indicate that they, like many New Women, considered marriage an inadequate expression of love because it excluded freedom. Yet their writing does not dispense with the institution, but modifies it. In contrast to traditional, heteropatriarchal models of marriage, Michael Field's textual representations of their relationship acknowledge and even celebrate each partner's various needs for freedom: differing opinions, interests, and desires which, over the years, are creatively and diversely accommodated.

The importance to Michael Field of an individual's freedom within a relationship is evident in a diary excerpt from 1892 where Cooper, with some guilt, reflects upon her beloved mother's death:

> [S]he did not understand my need of freedom. ... I suffered torments, struggles such as the hermits of the wilderness knew, under my [mother's] constriction. ...What a divine blessing it is to me I have my Love, who checks no self-expression, who brings beauty to my eyes and gladness to my life, who loves me and whom I love with strenuous force that is half-hidden by our caresses and humourous [sic] names and utter familiarity![20]

Notably, the extent to which Bradley and Cooper's relationship "checks no self-expression" includes an anti-heteronormative freedom to be honest about and explore attractions to other people. The diary does depict moments of jealousy, as when Cooper notes in 1894: "Lion [Lucy Fitzpatrick Phillimore] has a passion for my Love-she is rude and ignoring to me and takes caresses of my Love with a liberty that exasperates me."[21] Mostly though, representations of love between Bradley and Cooper accommodate the attentions of, and feelings for others, such as cousin Francis Brooks's ongoing infatuation for Bradley, Cooper's passion for art critic Bernard Berenson throughout the 1890s, and Bradley's lusty sharing of a fantasy with Cooper in 1887, when she remarked: "[t]ruly love, I would fain put the clock back thirty years and be loved by Robert Browning in his glorious manhood" (Donoghue 1998, 44). Bradley and Cooper spoke extensively about the latter's relationship with Berenson and wrote poems and soul-wrenching journal entries during these years, attended his lectures, entertained him at their home, and toured the Continent with him. In fact, during one visit with Berenson and his companion Mary Costelloe in Paris, when both Bradley and Cooper were miserable over Berenson's alternating attentions and cutting remarks, Bradley offered money to the penurious critic to give them art lessons, knowing it would make Cooper happy.[22]

In their journals, Bradley and Cooper often represent their attractions to other men and women as experiences to be had, and valued by the individual, then brought to the other partner to be shared and processed, ultimately enriching their personal and authorial relationship overall. Their appreciation of the correlation between difference and freedom has been eclipsed, so far, by literary critics' focus on their youthful "tropes of likeness." However, I would argue it is ultimately difference, more so than freedom, that keeps the Michael Field partnership fresh and vital.

Repeatedly, Bradley and Cooper remark that difference must be present for intellectual and creative exchange to bring forth interesting ideas and artful verse. This has significant implications for important choices the coauthors make as lovers, writing partners, and aesthetes. For instance, in 1897, Cooper, philosophises about a project she and Bradley were undertaking with Charles Ricketts and Charles Shannon, and equates art and relationships in order to lament that too much similarity ruins both:

> Two arts cannot marry on equivalents—one art must live in polygamy with the others if there is to be any combination. Wagner discovered that: the musician amorously used poetry, drama, painting, as lord of a harem. We are suffering from the equality of marriage between our drama and the Rickett's designing. Fools![23]

Likewise, the following poem from *Underneath the Bough*, with its repetitive imagery of two vessels side by side (similar not because of a "bond" but because of a "mortal alliance") should, in the context of its placement in the diaries, be theorised as a semi-autobiographical meditation on sameness. As such, it explores how the relationship between Cooper and Berenson was ill-fated, because they were too much the same:

> As two fair vessels side by side,
> No bond had tied
> Our floating peace;

We thought that it would never cease,
But like swan-creatures we should always glide:
And this is love
We sighed.
As two grim vessels side by side,
Through wind and tide
War grappled us,
With bond as strong as death, and thus
We drove on mortally allied:
And this is hate
We cried.

Sameness and difference continue to be recurring themes for the coauthors. In 1896, after Berenson enraged Cooper and caused a break with both women by insulting Bradley, Cooper refers to him as "the hateful tyrant of my blood-the man whose brain thinks the same thoughts as mine, whose fire is my fire, whom I adore to the point of self destruction."[24] She then clarifies that the threat to her sense of self, in part, is danger to herself-as-poet, something she had noted back in October, 1894: "[h]e would like me to be his Maenad; he has no intention of serving me."[25] Now, in 1896, Cooper comes to terms with the realisation that when she is away from Bernard she is very creative, but when she is with him her writing suffers: "I am a Satanic ant on my poetic side, and too captured physically to gain mental joy from exchanges of thought." Although she has experienced both joy and anguish—"to stand between Hell and Heaven, loving both, has been a crisis"—Cooper reflects upon the choice she has made, which, in retrospect, has been no choice at all, and concludes:

Thank life, the flames are where they should be now, and the sun atop, the dear, liberating passion by which I live! We don't think alike-for my Michael is in opposition to most of the thought I share with Bernhard [sic]; but that is of course our fascination for each other—difference found in one perfect feeling, one creative unity of nature.[26]

Significantly, this meditation evaluates the positive effects of difference but does not privilege biological difference. Her journals and verse make clear that Cooper experiences erotic, romantic, and intellectual desire for both Bradley and Berenson but only her feelings for Bradley are productive and consistently pleasurable. For Cooper, her relationship with Berenson, in contrast with Bradley, is plagued by sameness and thus is barren and destructive. Cooper ponders many factors, including writer's block; ultimately she remains with "Michael"—the lover with whom she can write.[27]

Thus, in Michael Field's ongoing representations of their relationship, which Donoghue calls a "strong evolving organism" (1998, 32), longevity and passion ultimately have less to do with the "twin hearts" and "shared souls" of their earliest days, than with a strategic recognition and celebration of the productive differences that exist within their union. For instance, in the same period as the "closer married" statements, Bradley describes Cooper to her cousin Francis as "a cross between a swan and a sloth. ... If I had her gifts and my own energy-but the two do sometimes meet, and then all is well. Would we were both in our places at your breakfast table to greet you."[28] This letter reflects upon difference with a teasing, yet admiring and accepting tone, speaks not of merging but of "meeting," as writers and lovers, and mentions each partner's individual claim to space.

A similar tone is present in the erotic and playful "The Bee and the Flower" (written for Cooper's birthday in 1897), which describes symbiosis but not sameness:

> Thou art a flower and I a bee
>> The sun is on high
> Thou wilt fade and I shall flee
>> The sun will lie down wearily
> But what love I!
> When the sun is on power
>> And the flower on the tree
> There follows the bee
>> To feed on the flower![29]

Fauna and flora are both of Nature; but they are different, nonetheless. Thus, a drama unfolds between lover and beloved, pursuer and pursued, as the bee is entranced and fed by the flower. The juxtaposition of eternally cyclic solar patterns with the fleeting life cycles but otherwise differing behaviors of the bee and flower heightens the tension of their differences; yet the sing-song rhythm of the poem tells, with simple, playful certitude, that the bee and flower will come together as surely as the sun will rise and fall. The more sophisticated "Stream and Pool" similarly advances an erotics of difference while it enacts a nuanced exploration of personality and desire through complex water images, parallel but contrasting movement, and, fitting for the aesthetes, analysis of music and light:

> Mine is the eddying foam and the broken current
> Thine the serene-flowing tide, the unscattered rhythm
> Light touches me on the surface with glints of sunshine
> Dives in thy bosom, disclosing a mystic river
> ....
> What is my song but the tumult of chafing forces
> What is thy silence, Beloved, but enchanted music?[30]

These poems are continued variations on the theme of eroticised and aestheticised difference-within-union that Bradley and Cooper had articulated from the very beginning of their career, and which they had made concrete back in 1886, with their adoption of the bramblebough insignia (see Figure 9.2). Cooper writes to Robert Browning upon sending him *Brutus Ultor* (1886):

> We have worked equally at it. My song-mate has entirely shaped Lucretia, I, mostly Brutus. You may like to know that she made the bramble-bough the emblem of our united life: that is why it is drawn on the cover. She wrote:
>
> My poet-bride, sweet songmate do I doom
> Thy youth to age's dull society?
> On the same bramblebough the pale-cheeked bloom
> Fondling by purple berry loves to lie;
> Fed by one September sunshine, there is room
> For fruit and flower in living unity.
>
> When we adopted this as our symbol, my father carved the berried and flowery sprays over our mantelshelf and we have them on our study-chair also.[31]

Figure 9.2 Bramblebough insignia from *Sight and Song* (circa 1886).

Like "The Bee and the Flower" and "Stream and Pool," this letter to Browning takes great care to delineate the two unique halves of Michael Field, even as it justifies their union. The bramblebough poem dispels any concern about their considerable age difference, transforming the contrast in age into a sensual artistic image that ultimately becomes a decorative element in their home. The bloom and the berry are of the same vine, grown under the same sun; yet paradoxically, the aesthetic appeal of the striking contrast of the pale flower nestled with the purple fruit justifies the attraction between the songmates in this poem. Through this image and the previous two lyrics, we see that even over the course of decades, and with each partner's frequent declaration that they are growing ever closer, there remains "room" for assertions of difference in both life and text. In fact, contrary to much existing Michael Field scholarship, difference seems to be as integral as, or perhaps at times even more of a driving force for compatibility, stimulus and creation than, the Spinozan focus on similarity.

As Bradley and Cooper play with difference in these poems, they negotiate what Psomiades and other feminist literary critics have observed as aestheticism's "tendency to think about the body of woman as mysterious surface accompanied by unknowable depth" (Psomiades 1997, 108). Because much of their verse performs the Michael Field collaboration, the contrasting bodies of *both* the lover and beloved are present in the poems' highly visual, sensual metaphors. This creates a productive paradox. On the one hand they employ natural rather than artificial images, accessible stories and familiar, often domestic or garden comparisons.[32] This quotidian turn departs from the male aesthetic tendency to "claim that the praxis of art is incompatible with everyday life" (Psomiades 1999, 109). On the other hand, these aesthetic impressions, which function as metaphor for relationship, *are* highly artful; and we can read them, vis-à-vis Halperin, as a queer site of becoming. Together, and often *because* of their differences, Michael Field both make and *are* art, locating the aesthetic impulse in each other and their union, through association with sensations experienced close to home.

Importantly, for Michael Field, unlike many male aesthetes, everyday life includes a matter-of-fact, yet worshipful attitude toward spiritual mysteries. The following journal entry typifies Bradley and Cooper's approaches to thinking about religion, art and everyday life; here, as elsewhere, we see a comfortable emphasis on their differences:

> A mild wholesome west wind—its noise and sun are about us. At Breakfast Michael and I were talking of our different attitudes toward the spiritual world. Michael sees it as an Umbrian Painter sees the sky, trees, with adoration in her eyes … I see it as Whistler sees this world through an atmosphere, and as long as I can keep within that atmosphere I have found the condition by wh: [sic] I can live in it. This atmosphere is what light is to our world—no more mystical-the dead are in it, as flowers and beasts and men are in the sunshine.[33]

Ultimately, Michael Field extend their strategies about life-in-art into representations of the afterlife, as seen in 1897 "The Art of Love," another lyric celebrating the strength that age difference can bring to love, this time via the Biblical example of Ruth and Naomi's devotion:

> Ah Dearest, Thou dost cleave to me
> Even as Ruth to Naomi
> Yet, see, great Love has grown in art
> At Death there is no need to part;
> Nor shall one sue for burial where
> The other crumbles into mould
> Past iron Time there is an age of gold-
> And hand in hand we will seek entrance There.[34]

Here, the loving permanency of Ruth and Naomi's intergenerational female marriage counters the fear that death would separate the Michaels. The poem posits a logic in which iron is not stronger than gold, nor Time and Death stronger than love in life, through the triple meaning of the phrase "great Love has grown in art." This phrase suggests that because "Love has grown," or matured, in the fertile environment of aesthetic surrounds and endeavors, Death cannot part the lovers; the speaker also implies that "Love has grown in art," or skill, like an artist who can transform ugliness (the power of Death to separate) into something beautiful. Finally, the phrase suggests that Love rendered into art has been proven to last and increase, as evidenced by many well known stories, including Ruth and Naomi's. The Love between speaker and beloved will thwart Death as well, in this and other poems that represent their life and love as art—indeed, that remake Love into an art object. These three possible readings do not contradict, but rather complement each other. Appropriately, understanding the relationship between Love, art and Death is articulated as seeing in line four's "Yet, see." The tone here is generously soothing and matter-of-fact, as if the relationship between the mysteries of Love and Death is perfectly visible, or understandable, once it is pointed out.

Finally, their diaries and poems illustrate that Bradley and Cooper's ongoing, erotic play with difference includes adopting a full range of gender positions and roles—such as Dionysian Maenads, Husband and "Wiftie," Michael and Henry, All-Wise Fowl and Pussie—along with an exploration of attendant power dynamics. Sometimes, play like this can emphasise their individual writing goals, such as letters from Autumn 1885 when Cooper was too obsessed with *Brutus Ultor* to work with Bradley on another project:

> The Pussie wants to finish catching its rat before it goes after the mouse. You see—for a King it may execute many things, but if a Cat is not concentrated at its prey it will come off badly. Let me go on quietly with *Brutus* (as I must, if I am to do anything masterly).[35]

Sometimes role play is just play, as an 1888 letter, where Bradley (here signing herself Mick) bawdily teases, "[w]ell Puss, dear Elizabethan man

I congratulate you: but what I am chiefly pleased to learn is that I am more vigorous than Pussie—the male part of Michael as beseemeth our relatives."[36]

Elsewhere, such experimentation with sex/gender fluidity inspires Michael Field to write some of their most intriguing poetry. *Long Ago*'s "Tiresias" (1889), for instance, depicts the mythological man turned into a woman and back again, only to conclude that woman "has more delight" in the passions of sex and love (86). This poem has led Chris White to remark, "Tiresias is a representation of the absence of any clear split between male and female in Michael Field's Utopian vision" (1996b, 155) and Prins, quite rightly to assert: "Tiresias becomes an interchangeably doubled self: both masculine and feminine, self-divided yet coupled together. His ... ability to cross between sexual identities and be receptive to the split also suggests the possibility of being *'closer married'* as Bradley and Cooper describe themselves" (Prins 1999b, 92).[37] In the same vein, the early "Caenis Caeneus," published in *Dedicated: An Early Work of Michael Field* (1914), tells how Neptune heard the prayer of a young woman, Caenis, who wished to be a man "in form and thought" (line 40). As the male Caeneus, s/he "loved and sailed and sang / And fought in battle with his peers / And laboured for his joy through glorious years;" but ultimately, s/he is killed while intervening in a rape. In the afterlife, and female once more, Caenis mourns that "Her life of shadow I resume" and greatly laments the loss of masculinity's privilege: "My maiden life could win no valid range, / Aye waiting impotent to win; But with my manhood's sovereignty / I struck where women's hopes begin" (178; 187–90). Interestingly, in 1900, Bradley muses, "the poem is her Tiresias. I decide for the bliss of woman-hood, for her it is shadow-land. Surely some day she will be a man."[38] Clearly, critical appeals to similarity within the Michael Field union, especially to texts about their shared womanhood, eclipse observations like those above about the role of difference in their partnership, and thereby obscure an important point of entry into their considerable oeuvre.[39]

These examples indicate Bradley and Cooper understood that erotic and intellectual play with gender transgression and the gaze would enable them to play with desire and power. It seems Bradley and Cooper found these dynamics intriguing, personally pleasurable, and artistically inspiring. For instance, in *Long Ago* as Michael Field "sings Sappho," they often acknowledge the passion of same-sex desire through an erotic gaze that, on the surface, may seem to reproduce the aesthetic tendency to objectify the beloved:

> Come Gorgo, put the rug in place
> And passionate recline;
> I love to see thee in thy grace,
> Dark, virulent, divine.
>
> (ll.1–4)

However, Bradley and Cooper invoke Sappho in order to recreate a fore-mother and the history and voices of the ancient Isle of Lesbos; thus, gazing upon the beloved's beauty in this same-sex environment does not signify as it might in the heteropatriarchal space of the artist's studio. If at times the object of the gaze is silent, Michael Field does not always equate passivity with being disenfranchised. Instead, the coauthors write of the utmost importance of the "power of the beloved as it reaches and envelopes and draws back into its depth. ... In all the great sonnets Michael has written she has been gained by the passion of the object."[40] Thus, a poem like "Unbosoming," speaking from the position of the beloved, compares "The love that breeds / In my heart for thee!" to an iris, tremulous with beauty, fertile and straining with the "harvest-secret" meant for the one who looks upon it. The beloved is filled with desire like a "thousand vermillion-beads / That push and riot and squeeze and clip," yet also experiences "great content" to "give thee, after my kind, / The final issues of heart and mind" (*Underneath the Bough* 1893, 99).

If Bradley is likely to fashion "himself" as lover and Cooper as beloved one year, "Henry" is just as likely to alter the dynamic the next, describing herself as Mars, desiring "Michael" as Venus,[41] or Zeus, lusting after the daughter of Acrisius, as she does in the conclusion of "Temptation" (1908), inspired by Bradley in a new nightgown:[42]

> But when he came
> Where sate the daughter of Acrisius,
> In her little house of stone,
> Clad in linen, all alone,
> Clad in linen finely wove,
> Straight he stared and plotted love.
> (*Wild Honey from Various Thyme* 57, ll. 13–18)

To desire and be desired, to gaze, to be gazed upon, and to return that gaze, all create sensation, pleasure, art; and Michael Field does not hesitate to explore each of these configurations. Similarly, it is noteworthy that the interlocutor in "Caenis Caeneus" employs an extremely aggressive gaze when speaking from the position of masculine privilege; yet juxtaposed with Caenis's less enfranchised gaze, the contrast seems to critically highlight how aestheticism takes traditional gender ideologies for granted. In other texts, especially *Sight and Song* as I have argued elsewhere, Michael Field speaks on behalf of the historically silenced object of the gaze, much as Christina Rossetti does in "In an Artist's Studio" (Ehnenn 2004, 219). If Bradley and Cooper have one irrefutable point in common, it is a queer-feminist penchant to fantasise about a multiplicity of gender embodiments, as lover, as lyric Poet, as interlocutor, and as subject *and* object of a poetic, aesthetic gaze.

Michael Field's queer-feminist eroticisation and aesthetisation of difference not only enlivens their relationship, it enables them to enter aesthetic conversations regarding art as authentic expression vs. reproducing convention as commodity. As they vary the theme of male artist painting the female body as beautiful but mute art object, Michael Field's disidentificatory play with the erotics of difference can be read as fixing the bodies of not only the beloved, but also the speaker, as art. Additionally, in keeping with aestheticism's tendency to render the impression through contemplation of surface, in much of Field's self-reflexive poetry, through artifice, both lover and beloved are constructed as objects. Yet both are authentic, desiring subjects as well—a claim made possible by aestheticism, but also critical of it. Here, what brings their complex queer-feminist aesthetic vision into being is their willingness to write into art the erotic charge of "lesbian" difference—not as an uncritical appropriation of heterosexual difference and gender roles—but as a queer exploration of multiple possibilities of lesbian gender, desire and mutually pleasurable power dynamics outside of a heteronormative framework, and the promise of those multiplicities for maintaining their relationship and their poetic creativity.

3. Necessary Fire

If the thyrsus eventually came to replace the bramblebough as formal logo, the ideas each symbol represented to Michael Field continued to intermingle in their writing until their deaths. The bramblebough—that early celebration of eroticised difference-in-symbiosis—continues to haunt their work, while the omnipresent thyrsus usefully performs Dionysian, passion-filled disidentificatory strategies of appropriation. However, the Dionysian thyrsus also informs Michael Field's positioning of themselves as aesthetes, and, I would contend, helps delineate the limits of their position in comparison to other aesthetic authors of their day.

Bradley and Cooper's fraught relationship to decadence, its French forbears and its *fin-de-siècle* British inheritors, is complex. They despised Zola's *Nana* (1880), yet admired Verlaine and Baudelaire, who are mentioned in *Works and Days* and are the subject of several lyrics. They were also very fond of Arthur Symons, who in "The Decadent Movement in Literature" (1893) defends and characterises the movement as "an intense self-consciousness, a restless curiosity in research, an oversubtlizing refinement upon refinement, a spiritual and moral perversity" and "a desperate endeavor to give sensation, to flash the impression of the moment, to preserve the very heat and motion of life" (138). Yet they were so offended by the *Yellow Book*, they refused to publish in it and returned their copy:

> One felt as one does when ... a wholly lost woman stands flaming on the pavement with the ghastly laugh of the ribald crowd in the air round ... the book is full of cleverness such as one expects to find in those who dwell below light and hope and love and aspiration. The best one can say of any tale or of any illustration is that it is clever— the worst one can say is that it is damnable.[43]

This is a far cry from how Symons describes Verlaine's decadence: "[The] poetry of sensation, of evocation which paints as well as sings. ... To fix the last shade, the quintessence of things; to fix it fleetingly; to be a disembodied voice, and yet the voice of a human soul" (2004, 140–41). But, it does echo the way Symons speaks of "the literature of a civilization grown over-luxurious, over-inquiring, too languid for the relief of action, too uncertain for any emphasis in opinion or in conduct. It reflects all the moods, all the manner of a sophisticated society; its very artificiality is a way of being true to nature" (136). How, then, are we to understand Michael Field's revulsion for decadence, and how might their attitude be related to the emotional economies of their own collaborative aesthetics?

Michael Field's verse sometimes, but not always, employs form and/or content in the same manner that contemporaneous male-authored poetry does. Bradley and Cooper certainly engage decadent tropes—much of their work is replete with fervor, death, corruption and decay, desire, and despair, and situated within gorgeous, exotic, and richly textured visual scenes. As we have seen, some of their verse negotiates traditional representations of sexually aggressive women as well as ambivalent narratives of poetic autonomy. Nevertheless, unlike female poets such as Graham R. Tomson, Bradley and Cooper do not feminise decadence (to use Linda K. Hughes's most useful phrase) in the way that perhaps they could be said to feminise aestheticism. Instead, it is at the vague divide between aestheticism and decadence that Michael Field found their stylistic parameter and literary goals. It is my assertion that because the coauthors were not willing to compromise their fierce dedication to the impassioned Dionysian impulse signified by the thyrsus, their poetic rendering of the Paterian impression could not accommodate decadent fascination with morbidity born of ennui.

Chris White and, more recently, T. D. Olverson have examined Michael Field's ongoing exploration of erotic Hellenism, with Olverson suggesting that the coauthors "replicate Swinburne's literary and philosophical premise, that it is the poet's (moral) duty to record one's passion for life and its potentially tragic cost" (2010, 124). Indeed, as the following meditation on Dionysian resurrection stories illustrates, Bradley and Cooper increasingly found ways to connect their early pagan rapture for the Bacchanal with their later passion for Catholic tradition and ritual, but only within a framework that insists upon intense engagement:

> It is sometimes said that shortly after his burial [Dionysus] rose from the dead and ascended up to Heaven or that Zeus raised him up as he lay mortally wounded or that Zeus swallowed the heart of Dionysus. ... It appears that a general doctrine of resurrection or at least of immortality was inculcated on his worshippers for Plutarch. ... The women of Elis hailed [Dionysus] as the Bull. They sang, "Come here Dionysus, to thy holy temple by the sea; dance with the graces to thy holy temple, rushing with thy bull's foot, O goodly bull, O goodly

bull." Therefore, in tearing live bulls and calves the Maenads were killing the god, eating his flesh, drinking his blood.[44]

This over-abundant and gory passage certainly does not shy from excess. However, it is motivated by a zest for sensation, not decadent economies of/ in languor. Indeed, in 1892 Bradley and Cooper recoil at Berenson's complaint that he is "bored bored bored," retorting, "ennui [is] made impossible by the multitude of thoughts and hopes. Ennui is the plague of life, punishing us when we refuse to be about our father's business-which is, we must always remember, 'that we should have life, and have it more abundantly.'"[45] Ennui is, in other words, contrary to the "light and hope and love and aspiration" that Bradley and Cooper sought, but found sorely lacking, in the *Yellow Book*. In contrast:

> At home in the evening Sim and I went over the larger fragments of Otho. Our brains struck fire each from each—we conceived his final exit, his farewell to Death, his joyous acceptance of everlasting anguish that is quick with life. We both felt it was the even of our resurrection as artists—as George Moore writes "To create soul is to accomplish the work of God."[46]

In this thrilling moment of collaborative *jouissance,* the Promethean and Judeo-Christian impulse coexist, and artistic agency is reborn. Ennui, that constant companion of the decadent aesthete, has no place in Michael Field's world.

The above consideration of Dionysian resurrection has significant implications for how Michael Field's characteristic engagement with both sacred and profane, made manifest in their pagan/Christian disidentification with the ringed thyrsus, plays out in their post-conversion devotional poetry, a topic beyond the scope of this project. It also begins to explain their rejection of the *Yellow Book* and of Hardy:

> *Jude the Obscure* (obscene) I could not read. Offal was thrown in my face. ... I turned away forever from the thrower. Hardy appears to me to be in Hell, not on Earth. He has no pulse for life—he blasphemes what he has never experienced. I felt this when I met him; he seemed less than an echimus, alive in the limitless seas-he was echimite—the mere petrifaction. ... The "still, sad music of humanity" played under the low roof of his pessimism becomes disgraceful noise. ... He is the Scribe of the Tragedy of Science—neither an Artist of Apollo nor of Dionysus.[47]

Here, Michael Field, with characteristic indignation, complicates Oscar Wilde's stance that "[t]he artist can express everything" (1988, 4), and they do so *not* on necessarily gendered principles, but rather on Dionysian ones.

Within Bradley and Cooper's aesthetic framework, things are not perverse in themselves, but representation without authentic and spontaneous intensity of experience becomes contrived, sterile, and blasphemous. Without a "pulse for life," there is no Paterian "gemlike flame." Without a place for the passion of the thyrsus, expression is not art.

§

This discussion has sought to illuminate some of the underexplored dynamics within Michael Field's representations of identity, desire, and sexuality, and to suggest direction for future study. For the coauthors, continuing attraction between lovers—sexual, emotional and intellectual—is clearly predicated upon a strategic practice of a fluid and changing performance of sexuality and subjectivity. On a strictly biographical level, this seems to have ensured that their individual freedoms, and in turn, their individual and collaborative creativity, were not curtailed; in Cooper's words, "the flames are where they should be." Yet Michael Field's self-reflexive textual performances of desire, difference, and disidentification also have theoretical implications for inquiry into women's literary collaboration and female writers' contributions to aestheticism. The authors who famously wrote "we are Michael Field" and "we are closer married" celebrate, at times, their shared experience of womanhood as well as tastes, interests, talents they held in common; but tropes of likeness, whether based on Spinoza, Shelley, Shakespeare or what we have come to call feminist principles provide only one point of interest in context of Michael Field's entire textual legacy. We must, therefore, continue to consider a full spectrum of sameness and difference, power shared and frankly contested, and subjectivities that may appear overlapping, individual, or queered. We must also consider where women like Bradley and Cooper drew their limits in such a way that their queer poetic and aesthetic vision was not compromised, even as their "brains struck fire each from each."

Notes

1. Here I refer to T. & D. C. Sturge Moore's 1933 edition, *Works and Days: From the Journals of Michael Field*. Quotations from the Michael Field journals at the British Library, London (Add MSS 46776–46804) will be cited by footnote with manuscript number, date, and folio. Quotations from the letters in the Michael Field Papers at the Bodleian Library, Oxford, likewise will be cited by footnote with manuscript number and date.

2. One of the earliest studies to complicate Michael Field's celebration of shared womanhood is Chris White's "Poets and Lovers Evermore: The Poetry and Journals of Michael Field." More recently, see, among others, Virginia Blain, "Michael Field, the Two-Headed Nightingale: Lesbian Text as Palimpsest" and Martha Vicinus, "Faun Love: Michael Field and Bernard Berenson."

3. I find these theorists useful for talking about Michael Field because they do not define queerness as a set category for radical or transgressive identity. Rather,

Halperin and Doty think of queer/queerness/queering as a fluid phenomenon dependent on shifting modes of being and perceiving the world. Although Michael Field may have had some transgressive ideas and were often considered a bit odd by their friends, I am not claiming they possessed a transgressive identity; after all, they were privileged women with enough private income to write, even when their writing was not popular.

4. The catchy title of Emma Donoghue's biography of Bradley and Cooper, *We are Michael Field*, can be misleading when read out of context. It refers to a journal entry from May, 1888, when Robert Browning visited Michael Field and expressed admiration for *Long Ago*'s "Tiresias." Browning reveals he had thought of treating the topic, but concludes it is better done by a woman. Bradley then writes: "He said to Edith he liked the 2nd series of poems even better than the first, and prophesied they would make their mark. But he refuses to write a preface. We must remember, we are Michael Field. Again he said, wait fifty years ..." In essence, Browning is saying, "You are Michael Field, and are best qualified to write your own preface. Don't worry, in time you will be famous." Add. 46777 (1888), 5.

5. Add. 46780 (1892), 46.

6. ALS Katharine Bradley to Robert Browning. Add. 46866 (1886).

7. Field, Add. 46779 (1891), 160.

8. Field, Add. 46785 (1896), 24.

9. Field, Add. 46781 (1893), 46 and Add. 46782 (1894), 28.

10. ALS Katharine Bradley to Edith Cooper, September 5, 1885, MS Eng. Lett c 418.

11. Bradley also calls Cooper Puss, Pussie or P, Field, and the Blue Bird. By 1892, her nicknames also included my Boy, Henry, Hennery, Henny, and Hennie-Boy. Bradley was Michael, Mick, Sim or S (from Simiorg, a mythological bird), and "the all-wise bird or fowl" (Donoghue 1998, 37).

12. Wayne Koestenbaum describes nineteenth-century male coauthors who perceive their joint work as a baby or child.

13. Field, Add. 46778 (1890), 107.

14. Field, Add. 46780 (1892), 59.

15. Field, Add. 46785 (1896), 63.

16. Bram Dijkstra's *Idols of Perversity* is a useful study of *fin-de-siècle* images of feminine evil. See also Yopie Prins on Michael Field as maenad in "Greek Maenads, Victorian Spinsters.".

17. Field, Add. 46780 (April 20 1892).

18. Field, 46780 (1892), 78.

19. In "What is an Author?" Foucault argues that the author, or person who has done the writing, is not the same as (and is less important than) the author-function, or set of beliefs, ideas, and even economic value that comes out of associating a particular text with a particular writer's name. See Foucault 1979.

20. Field, Add. 46780 (1892), 12.

21. Field, Add. 46782 (1894), 84. This episode with "Lion" made a strong impression, as "Michael" and "Henry" tell Ricketts and Shannon about it years later, when it became something the coauthors repeatedly tease each other about.

22. Field, Add. 46780 (1892), 126.

23. Field, Add. 46786 (1897), 22.

24. Field, Add. 46785 (1896), 35.

25. Field, Add. 46783 (1894), 94.

26. Field, Add. 46785 (1896), 39.

27. In 1903, when Berenson and Michael Field were again amicable, Cooper analyses the interactions between herself, Berenson, and Bradley: "[Bernard] said we draw him out and make him talk as no other people in the world. He almost does not talk at all. Michael is the fire that sets the saucepan boiling. Everything he [Bernard] has ever said I have understood—he does not believe there is anything I could not: but like Bertie Russell and he, we are in such fellowship of thought we almost bore each other. I do not challenge him to explain, as Michael does, to develop his ideas. We enjoy our understanding of each other through Michael's evocation. Without the content, our sympathy would merely be implicit." Add. 46792 (1903), 124. Here, the benefits of difference over similarity (fire over boredom) are clear. Yet, it is striking how the dynamic between Bernard and the two women creates pleasure for each dyadic permutation within the trio. Martha Vicinus explores similar ideas in "Faun Love: Michael Field and Bernard Berenson" (2009).

28. ALS Katharine Bradley to Frances Brookes 1884, orig. ital., MS Eng lett d 405.

29. Field, Add. 46786 (1897), 7.

30. Taken from the American version of *Underneath the Bough* (53) and reprinted in *A Selection from the Poems of Michael Field*, (20).

31. Michael Field to Robert Browning, Add. 46866 (1886).

32. "Sleeping Venus" from *Sight and Song* (98–105) represents autoerotic and homoerotic possibly for all women by beginning, "Here is Venus by our homes." Other Michael Field poems do employ exoticism and invoke less domestic imagery, especially the Whym Chow texts and their post-conversion devotional verses, also, much of their narrative poetry. See Ehnenn 2009.

33. Field, Add. 46789 (1900), 48.

34. Field, Add. 46786 (1897), 7.

35. ALS Edith Cooper to Katharine Bradley, September 1885, Eng lett. c419.

36. ALS Katharine Bradley to Edith Cooper, 1888, Eng lett. c 418.

37. See also Thain 2007. Wendy Bashant, in context of a discussion on *Bellerophon*, argues similarly that Michael Field depicts gendered categories as social constructs: "categories that must be dissolved" (2006, 85).

38. Field, Add. 46789 (1900), 123.

39. Here I disagree with Vicinus's argument that only Cooper alluded to their personal differences, while Bradley remained intent on their sameness and unity (2009, 762).

40. Field, Add. 46790 (1901), 53.

41. Field, Add. 46779 (1891), 98.

42. Cooper documents the genesis of the poem: "[W]hen we go to bed, my Beloved slips into the lawn night-dress designed by Kate Reilly; and grants me the loveliest vision of my eyes—she has the tender form of her family-youth is eternal in its small, delicate, generous colored outline; the Graces and Giorgione have been as patrons of her body. And now it is seen rosy as the hours and shadowly as they on the supple linen-a finer thing than a smile on a face or a touch—mere essential in the graciousness and its tingeing warmth. O this is Beauty—and it is fadeless and liberal; for I can never be as poor as I was before I had seen it whether I live or die. On Good Friday I have to write round my delight—Hence, 'Zeus in his sovereign heaven is wont to see' etc." Add. 46790 (1901), 51.

43. Field, Add. 46783 (1894), 38.

44. Field, Add. 46789 (1900), 103.

45. Field, Add. 46780 (1892). 135.
46. Field, Add. 46779 (1891), 27.
47. Field, Add. 46784 (1895), 25.

Acknowledgement

Many thanks to Marion Thain, Joseph Bristow, and Kim Q. Hall who each provided invaluable comments at various stages of this project.

Works Cited

Bashant, Wendy. 2006. "Aesthetes and Queens: Michael Field, John Ruskin and *Bellerophon.*" *Journal of PreRaphaelite Studies* no. 15, 74–94.

Blain,Virginia. 1996. "Michael Field, the Two-Headed Nightingale: Lesbian Text as Palimpsest." *Women's History Review* 5 (2): 239–57.

Dijkstra, Bram. 1986. *Idols of Perversity: Fantasies of Feminine Evil in Fin-de-Siècle Culture.* New York: Oxford University Press.

Donoghue, Emma. 1998. *We are Michael Field.* Bath: Absolute Press.

Doty, Alexander. 1993. *Making Things Perfectly Queer: Interpreting Mass Culture.* Minneapolis: University of Minnesota Press.

Ehnenn, Jill. 2009. "'Dragging at Memory's Fetter': Michael Field's Personal Elegies, Victorian Mourning, and the Problem of Whym Chow." *The Michaelian* 1. http://www.oscholars.com/Field/MF1/ehnennarticle.htm.

———. 2004. "Looking Strategically: Feminist and Queer Aesthetics in Michael Field's *Sight and Song.*" *Victorian Poetry* 42 (3): 213–59.

———. 2008. *Women's Literary Collaboration, Queerness and Late-Victorian Culture.* Aldershot: Ashgate.

Faderman, Lillian. 1981. *Surpassing the Love of Men.* New York: William Morrow.

Field, Michael. 1914. *Dedicated: An Early Work of Michael Field.* London: George Bell and Song.

———. *The Michael Field Papers.* MS, The Bodleian Library. University of Oxford.

———. 1892. *Sight and Song.* London: Elkin Matthews and John Lane.

———.1893. *Underneath the Bough.* London: George Bell.

———.1898. *Underneath the Bough* [American Version]. Portland, ME: T. Mosher.

———. 1923. *A Selection from the Poems of Michael Field.* London: Poetry Bookshop.

———. 1890. ALS to Vernon Lee. January 29. MS, The Vernon Lee Collection, Special Collections, Miller Library, Colby College, Waterville, Maine.

———. 1908. *Wild Honey from Various Thyme.* London: Fisher Unwin.

———. *Works and Days: The Journals of Michael Field.* Add. MSS 16776–46804. British Library, London.

Foucault, Michel. 1979. "What is an Author?" In *Textual Strategies: Perspectives in Post-Structuralist Criticism,* edited by Josué V. Harari, 141–60. New York: Cornell University Press.

Halperin, David. 1995. *Saint Foucault: Toward a Gay Hagiography.* New York: Oxford University Press.

Hughes, Linda K. 1999. "Feminizing Decadence: Poems by Graham R. Tomson." In *Women and British Aestheticism,* edited by Talia Schaffer and Kathy Alexis Psomiades, 119–38. Charlottesville: University of Virginia Press.

Koestembaum, Wayne. 1989. *Double Talk: The Erotics of Male Literary Collaboration.* New York: Routledge.

Laird, Holly. 1995. "Contradictory Legacies: Michael Field and Feminist Restoration." *Victorian Poetry* 33 (1): 111–28.

Muñoz, José Esteban. 1999. *Disidentifications: Queer of Color and the Performance of Politics*. Minneapolis: University of Minnesota Press.

Olverson, T.D. 2010. *Women Writers and the Dark Side of Late-Victorian Hellenism*. London: Palgrave.

Pater, Walter. 1986. "*The Renaissance* (1873)." In *Walter Pater: Three Major Texts*, edited by William E. Buckley, 219–20. New York: New York University Press.

Prins, Yopie. 1999. "Greek Maenads, Victorian Spinsters." In *Victorian Sexual Dissidence*, edited by Richard Dellamora, 43–81. Chicago: University of Chicago Press.

———. 1999. *Victorian Sappho*. Princeton: Princeton University Press.

Psomiades, Kathy Alexis. 1997. *Beauty's Body*. Stanford: Stanford University Press.

———. 1999. "Whose Body: Christina Rossetti and Aestheticist Femininity." In *Women and British Aestheticism*, edited by Talia Schaffer and Kathy Alexis Psomiades, 101–18. Charlottesville: University of Virginia Press.

Rubin, Gayle. 1993. "Thinking Sex." In *The Lesbian and Gay Studies Reader*, edited by Henry Abelove, Michèle Aina Barale and David M. Halperin, 3–44. New York: Routledge.

Symons, Arthur. 2004. "The Decadent Movement in Literature." In *Aesthetes and Decadents of the 1890s*, edited by Karl Beckson, 134–51. Rev. ed. Chicago: Academy Chicago Press.

Sturge Moore, T. & D. C. Sturge Moore, eds. 1933. *Works and Days: From the Journals of Michael Field*. London: John Murray.

Thain, Marian. 2007. *Michael Field: Poetry, Aestheticism and the Fin de Siècle*. London: Cambridge University Press.

Vanita, Ruth. 1996. *Sappho and the Virgin Mary: Same-Sex Love and the English Literary Imagination*. New York: Columbia University Press.

Vicinus, Martha. 2009. "Faun Love: Michael Field and Bernard Berenson." *Women's History Review* 18 (5): 753–64.

———. 1993. "They Wonder to Which Sex I Belong": The Historical Roots of the Modern Lesbian Identity." In *The Lesbian and Gay Studies Reader*, edited by Henry Abelove, et.al, 432–52. New York: Routledge.

White, Chris. 1996a. "Flesh and Roses: Michael Field's Metaphors of Pleasure and Desire." *Women's Writing* 3 (1): 47–62.

———. 1992. "Poets and Lovers Evermore: The Poetry and Journals of Michael Field." In *Sexual Sameness: Textual Differences in Lesbian and Gay Writing*, edited by Joseph Bristow, 26–43. New York: Routledge.

———. 1996b. "The Tiresian Poet: Michael Field." In *Victorian Women Poets: A Critical Reader*, edited by Angela Leighton, 148–61. Oxford: Blackwell.

Wilde, Oscar. 1988. Preface to *The Picture of Dorian Gray*. Edited by Donald L. Lawler. New York: Norton.

Contributors

Veronica Alfano is a faculty fellow in the English department at the University of Oregon, specialising in Victorian poetry, lyric theory, and gender studies. She has published articles on Tennyson, Christina Rossetti, and Robert Browning; along with Andrew Stauffer, she is co-editor of the essay collection *Virtual Victorians: Networks, Connections, Technologies* (Palgrave Macmillan, 2015). She recently completed a monograph titled *The Lyric in Victorian Memory*, which explores the links between mnemonic form and cultural nostalgia, and has accepted a visiting fellowship at Australian National University.

Matthew Bradley is a lecturer in English at the University of Liverpool, who writes principally on the relation between Victorian religion and culture. He has edited William James's *The Varieties of Religious Experience* for Oxford World's Classics and has recently co-edited a collection of essays on Victorian reading history, *Reading and the Victorians* (with Juliet John). He is currently writing a book about the end of the world in Victorian literature.

Catherine Delyfer is professor of Victorian studies at the University of Toulouse-Le Mirail, France. She is currently editor of the French journal of Victorian studies, *Cahiers victoriens et édouardiens*. She has published extensively on British *fin-de-siècle* culture and on neglected late-Victorian female writers such as Lucas Malet, Vernon Lee, Victoria Cross, and Marie Corelli, whose work bridges the gap between Aestheticism and Modernism. She is the author of a monograph on the pictorial poetics of Lucas Malet, *Art and Womanhood in Fin-de-Siècle Writing: the Fiction of Lucas Malet, 1882–1931* (London: Pickering and Chatto, 2011). In 2011, she edited a journal issue on female aestheticism which looks at the influence of non-canonical British women writers on proto-modernism (*Cahiers victoriens et édouardiens* 74, 2011). Most recently, she co-edited two collections of essays by leading critics entitled *Aesthetic Lives* (Rivendale Press, 2013) and *Beyond the Great Divide: Reconnecting Aestheticism and Modernism* (Pickering and Chatto, forthcoming 2015).

Jane Desmarais specialises in literary and visual Decadence. *Decadence: an annotated anthology* (co-edited with Chris Baldick) was published by Manchester University Press in 2011, and she is currently working on *Flowers of Evil* for Reaktion Press, a study of the metaphor of the hot-house flower in literature, art, and film.

Jill R. Ehnenn is professor of English at Appalachian State University where she teaches Victorian Studies and LGBT Studies/Queer Theory. She is the author of *Women's Literary Collaboration, Queerness, and Late-Victorian Culture* (Ashgate, 2008), articles on nineteenth-century women writers, especially Michael Field, and articles on queerness and contemporary popular culture. She is currently writing a book tentatively titled *Orienting the Victorians: Nineteenth-Century Progress Narratives, Sexuality, Disability and Nation*.

Jane Ford completed her Ph.D—which examined metaphors of economic exploitation and domination in *fin-de-siècle* literature—at the University of Portsmouth in 2013. Her publications include "Socialism, Capitalism and the Fiction of Lucas Malet: 'The Spirit of the Hive,'" *English Literature in Transition, 1880–1920*, 58.4 (2015) and "Spectral Economies at the Anglo-African Margin: Bertram Mitford's Predatory Politics of Consumption," *Victorian Network*, 1.1 (2009) (essay prize winner). She has co-organised two international conferences, including the AHRC-funded *Crossing the Line: Affinities before and after 1900* (University of Liverpool 2010) and *Enslavement: Colonial Appropriations, Apparitions, Remembrance* (University of Portsmouth 2011). Jane has taught across the undergraduate English Literature programme at the University of Portsmouth and, more recently, Keele University.

Kim Edwards Keates is sessional tutor at Liverpool John Moores University. Kim recently co-edited the *Victorian Periodicals Review* special issue, "Digital Pedagogies: Building Learning Communities for Studying Victorian Periodicals" (2015) and is Bibliographer (with Clare Horrocks) of *Dickens Quarterly*. She has research interests in digital pedagogy, Dickens, Victorian studies, the *fin de siècle*, gender and sexuality.

Kristin Mahoney is an associate professor in the English Department at Western Washington University. Her teaching and research interests include British aestheticism, Decadence, and queer studies. She has published articles in *Criticism, Victorian Studies, English Literature in Transition, Victorian Periodicals Review, Literature Compass*, and *College Teaching*. Her book *Literature and the Politics of Post-Victorian Decadence* is forthcoming from Cambridge University Press.

Sarah Parker is a lecturer at University of Stirling. She is the author of *The Lesbian Muse and Poetic Identity, 1889–1930* (Pickering & Chatto, 2013). Her other publications include "Fashioning Michael Field: Michael Field and Late-Victorian Dress Culture" (*Journal of Victorian Culture*, 2013), "Whose Muse? Sappho, Swinburne and Amy Lowell" in *Algernon Charles Swinburne: Unofficial Laureate* (Manchester UP,

2013) and "'A Girl's Love': Lord Alfred Douglas as Homoerotic Muse in the Poetry of Olive Custance" (*Women: A Cultural Review, 2011*). She is currently working on her second monograph, entitled "Picturing the Poetess: Women Poets, Celebrity and Photography (1880–1920)." An article entitled 'Publicity, Celebrity, Fashion: Photographing Edna St. Vincent Millay' is forthcoming from *Women's Studies*.

Patricia Pulham is a reader in Victorian Studies at the University of Portsmouth. She is author of *Art and the Transitional Object in Vernon Lee's Supernatural Tales*, (2008) and is co-editor of *Hauntings and Other Fantastic Tales* (2006), *Decadence, Ethics, Aesthetics* (2006), *Haunting and Spectrality in Neo-Victorian Fiction: Possessing the Past* (2010), *Crime Culture: Figuring Criminality in Fiction and Film* (2011), and of a Special Issue of *Symbiosis*, 'Decadent Crossings' (2012). Her most recent publication is a four-volume edited collection, *Spiritualism, 1830–1940* published by Routledge in 2013.

Ruth Robbins is professor of English Literature and head of the School of Cultural Studies and Humanities at Leeds Beckett University. She is the author of several books including *Literary Feminisms* (Palgrave, 2000); *Pater to Forster, 1873–1924* (Palgrave, 2003); *Subjectivity* (Palgrave, 2005); and *Oscar Wilde* (Continuum, 2011). She is also editor of a collection of reprints—*Medical Advice for Women: 1830–1915* (Routledge, 2009), and author, with Emma Liggins and Andrew Maunder, of *The British Short Story* (Palgrave, 2010).

Index